School for Young Children

School for Young Children

School for Young Children:

Developmentally Appropriate Practices

CHARLES H. WOLFGANG
Professor of Early Childhood Education
Florida State University

MARY E. WOLFGANG
Director
School for Young Children, SYC

ALLYN AND BACON
Boston   London   Toronto   Sydney   Tokyo   Singapore

Series Editorial Assistant: Carol L. Chernaik
Editorial-Production Service: Benchmark Productions
Cover Administrator: Linda Dickinson
Cover Designer: Suzanne Harbison
Manufacturing Buyer: Louise Richardson

Library of Congress Cataloging-in-Publication Data

Wolfgang, Charles H.
   School for young children : developmentally appropriate practices
   / Charles H. Wolfgang, Mary E. Wolfgang.
      p.   cm.
   Includes bibliographical references and index.
   ISBN 0-205-13122-0
   1. Early childhood teachers--Training of. 2. Early childhood
education--United States.   I. Wolfgang, Mary E.   II. Title.
LB1732.3.W65   1992
370'.7'3262--dc20   91-21427
                                              CIP

Printed in the United States of America
10 9 8 7 6 5 4 3 2 1   96 95 94 93 92 91

Dedicated to Gerry Brudenell
A friend to all those he met,
and a person that had the joy of playfulness

Contents

Preface

An overwhelming amount of research and a plethora of theories have been produced relating to the developmentally and educationally appropriate needs of young children—so much that the teacher trainer wonders where to begin with the instruction of potential teachers of young children. What must they know and what may be left out?

To give order to our thinking about what beginning teachers of young children should know, we may view teaching as a process having different levels. The first level is survival. How do I get through Monday morning with a group of 15 to 20 four-year-olds and give them worthwhile experiences? Only after this survival level has been mastered can teachers "keep their heads above water" long enough to ask questions related to more advanced concepts—to higher levels of performance. This book is to help the beginning teacher get past the survival level.

The School for Young Children (SYC), for ages 3, 4, and 5, was started a few years ago by the authors. Classrooms needed to be set up, teachers needed to be grounded in SYC philosophy, and problems related to day-in day-out practice with children and parents needed to be solved. There was little time to spend on theory and research because the children "appeared" each morning needing to be taught.

Gradually, however, in weekend training sessions and at weekly faculty meetings, teachers' needs for guidance in organizing classrooms and materials, methods of teaching, discipline, working with parents, etc., were met with practical ideas and constructs supported by theory and research. The chapters to follow contain syntheses of these practical methods and constructs, as well as some basic survival theory. Each chapter was written with the question in mind: what is absolutely necessary for the teacher to know related to this chapter topic? For example, an entire book could be written on playgrounds, and hundreds have been; what we have done is said simply, "Here is how we would design a playground for young children; here are constructs so that you, the reader, can design your own."

To follow, then, is a practical guide to what to do on Monday morning when 15 or 20 young children troop enthusiastically into your classroom. We hope it will help you survive—and more.

ACKNOWLEDGMENTS

A heartfelt thanks to many people who helped us make this book a reality. The teachers at SYC, Jamileh Mikati, a master teacher, Pam Phelps from Creative Preschool, a student who taught me as much as I tried to teach her. For reading the manuscript and giving useful feedback we thank Mark Koorland and Adrienne Herrill. Cathy Harrell for her photos. Sara Smilansky for her important research and ideas on sociodramatic play that is the genus for the developmentally appropriate play curriculum, and Nancy Curry for the University of Pittsburgh, who taught us so much about young children. Our children, Ellen, Ann, and Kate, who give us so much joy. And, finally, a special dedication to Gerry Brudenell, a friend and colleague whose presence enriched us all.

CHAPTER ONE

CHOOSING THE PROFESSION OF TEACHING YOUNG CHILDREN (DO YOU REALLY WANT TO BE A PRESCHOOL TEACHER?)

Why do you want to be a teacher of young children—3-, 4-, 5-, and 6-year-olds? Is it because you "love children"? Or is it because "Mother always told me I was good with children, and would make a wonderful teacher!" Or possibly because you want to be a teacher but can't see yourself teaching high school, where the "students are bigger than I am!" Or, because "I'm not good at math, science, and some of the other subjects, and in teaching young children I won't need to know all that stuff."

IS LOVE ALL YOU NEED?

Is it true that *all you need is love* to teach and care for young children? Do you picture yourself (if you are a woman) as being like the character Maria in the Sound of Music, tra-la-la-ing through the mountains with a brood of melodious children trailing behind you? The children are only slightly mischievous and, as "Maria," you know just the right song to sing at the right moment to comfort and calm them, winning their loyalty and cooperation. If you're a man, do you see yourself as a sensitive, controlled, caring "Mister Rogers," with cardigan, soft-soled shoes, and a smile? Or do you perhaps identify with

1

the jolly Captain Kangaroo, always ready to produce from a pouch items that will fascinate an audience of youngsters?

All we need is love?! Can you love Linda, who sucks two fingers constantly and eats crayons, producing a "rainbow of colored teeth"? Will you want to cuddle her on your lap late on a hot Monday morning, when a lax schedule of home hygiene becomes painfully apparent, forcing you to breathe through your handkerchief? Can you *love* Linda?

How about Oliver, who, for no apparent reason, turns on and viciously bites Andy's arm, leaving a set of bluish teeth marks? Andy's mother is president of the school parent group, and always has a plethora of "helpful" ideas for running your classroom.

No, unhappily, love is *not* enough; but it is a beginning. The love and affection that we give as teachers of young children are perhaps the most important part of what we do, and the love we receive in return is one of the greatest rewards of our profession.

Product vs. Process Love

We can think about love as being of two types: "product" love and "process" love. Product love is primarily a love that stems from the child's fulfilling a role defined by the teacher: "Oh, Carol, what a beautiful painting you have made me." "Come, Janie, you may sit on my lap because you have been my best little girl this morning." Product love requires children to "produce" for the teacher (Dreikurs, 1964). The classroom is the teacher's domain and kingdom, and the children are the subjects, performing for the teacher's pleasure. The unfortunate result of product love is that children learn helplessness and dependency.

The second characteristic of product love is the expectation that children behave as miniature adults:

As the sky darkens overhead and thunder crackles, Kathy's teacher orders the entire class inside; but Kathy, engrossed in her sandbox play, refuses to comply. So the teacher picks her up and carries her, protesting and wriggling, into the classroom.

Kathy: "I hate you—I hate you Mrs. Anderson! You are the meanest teacher in this whole school! No one likes you!"
Mrs. Anderson: "No, I will not have you talking to me that way, young lady. We will not have discourtesy in my classroom. You go immediately to the time-out chair and stay until I tell you that you may get up."

Thus, in the product-love classroom children such as four-year-old Kathy are expected to behave in certain ways, expected to "know how to act"; certainly their parents should have taught them how to behave toward adults.

Kathy is expected to follow the rules in the "kingdom," showing courtesy and deference to the sovereign teacher.

Process love is different. Here's how a teacher would express process love when confronted with the above situation:

Kathy: "I hate you—I hate you Mrs. Anderson. You are the meanest teacher in this whole school. No one likes you!"

Mrs. Anderson: "Sometimes I must ask you to do things that you do not want to do—and that makes you angry. It's OK to be angry. I still like you. Maybe tomorrow or the next day we may be friends again."

Thus, process love sees children not as finished products, but as constantly changing and growing. With process love children do not have to behave or act to please the kingly or queenly teacher and win favor. Process love holds that today the young child is like this, but tomorrow, with support, she will grow, and her daily progress will add up to real maturity and competence. In the child-centered kingdom of process love, performance-based praise and punishment have been banished.

Does your "I love little children" really mean "I love to be loved by little children"? If so, you will be disappointed! You may be looking for a classroom kingdom where you will reign; but little children do not make good subjects. You might try to maintain order by dispensing large quantities of praise and punishment, but in the end little love would be found.

You might think now about the type of love that motivates you to become a teacher of young children. Spend some time in a daycare or preschool center! Get there early and stay late. Go for three or four days in a row so that you can feel the amount of energy it takes to work in the "real world." Find a child who, like Kathy, appears difficult to handle. Watch her closely. How do you feel toward her? What type of love do you have for her—product love or process love?

My Mother Told Me That . . .

Not only are the young children that you will soon teach growing, developing, and changing, but so are you. Whether you are an undergraduate at 19, 20, or 21 years of age, or a person seeking a career change, you are still developing and changing (Chickering, 1975; Gould, 1978; Havighurst, 1976; Levinson, 1979).

In this period of your life you are making some critical decisions about your future: whether to go to college, which profession to choose, whom to marry, etc. How do you make these decisions? Does your brain act like a computer that whirls and clicks and finally spits out the "correct" answer? Actually, logic plays only a part in the process of making big decisions. Such decisions are made also in part through our dreams!

In the quiet of the night as we sleep, we "live" out dreams in which we see ourselves being successful (or unsuccessful if it is a nightmare) in a profession or in other aspects of life. We may see ourselves as a teacher, a parent, a secret agent, an arbitrager.

Where do these dreams come from? Sometimes they develop from the perceptions and expectations of our parents and other adults who may have told us, "You would make a wonderful teacher," or "You'll make someone a good husband (or wife)." They may come indirectly by seeing others in roles that we admire and respect: "Mr. Thompson, the teacher who truly knew me, would take the extra time to explain the answer in the way that only he could. I'd like to become like Mr. Thompson!"

These dreams, these subconscious impressions, weigh powerfully on our decisions, big and little (what courses to take, what people to date, what career and other interests to pursue, whether to marry). In fact, the major task in deciding on a career is to determine whether the dreams one is following are one's own or those of someone else (Erikson, 1950).

A parent may transfer his own dream to his child; for example, the father who dreamed of learning to play the piano asserts: "My child is going to have the opportunity to take piano lessons, something I never had!" He buys the Steinway and pays for the lessons, and then awaits the unfolding of the musician. Unfortunately, the child may despise the Steinway, preferring to blow on Uncle Ike's old tuba, or to shatter the family's nerves with a set of drums.

Deciding what dream is really your dream and what dreams belong to others is crucial. Getting up each morning to face your choices will be your responsibility. If you follow someone else's dream, you may end up thinking, "Maybe Mother, who "loves" little children so much, should be here wiping their noses. *I* don't like this!"

How can you decide if it truly is your dream to become a teacher? The acid test is "time in the saddle!" Just as people can tell you how much you would enjoy riding horses and describe in glowing terms how beautiful and loving horses are, to decide for yourself whether you want to ride, you must have firsthand experience. You must get on and ride. In a few minutes, you will either feel a joy in cantering along on the back of the powerful beast, or you will think, "If I ever get down from here alive I will never get on another horse as long as I live!"

It is hoped that your introductory early childhood education class will provide opportunities to work directly with young children full time in real day-care or school situations. If not, don't wait! Volunteering part time in a classroom, teaching Sunday school classes, or babysitting *do not* give you a real idea of what full-time teaching is!

After your "in the saddle" experience, spend time "dreaming" or thinking about your reactions and feelings. Talk to experienced teachers, express your feelings to them and see if they have thought and felt as you do. If you should decide that the dream of becoming an early childhood teacher is not yours, that you prefer to follow another dream, you might feel a bit guilty at first, but this is not a sign of failure—it is a sign of growth. To find your own fulfillment in life, you must reject those roles which don't really seem to fit, and find the ones which do.

Fortunately, some of us do truly believe that the dream of teaching young children is ours. We find Kathy standing before the easel using the long brush covered with paint to "stab" other children as they pass by, and we move close to her: "Paints are exciting to use! What will you make next in your painting?" And, if need be, "Keep the paint on the paper!" We tell the child what *to do*, not what not to do. We have discovered that we can, without using manipulative praise or punishment, guide Kathy to take one more step toward mature behavior. If you become a teacher, you will have found a professional home which will enable you to find excitement, joy, and even love in nourishing those seeds of goodness and talent that children have inside them. Welcome to *teacherhood*!

I'm not good at——, and early childhood teachers don't need to know all that stuff!

The public (and possibly you) are burdened with many educational "myths." For example, a father, having introduced his son to his co-workers, proudly announced, "My son is going to be a teacher!" "Oh, what grade?" one of the co-workers questioned with a smile. "Kindergarten!" he responded. "Kindergarten?" echoed the co-worker, whose smiling face had taken on a look of wrinkled confusion, "Kindergarten? Well, I guess you have to start out somewhere; maybe after you learn more you will be able to move up to high school." Bizarre thinking? Yes, but not uncommon! The public has a host of such mistaken ideas which they hold as absolute truths: "*I* know about teaching and schools. After all, I spent 12 or 13 years of my life there. I know what they are like."

In certain areas early childhood teachers need to know much more than high school teachers. A high school teacher might be hard-pressed to respond to students who ask, "Why does the moon follow me everywhere I go? Where does my poopie go when we flush the toilet? Why does big people's breath stink? What is this rock (or insect) that I found on the playground?" The Early Childhood Education (ECE) teacher needs a whole smorgasbord of knowledge of the so-called solid-content areas of science, such as biology, chemistry, physics, and mathematics.

Usually, the young children's curriculum will not be in the student's textbook, or in the teacher's manual. It will come from real life experiences—digging in the ground, rooting through leaves, rocks, or even waste materials. In these ways children make discoveries and ask questions which would challenge a Rousseau or an Einstein. Early Childhood Education teachers must have a scientific knowledge of how children think and feel, along with a real understanding of the physical and biological world around us.

Children are dramatists and musicians; we will need literature and the classics. They are scientists and mathematicians, wondering about, ordering, seriating, and classifying their world; their teachers need science and mathematics. We begin to see that, unlike the high school teacher who knows much about a narrow subject or field, we must have a great deal of knowledge about nearly everything! Quite a requirement, isn't it?

WHAT ARE EARLY CHILDHOOD EDUCATORS GENERALLY LIKE?

Although there is no mold for early childhood educators, researchers in the field of vocational planning have found some characteristics which childhood educators generally share. "The Occupations Finder," developed by John L. Holland, lists the field of early childhood education under the heading **Social-Artistic-and-Enterprising** occupations. **Social** competencies include the following: ability to explain things, ability to entertain others, ability to work well with others, participation in charity events, ability to teach children, ability to judge personalities well, experience volunteering or helping others in need. The social personality likes many of the following activities: writing to friends, attending church or synagogue, social clubs and meetings, going to parties, dances, and sports events, making new friends, and helping friends with problems.

Artistic competencies include: ability to play a musical instrument, sing, or dance, ability to act or do interpretive reading, ability to draw, paint, or sculpt, ability to design clothes or environments, and ability to write. Activities which the artistic personality enjoy include: reading books and plays, attending plays and concerts, playing musical instruments, arts and crafts, photography, and writing poetry or prose.

The **enterprising** characteristics include: having been elected to an office in school, high energy level, persuasiveness, salesmanship, experience in organizing groups, having been a leader for others, ability to debate. The enterprising person enjoys: selling things, influencing others, participating in politics, giving talks, serving as an officer or leader of a group, supervising others, and meeting important people.

Now, no one person is a composite of all these characteristics, but if you find yourself identifying with many of them, you will probably fit in well with other early childhood educators. For a more thorough exploration, contact your college's career counseling center, and seek an assessment measure, such as Holland's *The Self Directed Search*.

BEYOND THE CLASSROOM

Although some gifted teachers spend their lives guiding children's growth and development, many persons in this era change jobs and careers several times. Training in education is often a door opener. A professional educator has experience in planning, organizing, writing, evaluating, interpersonal relations, management skills, and counseling, as well as basic teaching and training abilities.

Preschools, daycare centers, and public school early childhood programs are just a few choices. A career path in early childhood could include administration, state programs, or community college-university early education. In addition, ECE training and experience can qualify a person for options in business or government, or in self-employment.

Activities   *Activities to evaluate your career choice*
1. Write a diary. Include as many activities, competencies, and experiences as you can remember, from as far back as you can remember. When you are finished, go back and make lists of these experiences in two columns.

    List 1: Items I would definitely like in a career

    List 2: Items I would definitely not like in a career

2. List at least five occupations you have considered when daydreaming about your future. List the pros and cons of each. Number them in reverse chronological order, with the most recent daydream first.

3. Interview an early childhood educator who has worked in the field for at least five years. Some questions to include:

    —What has been most rewarding?

    —What has been most difficult?

    —What would you change or do differently?

    —What are your future career plans and why?

    —What influenced you to choose ECE?

4. Remember those teachers who taught you. List your two most favorite, and your two least favorite. List the positive and negative qualities of each.

Books About Jobs, Work, And Careers
BEST, F., ed., *The Future of Work*. Englewood Cliffs, N.J.: Prentice-Hall, 1973. Describes the growth and decline in future kinds of jobs.

BOLLES, R.N., *What Color Is Your Parachute?* Berkeley, Calif.: Ten Speed Press, 1976. A do-it-yourself guide for job hunters or career changers.

CAMPBELL, D., *If You Don't Know Where You're Going, You'll Probably End up Somewhere Else.* Niles, Illinois: Argus Communications, 1974. A self-help book on planning a career.
DREIKURS, RUDOLF, *Children: The Challenge.* New York: Hawthorn Books, 1963.
HOLLAND, J.L., *Making Vocational Choices: A Theory of Careers.* Englewood Cliffs, N.J.: Prentice-Hall, 1973. Gives a description of personality types and attempts to help the reader compare these types to job decisions.

References

CHICKERING, ARTHUR W., *Education and Identity.* San Francisco: Jossey-Bass, 1975.
ERIKSON, ERIK H., *Childhood and Society.* New York: Norton, 1950.
GOULD, ROGER, *Transformations: Growth and Change in Adult Life.* New York: Simon & Schuster, 1978.
HAVIGHURST, ROBERT J., *Developmental Tasks and Education.* New York: David McKay, 1976.
LEVINSON, DANIEL J., *The Seasons of a Man's Life.* New York: Alfred A. Knopf, 1978.

CHAPTER TWO

THEORIES AND MODELS FOR TEACHING: WHAT GOOD ARE THEY?

Once you decide that you do want to become an early childhood teacher, you must decide just what kind of early childhood teacher you want to be. Let's visualize two different types of early childhood classrooms. In one classroom we see a teacher seated on a chair at the front of the room, with a half circle of young children seated around her. Other children are quietly working in a row of desks.

"Class, today we are going to learn the number THREE. (Teacher holds up a card with the numeral 3 on it.)

"Class, could you say three? (Teacher points to card.)

"Say, three!" (Children respond in unison—"three.")

"Now, class, on this card are three baby kittens. Count them with me, please. Ready—one, two, and three." (Teacher points to each kitten, and children respond in unison.)

"Now, here is another card with balloons on it, how many balloons are there, class?" (Children in unison respond, "three.")

"Yes, there are three! Count with me, 'One, two, three." (Children do as asked.)

(Teacher repeats this with cards containing ships, dogs, horses, and rabbits. Teacher then selects four cards containing six cats, one dog, two rabbits, and three bears.)

"Now, look carefully, I am going to ask one of you to come up and pick the card that has three animals on it. Look carefully. . . . Johnny, come up and pick the card that has three animals on it."

FIGURE 2.1   Direct Instruction Lesson

"Good, Johnny, you have picked the card with three bears; please use your finger and count them out loud for us." (Johnny points and says—"One, two, three.")

"Good boy, Johnny. Class, count with Johnny as he points to each bear. Ready, class, one, two, three. (Class responds.)

(Teacher scatters 10 pencils over the top of a small table in front of the children.)

"Now, watch closely. I am going to ask one of you to come up and pick out three pencils. Ready, Carol." (Carol selects three pencils, and the teacher turns her to face the class.)

"Count them out loud to us, Carol." (Carol responds as directed.)

(Teacher repeats this sequence with care to enable each child to stand up and select.)

"Class, now you count out loud with Carol as she holds up each pencil. Ready, one, two, three." (Class responds.)

(Teacher repeats this sequence, changing the items each time and permitting each to stand up and select.)

"Now, open your workbooks and use your pencil, mark an X over three flowers in the first question." (Teacher points at the row of four boxes available, and places an X over the correct box. She then checks to see that all children have done the same.)

"Let's do a second one." (Repeat with item 2.)

"Now, I want you to return to your seat and work on this page doing the problems. Remember, put X on those that have three things in the box." (Children scatter to their seats.)

Now, let's look at a very different classroom, where at first we are disoriented. We have just come from an orderly, arranged classroom, whereas the room we're now surveying seems to be almost chaotic. At first we can't even see the teacher, and it is difficult to determine what is the front or back of the classroom. What we do see is many children involved in block building, painting, "reading" books, looking at the fish in the aquarium, and a host of similar activities. Finally, we see the teacher sitting with a group of five children. The children are "playing" store, while the teacher appears to be merely watching.

First child (as she balances precariously in a pair of woman's high-heeled shoes, straightens her "wedding gown," and pillbox hat): "I want to buy three cans of soup, two boxes of cereal, and bananas."

"Storekeeper" (fingering the keys on his toy cash register): "That is three dollars—pay me three dollars."

First child (rummages through her patent leather purse, produces a fistful of play "dollars." There are ones, fives, and tens. She holds out a five.)

Second child (after waiting "patiently" in line to pay for his groceries): "No, that's not right, that's not right, that is five, five dollars. Give three, give three."

First child: "This is my money! Don't touch my money!"

"Storekeeper": "Hurry up, Janie, give me three dollars."

Second and third child: "Hurry up, Dummy."

(Teacher leans forward and speaks.)

Teacher: "Janie, you are selecting three dollars from your money to pay." (Janie puts down her purse and spreads her money on the "counter.")

Teacher: "What number is on these dollars, Janie?"

Janie: "Ten!"

Teacher: "What number is on these dollars?"

Janie: "Five."

Teacher: "And these?"

Janie: "One."

Teacher (as all children focus closely to watch): "Let's count out three. Ready?"

(Teacher points to each "dollar" and children respond in unison): "One, two, three."

Janie: "Here is three dollars." (She hands the bills to the "storekeeper," throws her groceries into her shopping cart, and with great "airs" pushes off to her "home.")

(Later, we see Janie setting the table for "three" people, making a block arrangement with series of three blocks, and finally, in her painting, making three "boats.")

FIGURE 2.2   "Looking On" at Dress Store Play

TABLE 2.1   Child- vs. Teacher-Centered Models

CHILD-CENTERED	TEACHER-CENTERED
Developmentally oriented	Behaviorally oriented
Play oriented	Skill oriented
Process based	Content based
Open	Structured

In these very different classrooms, which teacher is using the correct approach? In order to think and talk about these two classrooms, we need labels. Classroom 1 can be thought of as a teacher-centered model, while we may call classroom 2 a child-centered model (see Table 2.1).

There are many different educational "models," or programs that have very specific philosophies about how children learn, very specific ways of teaching, and very specific types of learning materials. You may have read of such models as the Bank Street model, the Montessori model, the Distar model, the British Informal model, Weikart's cognitive model, and others; but for the moment let's consider the teacher-centered model and the child-centered model as two opposites on a continuum. Other "educationese" that is important for you to know can be clustered under these two labels—child-centered and teacher-centered.

The child-centered models are generally based on the writings of the psychologists Jean Piaget (1960 and 1962), Erik Erikson (1950), and Susan Isaacs (1963 and 1968), while the teacher-centered models are based on the theories of B.F. Skinner (1956, 1962, and 1968) and other behaviorists. You may remember Piaget, Erikson, and Skinner from Psych. 101. You probably stayed up all night trying to memorize their theories so you could pass that test. Well, they're back to haunt you: you'll need those theories in teaching young children.

What good are theories? Consider an everyday situation which illustrates the usefulness of "theory." Tuesday morning your alarm fails to go off, and you have an 8:00 A.M. class in which a major test is to be given. You turn the car key but nothing happens. You open the hood and peer down thoughtfully on the engine—but unhappily admit to yourself that you don't know what in the world you're looking at! You're hapless and helpless *because you've got no theory!* No theory to tell you how the fuel system works, no theory to explain the electrical system, and most important, no theory about how all the systems work together. You are beginning to have doubts about whether buying the Mercedes was wise—shouldn't you have taken the Maserati instead? Solution—slam the hood shut, kick the tires, call the professional, and sell your stereo or take out another loan to pay the bill you are about to get.

Now, in order to be able to teach young children, one must have expertise—be a professional—as well. For instance, when Carol knocks over Jim's block tower, Jim kicks Billy, Billy grabs the paint brush from Sally, and Sally throws up ... things are not going well, and *something* must be done! We need someone who understands the theories about young children's socialization, about aggression, about how young children learn. A teacher who doesn't understand them will feel just like the non-mechanic in our example—lost and helpless.

In dealing with theories which might be helpful to us as teachers, we must first realize that the authors of these theories see growth and development in very different ways. On one side are those psychologists who believe primarily in using the techniques of behavior modification. On the other side are those broadly known as developmental psychologists. Table 1 depicts the former as teacher-centered and the latter as child-centered.

The opponents of behavior modification call it the "hoop-jump-biscuit" theory:

> As students see it, schools require them to play a game, which John Holt, in his provocative book Freedom and Beyond, calls the 'hoop-jump-biscuit' game. Teachers hold up a hoop and say 'Jump.' Again, another biscuit if they make it. Raise the hoop still higher, and another biscuit if they make it, and so on.
>
> This is not only the way most schools try to get students to perform, but it is commonly accepted in our society as 'the way it's s'posed to be.' Schools reflect the traditional ways of thinking in the society. Using rewards to motivate students to learn what some teacher or principal or school board or state has decided would be best for them to learn is deeply ingrained, both in teachers and in the other adults in our society. After all, it is the same game they had to play when they were in school, and the game their parents had to play, and their parents' parents. What other way is there? Why change? (Gordon 1974, pp. 11-12)

What is it that would get someone so worked up as to hurl insults at the "hoop-jump-biscuit" theory? Maybe the fact that the early research from which the "behavioral" theories were developed was done on dogs, rats, and pigeons. However, before we relegate behavioral methods to the local pet store operator, let's closely examine the background and findings of the behaviorists.

THE BEHAVIORAL POSITION

The idea of using behavior modification techniques originated with the experimental work of Pavlov with his famous (or infamous) salivating dogs. Over a period of time he consistently had a bell rung just as the dogs were about to be fed. Eventually, he found, when the bell rang, even in the absence of food, the dogs began to salivate! They were "conditioned" to salivate at the sound of a bell. Through this somewhat fractured version of Pavlov's experiments, we can see that his point was that animal behavior can be explained in terms of stimulus and response; thus, an animal's actions can be traced to an occurrence in the animal's environment.

B. F. Skinner (1956), the experimental psychologist, philosopher, and Utopian visionary, is now the recognized leader of the behaviorist movement. He, more than any other, took the stimulus-response theory of Pavlov, verified it with experiments on other animals (pigeons and mice), and applied it to the human condition. All human behaviors can be explained as responses modified by the stimuli (such as praise or disapproval) that follow them. The behaviorist position does not acknowledge an inner rational person. Any student who behaves rationally does so because of adults who have rewarded rational behavior and ignored (or punished) irrational action.

THE DEVELOPMENTAL POSITION

Developmental psychologists see the child motivated from birth by his own internal drive to become competent. Watching the year-old child learning to walk, we see him, with much effort, pull himself upright using a chair. No sooner is he up than he falls with a thud, his face showing his discomfort. The struggle for competence at walking continues as, little daunted by repeated falls, the child makes herculean efforts to get up and stay up. There is an inner drive, an intrinsic motivation that pushes him on until one day he stands upright and walks! Where does he go? Nowhere! This movement happens for the sheer joy in being able to move. This "competency motivation" idea has led the child-centered early childhood educators to come to respect the inner processes of young children and to attempt to "go with the flow," creating environments with a wide variety of materials and equipment to enable children to learn, at their own speeds, and with guidance from teachers, by challenging themselves and by doing.

Developmental psychologists have attempted to discover the patterns and sequential stages of behavior produced from this inner drive in the domains of cognitive, social, emotional, and physical growth. With this knowledge we may create play-based learning environments for young children, which support and encourage the self-initiated activities of children.

THE USEFULNESS OF THEORIES

The professional needs psychological theories of children's behavior to understand human and classroom dynamics, and to be able to decide what teacher actions are needed. Theoretical knowledge helps us to keep our classroom activities purposefully humming along, whether through direct teaching (as in the numeral "three" example) or in the child-centered classroom (where children may learn the concept of "three" in dramatic play, block building, and the like).

We have stated that behaviorists (whose theories underlie directive-instruction) and developmentalists (whose theories underlie child-Centered Teaching) differ dramatically in how they view growth and development, which leaves us, as practicing teachers, feeling confused. Which theories should we follow?

The School for Young Children maintains that both theories can contribute to the teacher's "getting the Mercedes running," and that therefore we can make use of both. But, as more and more programs nationwide are started for young children, especially in public school, the direct instruction strategies traditionally found in elementary school are simply being moved down into the kindergarten and programs for children aged 3 and 4. It doesn't take a child psychologist to understand that the direct-instruction methods will not be generally applicable with the young child. Young children have a limited attention span, and a direct teaching program would place him under great pressure and stress. Let's look at these two methods in more detail.

Teaching Method 1: Play-Activity

The play-activity method of teaching permits young children the freedom to act on their own ideas—they originate the ideas and they initiate the action. Thus, from the children comes the *curriculum*.

Remember our opening example, in which we discover the children "playing" store while the teacher appears to be passively watching.

First child (as she balances precariously in a pair of woman's high heel shoes, straightens her "wedding gown" and pillbox hat): " I want to buy three cans of soup, two boxes of cereal, and bananas."
"Storekeeper" (fingering the keys on his toy cash register): "That is three dollars—pay me three dollars."
(First child rummages through her patent leather purse, produces a fistful of play "dollars." There are ones, fives, and tens. She holds out a five.)
(Later, we see Janie, the first child, setting the table for "three" people, making a block arrangement with a set of three blocks, and finally, in her paint she makes three "boats.")

Make-believe dress-up play, block building, painting, and similar activities originate with the children, and constitute a play-activity curriculum. The teacher's method looks passive (just "life-guarding") at first, but we later see her making nondirective statements (I see that your money has fives, threes, and ones); directive statements (put this dollar down and count these); and modeling (let me show you this). The most important aspect of the play-based method is the child's total freedom to initiate play; thus it is found along the "child-centered" end of the continuum.

Advocates of the play-activity curriculum see the needs of the developing child as unique to each individual. Thus the child's self-initiated ideas are most valued. The goals are related to developmental theory, and are longer-term in nature than those of the direct-instruction curriculum. Newborns arrive nearly helpless into this world, but by age three they can express their needs through language, solve simple problems, and physically move themselves about. The child-based curriculum aims to facilitate the growth of these adaptive abilities.

Teaching Method 2: Direct-Instruction

Let's review our beginning example of directive-instruction:

"Class, today, we are going to learn the number 3. (Teacher holds up a card with the numeral 3 on it.)
"Class, could you say 'THREE'? (Teacher points to card.)
"Say, 'THREE'!" (Children respond in unison—"THREE")
(Teacher now selects four cards containing six cats, one dog, two rabbits, and three bears.)
"Now, look carefully. I am going to ask one of you to come up and pick the card that has three animals on it. Look carefully."
"Johnny, come up and pick the card that has three animals on it."

This example demonstrates direct-instruction teaching, through which the instructor requires the students to perform in a certain way and then evaluates the performances. The general procedure for this direct teaching is Show, Say, and Check:

Show: "Children this is a three!"
Say: "Class say 'three'."
Check: "Pick out the card which has three animals on it."

TEACHING CHARACTERISTICS

The continuum below presents the two methods, play-activity and direct instruction, that have been discussed as they relate to various model characteristics.

As Table 2.2 shows, the goals of a direct-instruction curriculum are narrow, relating to a specific behavioral or motor action that the child will be able to perform once a task is taught effectively: "At the end of the lesson, the child will be able to verbally label numerals 1 to 5." With this method the skill

TABLE 2.2   Teaching Characteristics

PLAY-ACTIVITY	DIRECT-INSTRUCTION
CHILD-DIRECTED	TEACHER-DIRECTED
Time, Space, and Materials Free to use.	Teacher determines.
Teacher's Role Follow child's lead and interest. Clarify experiences. Aide, resource to child.	Direct, initiate, evaluate, determine, and redetermine child's performance.
Instructional Framework Activity oriented: experiments, explores, questions.	Step-by-step sequence based on preplanned goals.
Motivation Intrinsic desire to learn.	External, tangible rewards.
Concept of Learning Direct experience with knowledge used to accomplish play or real functional task.	Drill in practice repetition for skill.
Individual vs. Group Focus Individual child's needs.	Group needs as a whole. Ability grouping.
Methodology Maximum freedom to use teacher intuition, feelings, judgment.	Defined by model.

to be learned is decided first (usually related to beginning reading, math, language, and motor skills) and is then sequentially presented to the child. Thus, the skills are externally determined and presented and the child gradually internalizes the new learning with practice. The student's time and focus are controlled with the use of reinforcement (rewards), and the same concepts are taught to an entire group of children (usually placed according to ability).

DEVELOPMENTALLY APPROPRIATE PRACTICE

If you are wondering which method of teaching is best, direct instruction or play-activity based, you are not alone. Nationally, schools, school agencies, and governmental agencies that set policy for educational programs for young children are all attempting to answer this question. One stab at answering the question is to change it slightly and ask, "Which methods are developmentally appropriate practice in early childhood programs serving children from 3 to 7 years of age?"

In 1986 the National Association for the Education of Young Children (NAEYC) published the findings of a commission that involved hundreds of early childhood educational experts to answer the question as to what is developmentally appropriate. Their second report asserts the following:

> "In recent years, a trend toward increased emphasis on formal instruction in academic skills has emerged in early childhood programs. This trend towards formal academic instruction for younger children is based on misconcepts about early learning (Elkind, 1986). Despite the trend among some educators to formalize instruction, there has been no comparable evidence of change in what young children need for optimal development or how they learn. In fact, a growing body of research has emerged recently affirming that children learn most effectively through a concrete, play-oriented approach to early childhood education." (Bredekamp, 1987, p.1)

In keeping with developmentally appropriate goals the NAEYC guidelines, the chapters that follow show the beginning teacher, or the mature teacher with a limited understanding of *young* children, how to go about creating developmentally appropriate practices based on play, and concrete activities by (1) defining a play-activity curriculum, (2) detailing how to set up classrooms and classroom procedures, (3) describing methods of how to teach, (4) offering suggestions on relating to parents, and finally, (5) explaining how to evaluate learning in a play-based curriculum.

Even when there is an agreement on what is developmentally appropriate and that play-activities are the central method of learning for young children, early childhood teachers will vary dramatically as they set out to implement a play curriculum. They will differ on what is put into the classrooms, on materials arrangement, on how discipline is done, and on a multitude of other practical decisions. Here, we boldly set forth in great detail what a classroom teacher would need if she or he were hired in August by the School for Young Children to begin teaching in September. The chapters that follow are practical procedures and techniques for helping such a teacher get started and run a developmentally appropriate classroom. No time is taken to debate a wide variety of methods, which might be equally effective and appropriate. This book guides the teacher practitioner on one successful approach to providing best practices; once the teacher is "up and running," other individual, creative differences may be added. We believe the SYC model that follows provides fundamental guidelines for good developmental practices.

Activities

1. Visit two classrooms for three-, four-, or five-year-old children, and observe the (1) teacher's use of time, space, and objects, (2) teacher's

role, (3) instructional framework, (4) motivation, (5) concept of learning, (6) individual vs. group focus, and (7) methodology. Rank each of the classrooms on the two methodologies: play-activity or direct-instruction models.

2. In a small group of teachers share your feelings. Do you feel strongly that one model is best? Why? Which model is more widely used in daycare? Public school? Church schools? Private preschools? Handicapped programs for young children? At-risk programs? Head Starts? Why?

3. In a small group of teachers define why they chose to teach as they did (direct vs. play-activity instruction). Use value-clarification questions such as the following (Raths, 1966) to think through your attitudes or values:

   Choosing freely: Where do you suppose you first got these ideas? Is there rebellion in your position?

   Choosing from alternatives: Did you consider another alternative?

   Choosing thoughtfully and reflectively: What are the consequences for the children who will be in your class based on your position? Will all children fit into your orientation?

   Prizing and cherishing: Are you proud that you view learning and children in this manner? Is it clear that those in teaching authority have a different philosophy from you?

   Affirming: Would you be comfortable telling other teachers how you feel?

   Acting upon choices: What actions would you take to do your best within the frame of your preferred model?

   Repeating: Do you think your courses in early childhood have been worth the time and effort in working toward your teaching goals? Will you continue?

References

BREDEKAMP, SUE, ed., *Developmentally Appropriate Practice in Early Childhood Programs Serving Children from Birth Through Age 8*. Washington, D.C.: NAEYC, 1987.

ELKIND, DAVID, "Formal Education and Early Childhood Education: An Essential Difference," *Phi Delta Kappan*, May 1986, pp. 631-36.

ERIKSON, ERIK H., *Childhood and Society*. New York: Norton, 1950.

GORDON, THOMAS, *T.E.T.: Teacher Effectiveness Training*. New York: David McKay, 1974.

ISAACS, SUSAN, *Intellectual Growth in Young Children*. New York: Schocken Books, 1968.

PIAGET, JEAN, *The Psychology of Intelligence*. N.J.: Littlefield, Adams, 1960.

——, *The Origins of Intelligence in Children*. New York: Norton, 1962.

——, *Play, Dreams, and Imitation in Childhood*. New York: Norton, 1962.

RATHS, LOUIS E., Merrill Harman, and Sidney B. Simon, *Values and Teaching: Working with Values in the Classroom*. Columbus, Ohio: Charles E. Merrill, 1966.

SKINNER, B.F., *The Science of Human Behavior*. New York: Macmillan, 1956.

WOLFGANG, C.H., B. Mackender, and M. E. Wolfgang, *Growing and Learning Through Play*. Paoli, Penna.: Instructo/McGraw-Hill, 1981.

CHAPTER THREE

UNDERSTANDING THE YOUNG CHILD'S PLAY

Play-activity learning is basically a child-initiated play curriculum, permitting the young child to select from a well-chosen variety of play materials. These would include clay, paint, drawing materials, blocks, puzzles, and make-believe or socio-dramatic play materials. The role of the teacher is to design a well-balanced play area, evaluate the level of play of each child, and use methods and techniques to promote the play to more advanced levels. The Chapter 2 example of "playing store" demonstrates the play-activity curriculum. Following is a case for the value of children's play, a thorough description of young children's development, and instruction on how to apply theory to real life.

"Wait just a minute! Play? What's this play stuff? I'm interested in being a *teacher* of 3- to 6-year-olds, not in letting these kids waste their time by playing all day. They can do that at home. . . ." Often, parents and elementary teachers express similar thoughts: "You're 'ripping off' those children. All they are doing is playing all day! When are they going to learn something?"

In a competitive, upwardly mobile society where all parents expect the best for their children (and the best is often interpreted as "my child must be first . . . , competitive . . . , able to do better than others"), we have the expectant father reading to his unborn prodigy so that the newborn will be ready to read sooner than any of his peers on the block; we have the preschool teacher's recommendation that the slow-to-develop child stay another year in the 4-year-old class before entering public school kindergarten met with the parent's objection: "But he will be later in taking the qualifying exams for med-school."

In such a society, play is held by most of the public and many educators as not only the most useless of activities, but as even sinful. The myth that "idle hands do the devil's work" is a hard one to slay. Perhaps the public will never understand the value of play, but what about you? Do you yourself question its value?

Think again of the two classrooms described in the previous chapter, where the concept of "three" was being taught. The direct-instruction model is probably familiar to you; this is the way you were most likely taught during most of your schooling. We tend to teach the way we were taught, and if we put you in a classroom for young children tomorrow you most likely would put on the familiar, teacher-directed shoes and proceed in the manner in which you were taught.

I had taught for many years in an elementary school, junior high school, and boarding high school, and had been an elementary principal, when I decided to return to graduate school to study early childhood education and child development. The very first day my professor sent me out to the playground to observe and I found five 3-year-olds "playing." Having just come from working with older students, I wondered how I would even be able to talk to these small creatures. I soon found out, when one rode his tricycle up to me and inquired with a smile, "What's your name, Mister?"

"Ha!" I thought, "this is not going to be so hard after all!" I announced in a clear voice, "My name is Mr. Wolfgang," bending over to be sure he heard me, and returned his smile. But suddenly his face went blank and his body froze . . . and then, like a bat-out-of-heck, he jumped from the tricycle screaming, "Wolf! Wolf!" and ran to the other four children to tell them that Little Red Ridinghood's assailant had abandoned the woods for their playground. Quickly they found a branch lying nearby and, using it for a woodcutter's axe, advanced courageously upon the evil wolf, driving him from their sanctuary.

Thus, I quickly learned that the child under six is a very different "breed of cat" from the elementary school student. The assumptions about learning in the elementary school (where I had been using a teacher-centered model) did not necessarily hold for the preschooler.

Now, you can imagine how the "big bad wolf" felt when assured by his professor that it was safe to come out of the storage shed and join not just the "woodcutters" but 15 of their compatriots—in their classroom. What was really terrifying was that I did not find them all safely deposited in chairs or desks, but rather moving about uncontrolled, some in a housekeeping corner playing mommies and daddies, some painting at easels, some building with blocks, and some doing apparently nothing. Good grief, I thought, what if the woodcutters tell the other 15 that the wolf is among them? I might be set upon, my stomach cut open, filled with rocks, and sewed shut!

Joking aside, the experience was disturbing. In a teacher-centered class-room I had been comfortable because I was "the boss" or king in my kingdom. The children were seated and moved only with permission; children were moving about at will, and I was afraid that chaos would erupt at any moment. However, after about 40 minutes I began to realize that no one was in imminent danger, especially me, my heartbeat began to return to normal, and I made it through the morning intact!

THE BASICS OF THE PLAY-ACTIVITY CURRICULUM

In the direct-instruction classroom what is to be learned is clearly defined, a system for teaching is clear, what materials to use and when are specified, and criterion testing is used to indicate what learning has occurred. Historically, this degree of specificity has not been true for play-oriented curricula. "Play" had been difficult to define, and a system for teaching through play was nonexistent; in fact, there were those who believed that adults did not belong in children's self-initiated play.

As play-oriented curricula began to emerge, beginning teachers were trained by working or "apprenticing" with an expert who knew from experi-ence what to do and could ignite others' enthusiasm for similar methods of teaching. However, the limitation of this apprenticeship system was that very few people could be trained at one time. Today there are some publications available which describe this type of teaching, and we hope that what follows will be a complete and useful summary of this method. In the following sections we will (1) define play, (2) demonstrate how play changes as the child develops, and (3) explain the value of play as a process for facilitating the child's emotional, social, intellectual, and physical development.

PLAY: HOW DO WE KNOW IT WHEN WE SEE IT?

Developmental observers have noted four large categories of play: (1) senso-rimotor play, (2) symbolic play, (3) construction, and (4) games with rules. Let's look at each of these forms to learn the subcategories and developmental sequences of each.

Sensorimotor Play

Sensory play.   The infant from birth learns about the world through sen-sory play—tasting, touching, smelling, and hearing. Later, any new play item given to a child three or older is first explored through sensory activities,

FIGURE 3.1 Fluid Construction or Finger Painting

sometimes called 'tooling-up.' For example, when children get fingerpaint for the first time they enjoy smearing it (touch), smelling it, and even sneaking a small taste of it before they begin to make markings or "pictures" in the paint.

FIGURE 3.2 Sensori-Motor Play

Motor play.   Fine-motor activity, the use of fingers and hands to manipulate objects and materials, begins formally with the 8-month-old infant's pincer grasp (use of thumb and forefinger to pick up small objects) and continues to develop into such finger activities as cutting with scissors and holding a crayon or pencil. Plastic manipulative materials such as interlocking blocks are first used in a motoric way and later in more advanced forms of play. Gross motor play (walking, climbing) and the use of the large muscle and skeletal systems begins formally between 10 and 15 months, when children generally learn to stand upright and walk.

The child climbing up and over the climbing frame is deliberately moving his center of gravity and using the muscle system to maintain balance and movement. Simply put, motor play is practicing body skills in a gravitational field (Gerhardt, 1973). With increased abilities the child will learn such physical skills as balance, climbing, and throwing.

It is general agreed that six fundamental motor pattern develop during the early ages and reach maturity and coordination by age five: walking, running, jumping, kicking, throwing, and catching. Table 3.1 summarizes the initial attempts at these skills and the mature levels.

FIGURE 3.3   Micro-symbolic Play

TABLE 3.1   Fundamental Motor Patterns

INITAL	MATURE
Walking	
Short steps.	Increased step lenghth.
Flat-foot contact; knee bent as foot touches ground, then quick knee straightening. Relatively no ankle movement; leg bent excessively.	Heel contacts ground with the knee straight; weight rolls forward so toe pushes, then knee bends as it is lifted off the ground.
Toes point out.	Toes generally point straight ahead.
Feet spread apart wide.	Feet are placed closer together, narrowing the base of support.
Slight spread slightly apart.	Feet are placed closer together, narrowing the base of support.
No hip rotation.	Hip rotates back to the support leg, then forward to the side of the moving leg.
Arms held up with elbows bent for protection against falls (high-guard position).	Arms held straight, swing easily at sides of body.
Running	
Arms held straight, very little movement—mainly to help maintain balance.	Arms bent and swing in diagonal pattern in opposition to the leg action—that is, right arm forward when left leg is forward. Elbow brought up parellel with shoulder.
Short stride.	Increase in stride length.
Slow running speed.	Increase in running speed.
Support leg (back leg) straightens slowly as child takes off.	Support leg pushes off forcefully by straightening behind the buttocks.
No trunk lean.	Slight forward trunk lean.
Leg is bent at low level as it comes forward. Motion of knee is out to the side and then forward.	Knee lifted high as leg comes foward, and the heel of the foot is brought close to the buttocks.
Toes point out.	Toes point forward.
Jumping (vertical)	
Very minimal crouch.	Knees, hips, and ankles bend in crouch in preparation for jumping.
Arms are raised to side as jump starts. Arms may swing out to back if not given target to reach for.	Arms forcefully lift body.
Hips and knees bend in air on takeoff.	Hips, knees, and ankles straighten forcefully as body goes up.
Slight forward lean during pushoff.	Body remains straight until landing, then hips, knees, and ankles bend to absorb the shock.
Stepping or one-foot landing.	Two-foot landing.

Throwing
Stage 1
1. Feet are stationary.
2. Ball is held near ear. Child pushes ball straight down.
3. No rotation of body or step forward.
Stage 2
1. Some body rotation to side opposite throwing arm.

2. Hand holds ball cocked behind the head.
3. No foot movement.
Stage 3
1.Arm and trunk movements are the same as in Stage 2.
2. Child steps forward on foot that is on **same** side of body as throwing arm.
Stage 4: Step-turn-throw
1. As movement is begun, body weight shifts to side with ball.
2. Arm is brought up and back behind head.
3. Weight is transferred by a step to foot that is on the **opposite** side of body from throwing arm.
4. Trunk rotates to opposite side.
5. Ball is released as elbow is straightened with a whipping motion.

Catching
Stage 1
1. Arms are held out straight in front of the body, with palms up.
2. When ball makes contact with arms, elbow bend. Child tries to trap ball against chest. May clap at ball or use hands like vise if ball is small.
3. May turn head to side and lean back.
Stage 2
1. Arms are in front, with elbows slightly bent.
2. As ball approaches, arms encircle it aa chest.
3. Robotlike performance.
Stage 3
1. Arms are bent.
2. Ball bounces on chest, then is controlled with arms.
3. Tries to catch with hands but may resort to using chest.
Stage 4
1. Hands are positioned to intercept ball.
2. Grasps and control ball.
3. Gives way to force of ball by bending at hips and knees.
4. Absorbs force by continuing to move and give way in direction ball came from.

Kicking
Stage 1
1. Kicking leg is straight, moved up, and foward.
2. No accompanying body movement.
Stage 2
1. Lower part of kicking leg is lifted up and behind body to prepare for kick.
Stage 3
1. Upper leg is brought back, with knee bent.
2. Leg swings through greater arc than in stage 2.
3. Some body adjustments.
4. Leg may be overcocked resulting in loss of mechanical advantage.
Stage 4
1. Hip and knee are cocked effectively.
2. Trunk leans backward.
3. Leg moves through greater range of motion.
4. Knee straightens as leg swings through to contact ball.
5. Arm and body adjustments are make during follow-through.
6. Starts farther behind ball and moves total body into it.

Symbolic Play

Symbolic play (Millar, 1968; Piaget, 1962; Weikart, 1971) is fantasy play, whereby the child expresses or represents her ideas with gestures (stirs the batter of a pretend cake), or with objects (uses a block for a walkie-talkie). When this pretending becomes well-developed, the child will play out "stories" with themes, characters, and beginnings and endings. We call this **dramatic play** when it contains these three criteria:

> 1) The child imitates a role.
> 2) The child must sustain the theme for many minutes.
> 3) The child uses gestures and objects or represents imaginary objects or people.

Later, the child develops the ability to play with other children in theater-like make-believe dramas, an advanced form of dramatic play called sociodramatic play (Smilansky, 1968, 1990). In addition to meeting the three criteria of dramatic play, socio-dramatic play must also include these elements:

> 4) The child must interact with others.
> 5) The child must use verbal exchange.

Examine the following examples of sociodramatic play:

Medical World   The playhouse has been moved into the center of the room and arranged so that it can be entered from all four sides. On one side of the playhouse is an imaginary ambulance, complete with a steering-wheel toy, walkie-talkies, and a blanket for a stretcher. On the opposite side is what looks

FIGURE 3.4   Sociodramatic Play

like an operating table. In another part of the room is a combination doctor's office/hospital room with a bathroom scale, a yardstick for measuring height, and a bed with a tray. The play store in the classroom has become a pharmacy. In each of these areas is a doctor's kit and a few pieces of specialized equipment.

Doctor's kits:
-A stethoscope
-Shot needles (made from construction toy sticks)
-A flashlight
-Cotton balls and masking tape (for bandages)
-Tongue depressors
-Medicine bottles

Specialized equipment:
-A rubber knife and large plastic needles (for operations)
-A black box with two tin cans attached to the sides by electrical wire (for starting a heartbeat)
-White jackets, masks, and rubber gloves
-Blankets and towels
-Ace bandages and slings
-Plastic medicine bottles and spoons
-Prescription pads
-A plastic catsup bottle with a hose attached (for giving blood transfusions)

The children fan out quickly across the room and soon are playing in pairs and trios. One child stands on the scale, while a second child administers a shot and dabs the immunized spot with a cotton ball. Another pair is involved in a makeshift operation. The patient lies on the operating table while the doctor pretends to amputate an arm. The doctor presses a flashlight against the arm, makes a buzzing noise and says, "Now I make you a bionic arm." Still another pair is sitting at the steering-wheel toy, pretending to drive somewhere, making siren noises and talking excitedly into their walkie-talkies. The play episodes are short and disjointed.

Two girls approach the doctor's office: "My daughter is sick," the older girl says to the doctor. "I guess she'll have to go to the hospital," the doctor replies, motioning with his arm toward the nearby cot. The mother helps cover up her daughter with a blanket and then watches as the doctor puts his stethoscope on the girl's forehead "She has lots of germs," he advises, "She will have to stay here three weeks." The "sick" girl giggles quietly to herself. In a matter of minutes the three weeks pass, and the mother takes her daughter home. In just a few more minutes she is back with another family member who needs to be hospitalized.

As the family members take turns going to the hospital, a boy rushes into the playhouse, announces loudly that he is dying, and then collapses dramatically on the floor. The teacher directs the attention of the driving pair to this catastrophe: "Hey, ambulance drivers, someone just died over there. Better get him to the doctor." In due course the victim is carried and dragged to the operating table. Several doctors converge on the scene. "What happen to him?" the teacher asks. After some discussion the doctors agree that the boy was shot. "Looks pretty serious," the teacher agrees, as she picks up the empty catsup bottle. "Maybe he needs some more blood." She inverts the bottle and touches the attached tube to the patients's arm. The doctors poke and probe the patient with their operating tools. "I think he's alive now," one of them finally says. "No, I'm still dead," the patient insists. "What do you do with dead people?" the teacher wonders. "Let's throw him in the river," suggests a doctor. Unable to cure the patient, the doctors and ambulance drivers haul him away to the river. But as they struggle to dispose of the corpse, it scrambles back to life and runs away laughing, "I'm OK, I'm OK."

Note: From Don Adcock and Marilyn Segal, *Play Together/Grow Together*. (White Plains, New York: Mailman Family Press, 1983.)

Construction Play

The third form of play (after sensorimotor and symbolic play) is construction. Construction has historically been referred to as "arts and crafts," which includes, among other activities, painting, clay modeling, crayoning,

FIGURE 3.5   Easel Painting or Fluid Construction

and building with blocks and interlocking blocks. Construction play occurs when a child has an idea and represents it through some media (such as paints or clay) to produce a product: Carol paints a "doggie" at her easel; Jim sculpts an elephant out of clay. The child has produced *symbols* to represent these animals (Kellogg, 1970; Millar, 1968; Piaget, 1962); that is, one thing (the child's marks on the paper) stands for another (the real object). These symbols go through a number of developmental stages as the child's intellectual capacity grows. For example, in drawing and painting, the symbols generally develop in the following manner:

 1-2 years: random scribbling. The child uses random scribble marks simple as a sensorimotor activity.

 2-2 1/2 years: controlled scribbling. The child begins to develop some control of his fine motor abilities, and the scribbles gain some direction and control. After some experience with controlled scribbling, you may hear a child name his picture a "motorcycle" or a "big wheel," although there appears to be no resemblance. This is an intellectual accomplishment for the child, an indication that he is taking his first step towards being able to do representation.

 2 1/2-3 years: the face. The next major development is for the circle to become a face.

 3 1/2-4 years: arms and legs. The circle "person" develops stick arms and legs, which protrude from the circle, or the head; there is no body as yet.

 4 years: the body appears. The human figure begins to acquire a body. Gradually, more and more body parts are added (hands, feet, hair, ears, etc.).

 5 years: floating house. First "house" drawings usually resemble a face, with windows placed like eyes and door like a mouth. These first houses are usually somewhere in the middle of the paper and seem to be floating in space.

 5 1/2 - 6 years: house on bottom line. The bottom of the paper is used as a baseline and the house rests on it.

 5 1/2 - 6 years: baseline supports house in drawing. A base line appears within the drawing and the house rests on it.

 6-7 years: two-dimensional drawing. The baseline begins to take on the quality of a horizon, which indicates the child's awareness of two-dimensional space.

The human figure, which evolves into the face-like house, is given as an example above and does appear in the symbolic development of many children. However, each child will express the symbolic objects which are most meaningful for him, and some might not draw the human figure or the house. What is important to understand is that no matter which symbols children draw, they will progress through very similar stages. Therefore, when we, as teachers, keep a record of symbolic development in construction (artwork), we can evaluate each child's progress in representational skill, and we can better facilitate the child's further progress (Goodnow, 1977; Kellogg, 1970).

It is important to save samples of the child's artwork over a period of many weeks. Marked with the date and placed in sequence, they form a record of the child's progress in symbolic representation.

Three-dimensional materials, such as clay, are the objects of a similar line of development (Smilansky, 1988). When children work with clay, expect to see (1) random pounding (sensorimotor play), (2) controlled pounding (sensorimotor), (3) rolling clay into snake-like rolls and later into circles, (4) adding pieces to the rolls and circles (facial features and body parts), and (5) combining products, such as people in cars or a boy on a horse. Development in this three-dimensional artwork could also be shown in the child's chart or in photographs of the three-dimensional products.

Using the above categories of play (Sensorimotor, Symbolic, and Construction), we outline below the types of materials used with these forms of play.*

FORM	MATERIALS
Sensorimotor Play	Slides, tricycles, balls, and similar items.
Symbolic Play	
Microsymbolic Play	Miniature toys (replicas of furniture, people, animals, etc.) and puppets.
Macrosymbolic Play	Child-sized furniture, toy eating utensils and food, dolls, toy telephones, and similar items.
Construction Play	
Construction—Fluid	Clay, easel paints, drawing tools. (Fluid materials have a high sensorimotor quality and easily transform their shape and generally have little or no form.) (Wolfgang, 1977, 1981)
Construction—Structured	Carpentry materials, interlocking blocks, and puzzles. (These structured materials maintain their shape and have a more work-like quality.

*Note: The two common forms of symbolic play materials include toys used for microsymbolic play and macrosymbolic play (Erikson, 1950). Looking at a storybook or reading a book could be viewed as a related form of passive-symbolic play.

GAMES-WITH-RULES

Games-with-rules include baseball, softball, and such board games as "Chutes and Ladders," "Candyland," Monopoly, and checkers. It will be at age 6 or 7, or even later, that the child will be able intellectually to grasp the "point of view" of others. Therefore, games-with-rules should usually not be included as play activities until elementary school (Piaget, 1962; Smilansky, 1990).

THE VALUE OF PLAY

As mother is taking the groceries from the car to the kitchen, the 3-year-old sees the ice cream on top of the grocery.

"Mommy, I want some ice cream!"
"No, not now, dear, you will spoil your appetite for dinner. You may have some for dessert, after dinner!"
"No, Mommy, I want it now!"
"After dinner, dear!"

(The three-year-old screams, "No, now, Mommy" and begins a major temper tantrum). Mother "scoots" the young child outside to her sandbox to play and begins to prepare dinner. At first the child crosses her arms and "pouts;" next, in one last rage she kicks the sand bucket. Then she begins to pick up handfuls of sand and let it slip through her fingers—until she appears to "have an idea." She begins lining up small cups that she has found, carefully forms wet sand into well-shaped balls, and positions a ball on top of each cup (construction play).

Finally, after exhausting her supply of cups and making 15 to 20 sand balls, she carefully leans back to admire her creations. With a giggle (and a sideways glance toward the kitchen window where mother is working) she carefully picks up one of the cups with a sand ball on top and pretends to lick the ball. Right under the eyes of her unsuspecting mother she pretends to devour, in a beginning form of dramatic play, all the ice cream she wants, without concern for ruining her appetite! Later she will set the table for each of the baby dolls and act out the serving of a three-course imaginary dinner (a fully developed form of dramatic play).

Emotional Development

Just what does the above anecdote illustrate? Because of young children's limited language and intellectual abilities, it is difficult for them to deal with frustrating, scary, or stressful experiences—such as "no ice cream until after dinner," or being frightened, or being given an injection by a doctor. It is through symbolic or representational play, including construction, that the child can digest, a little bit at a time, larger emotional experiences which are too hard to "digest" all in "one bite" (Erikson, 1950; Moustakas, 1974; Piller, 1959).

A clear illustration of the emotional value of play can be seen in the experience of a child who visits the doctor's office and gets "shots" from a scary man in white clothing. When the child returns home she retreats to her toys, dresses one of her dolls in white, uses a pencil as a hypodermic needle, and gives the doll-doctor a "shot" with full vengeance. We will see the child playing doctor for the next few weeks until the scary incident becomes emotionally "digested."

In symbolic or fantasy play the child can change from a helpless victim to an aggressor (and get revenge), or she may obtain what she wants in fantasy when she cannot get it in reality (ice cream cones). And after all, don't we do this as adults? Remember, perhaps, the ride home after work, on the day the boss reprimanded you unfairly, when you mentally tongue-lashed him, setting him straight in no uncertain terms? We adults do this emotional self-healing fantasizing in our daydreams, while preschool children "play out" what is bothering them (Peller, 1959). Some parents or other adults who see these sometimes violent themes in the child's play worry that their offspring might be emotionally disturbed. Generally the opposite is true. Symbolic-fantasy play is nature's built-in method of self-healing and it is more likely that the child who *cannot* fantasize or play is not emotionally healthy (Singer, 1973).

Social Development

Children are not born with the ability to be "social." How is it acquired? Some teachers define "being social" as waiting in line to take a turn, or saying "please" and "thank-you." Actually, these are only narrow customs; true social competence involves the ability to "play" a social role.

Let's imagine a three-year-old coming down the preschool hallway wearing a man's hat, a woman's skirt, and carrying a baby bottle. This image symbolizes the pivotal developmental stage of the three-year-old. He is experimenting with the role that he "is not," learning the role that he will accept and become, and still clinging to the role of infancy that he must give up.

Being social requires that one have a repertoire of roles to move into and out of daily. At one moment I am a driver of a car; next, a customer in a restaurant; next, a teacher, etc. This role-changing is constant and ongoing. In fact, the persons we find institutionalized as social misfits are those who cannot understand roles or who have defined for themselves nonsocial roles.

It is through sociodramatic play that the young child learns to be a role player, enabling him to become socially adaptive as an adult. It is this role playing that will permit him, at age 6 or 7, to play the game of formal schooling in first grade (Smilansky, 1968, 1990); it is the non-role players who are found by teachers as "not ready for school" or "still immature for his age." Thus, sociodramatic play helps a child develop social readiness for formal schooling—to become a cooperative worker with others (Smilansky, 1968; A. Freud, 1968).

A number of social skills must be mastered before sociodramatic play is acquired. The following are stages of increased social ability (Parten, 1933, pp. 249-251): unoccupied behavior, solitary play, onlooker behavior, parallel play, associative play, and cooperative or organized supplementary play.

Unoccupied behavior—"The child apparently is not playing, but occupies himself with watching anything that happens to be of momentary interest. When there is nothing exciting taking place, he plays with his own body, gets on and off chairs, just stands around, follows the teacher, or sits in one spot glancing around the room" (Parten, 1933, p. 249).

Solitary independent play—"The child plays alone and independently with toys that are different from those used by the children within speaking distance and makes no effort to get close to other children. He pursues his own activity without reference to what others are doing" (Parten, 1933, p. 250).

Onlooker—"The child spends most of his time watching the other children play. He often talks to the children whom he is observing, asks questions or gives suggestions, but does not overtly enter into the play himself. This type differs from the unoccupied in that the onlooker is definitely observing particular groups of children rather than just anything that happens to be exciting. The child stands or sits within speaking distance of the group so that he can see and hear everything that takes place."

Parallel Activity—"The child plays independently, but the activity he chooses naturally brings him among other children. He plays with toys that are like those which the children around him are using, but he plays with the toy as he sees fit, and does not try to influence or modify the activity of the children near him. He plays beside rather than with the other children. There is no attempt to control the coming or going of children in the group."

Associative play—"The child plays with other children. The conversation concerns the common activity; there is a borrowing and loaning of play materials; following one another with trains or wagons; mild attempts to control which children may or may not play in the group. All the members engage in similar if not identical activity; there is no division of labor, and no organization of the activity of several individuals around any material goal or product. The children do not subordinate their individual interest to that of the group; instead each child acts as he wishes. By his conversation with the other children one can tell that his interest is primarily in his associations, not in activity. Occasionally, two or three children are engaged in no activity of any duration, but are merely doing whatever happens to draw the attention of any of them."

Cooperative or organized supplementary play—"The child plays in a group that is organized for the purpose of making some material product (construction), or of striving to attain some competitive goal, or of dramatizing situations of adults and group life (sociodramatic play), or of playing formal games (games-with-rules). There is a marked sense of belonging or of not belonging to the group. The control of the group situation is in the hands of one or two of the members who direct the activity of the others. The goal as well as the method of attaining it necessitates a division of labor, taking of different roles by the various group members and the organization of activity so that the efforts of one child are supplemented by those of another." (Parten, 1933, pp. 249-251)

Parten's substages help establish criteria for determining where children are in their social development, so that the teacher can intervene and help the child move to more advanced stages of development, and finally to sociodramatic play.

Cognitive Development

The direct-Instruction models of early education are based on the idea that learning is an input-output process based on words and language (Bereiter, 1966; Engelmann, 1980): "Children, this is the numeral 3. Show me the numeral 3." But, the play-based play-activity models reject that position and purport that children must first have direct physical experiences with objects and people in their world (Biber, 1977; Piaget, 1962; Weikart, 1971). During these experiences, problems will occur, and solving these problems will entail getting, using, and assimilating (or digesting) information. We can recall the early example of the "store" play, in which the child needed to use the numeral 3 in real problem-solving.

Play, especially high levels of sociodramatic play, has been demonstrated to be related to a host of other developmental growth aspects such as language development (Marshall & Hahn, 1967; Smilansky, 1969), imaginativeness or creativity (Freyberg, 1973; Feitelson & Ross, 1973; Dansky, 1980; Udwin, 1983), group prospective taking and social skills (Rosen, 1974; Burns & Brainerd, 1979), and various cognitive task (Saltz, Dixon & Johnson, 1977; Golomb & Bonen, 1981).

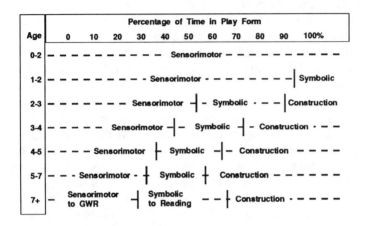

FIGURE 3.6   Developmental Play Abilities of Children

Developmental Play Capacities of Young Children

The play forms, sensorimotor, symbolic, and construction, and later, games-with-rules will change in complexity and duration as the child matures. In the elementary school years, sensorimotor play becomes absorbed in games-with-rules, symbolic play is replaced by the fantasy images evoked in reading (Smilansky, 1990), and construction play develops into hobbies and projects for school (Hurlock, 1972). The bars running from left to right in Figure 3.6 suggest the prevalence of the play abilities (Engstrom, 1971) from birth to age 7.

Figure 3.6 gives an approximation of the amount of time and space we as teachers would give to a classroom full of children of various ages. For example, the young 3-year-old will have some success with construction using media such as crayons or paints, but will find working with clay, or three-dimensional media difficult. This will change as the child matures and gains experience with these materials.

The figure suggests that large amounts of time and space should be given to the 3- to 4-year-old sensorimotor play (approximately 40%), a lesser amount to symbolic play (30%), and a similar amount to construction (30%). The 4 to 5-year-old would have sensorimotor (approximately 30%), and continued large amounts of time and space (40%) for symbolic play, while construction play would increase (30%). This trend would continue for the 5- to 7-year-old child with sensorimotor play (20%) dropping, continued large amounts of time for symbolic play (40%), and construction (40%) increasing.

At age seven the child enters a new stage of development called "middle childhood;" she becomes a "school-age" child. During this period the energies once directed toward sensorimotor play are now directed toward games-with-

TABLE 3.2   Materials Preference Inventory

The following is a preference inventory requiring you to make forced choices between two competing play materials. Once completed, you will know more about your own feelings and preferences for various types of play and play materials. Take the instrument below without more explanation.

PART I. FORCED CHOICE

INSTRUCTION: For each item below, there are two types of play materials, A and B. Choose the materials that you feel a 3, 4, or 5-year-old would gain most from using. You might like or not like either choice, but you must choose one. Circle either A (left example) or B (right example), but not both. Please be sure to answer all 20 items. Circle the letter following the number of each item, based on your choice between two play materials.

(1) A. Toy farm animals vs. B. Water play	(11) A. Easel painting vs. B. Dress-up costume play
(2) A. Legos vs. B. Balance beam	(12) A. Tricycle vs. B. Color shape matching board
(3) A. Puppets vs. B. Number steps	(13) A. Number cards vs. B. Child-sized toy kitchen
(4) A. Playhouse/furniture vs. B. Carpentry table	(14) A. Color pegboard vs. B. Doll with furniture
(5) A. Large playhouse vs. B. Climbing and sliding	(15) A. Swings vs. B. Miniature toy people/furniture
(6) A. Clay modeling vs. B. Number puzzles	(16) A. Number matching vs. B. Play dough
(7) A. Finger-painting vs. B. Unit blocks	(17) A. Cardboard blocks vs. B. Crayons/construction paper
(8) A. Sand play vs. B. Climbing structure	(18) A. Climbing structure vs. B. Easel painting
(9) A. Puzzles vs. B. Letter game	(19) A. Color puzzles vs. B. Large wooden blocks
(10) A. Rocking boats vs. B. Letter stencils	(20) A. Magnetic board/nos. & letters vs. B. Climbing hoops

PART II. SCORING

Step 1. Circle your response, from above, on the following tables, below, and add to get a total for each table:

No. 1	No. 2	No. 3	No. 4	No. 5
1A 3A 4A	1B 6A 7A	2A 4B 7B	2B 5B 8B	3B 6B 9B
5A 11B 13B	8A 11A 16B	9A 12B 14B	10A 12A 15A	10B 13A 16A
14B 15B	17B 18B	17A 19B	18A 20B	19A 20A

Step 2. Place the totals from the above tables on the following blanks and divide.

Total responses in Table 1_____divide by 8=_____%
Total responses in Table 2_____divide by 8=_____%
Total responses in Table 3_____divide by 8=_____%
Total responses in Table 4_____divide by 8=_____%
Total responses in Table 5_____divide by 8=_____%

Each of the tables above has clustered together similar types of materials to do specific types of play, and are: Table 1 Make Believe Toys for Symbolic Play, Table 2 Fluid Materials for Construction, Table 3 Structured Materials for Construction, Table 4 Equipment for Sensori-motor Activities, and Table 5 Academic Materials for Learning Numbers and Letters.

QUESTIONS TO CONSIDER: In understanding your results it is important to see how you scored related to your extremes in likes or dislikes. What was your number one choice of play and play materials? Would you include more of these materials in your classroom and encourage young children to spend more time playing and using these materials? What did you not prefer? Do you dislike these materials? Would you not put them into your classroom, and unknowingly discourage children from doing such play? Did you pick as your first choice Academic Materials? Would you design a classroom that is too academically oriented and not developmentally appropriate? In the chapters to follow you will learn to design a classroom that will create a balance of all these types of play and play materials.

rules (which, if we look closely, are sensorimotor play held together by socially agreed-upon rules.) Symbolic play tends to dissipate but its mechanisms are seen in reading and the shared fantasy of books. Construction continues to grow in importance, with the school-age children making clubhouses, models, collections of rocks, and generally doing "craft" activities. Middle childhood children are project oriented.

SUMMARY

What have we learned? Let's return to the play-activity classroom, where we could not find a front or back to the classroom, and at first could not find the teacher. The room looked confusing to us, but now, understanding the play concepts, we can make sense out of the activities going on. We see the "store" play again (sociodramatic play!). We see a child painting at the easel and another making and "alligator" with clay (fluid construction!). We can now watch the children painting and sculpting to see where they are developmentally, and we know how to begin to chart their progress in symbol development in construction. We see two boys in the block area, each making a castle (structured construction), and (from Parten's stages) we recognize parallel play.

In the play-activity environment, the "lessons" are created by the child-initiated play activities. Child-centered learning is guided by the teachers' (1) understanding of play forms, categories, and developmental stages, (2) knowledge of the classification of materials and equipment, (3) diagnosis of the child's play abilities (See Chapter 10, Methods of Evaluation and Assessment), and (4) appropriate intervention (see Chapter 5).

Having taken the Materials Preference Inventory (MPI) the teacher can better understand his or her own preferences and lack of preference for certain materials. In organizing a classroom full of materials this may lead to over-including and under-including those materials preferred or not preferred in the classroom. SYC would suggest a balance of all appropriate materials; in Chapter 4, Organizing Classroom Space and Play Materials, you will find how to do just that.

Activities

1. Visit a well-designed play-oriented school for children ages 3 to 5, and seat yourself passively either in a corner in an indoor classroom or similarly in an outdoor playground. Observe three children for a 30-minute period. From your observation determine what percentage of their time was spent in sensorimotor play, symbolic play, or construction. In your judgment what facilitated these forms of play? Note the abundance of materials that support each particular play form, including the teacher's control, intervention or non-intervention, and the arrangement of space?

2. Observe two 3-year-olds, two 4-year-olds, and two 5-year-old children of the same sex in active physical play on the playground. Using the Figure 3.1 Fundamental Motor Patterns, analyze each of these six children's fundamental motor abilities with regard to walking, running, jumping, throwing and catching, and kicking. If they did not demonstrate these actions, try to encourage them with each child, by supplying objects to throw, catch, or kick. Did you see an increase in the maturity of the child's action based on age?

3. For the same children you observed in activity 2, take a sample of the children's drawings or paintings and use the developmental sequence of symbolic development analysis to describe where each child is in his or her construction from "random scribbling to two-dimensional drawing." How would you facilitate the next stage in symbolic development for each child?

4. Observe two or more children in the sociodramatic play corner, and analyze their play based on Smilansky's five criteria. Which of the five elements of the sociodramatic play were missing? How would you facilitate the missing elements in each child's play?

5. Select three 4-year-old children, and introduce (without coercion on your part) a simple game-with-rules, such as the board game "Candyland." Were they able to grasp the rules and play the game? Interview them as to what "winning" means, and what is a "rule" as it relates to this game. Are games-with-rules appropriate for your age children?

6. Give the Materials Preference Inventory (Table 3.2) to an experienced early childhood teacher, an elementary teacher, and a parent with a child in an early childhood setting. What might each person's score indicate among these people regarding their view of play as academics (number and letter teaching)? Interview the adults about their first and last choice and have them explain why they chose as they did. What aspect of their answer related their philosophy of how young children learn?

7. Using the Materials Preference Inventory cut pictures of these toy materials from supply catalogues listed in Chapter 4 (Table 4.3) and place the picture in sets of two on sheets of cardboard. Now present these 20 cardboard-mounted dichotomous pictures to children ages 3, 4, and 5 and ask them to indicate which materials they like best from the two choices. Now score their preferences. What materials do young children prefer and not prefer? Are there differences between boys and girls? Are there differences based on age?

References

ADCOCK, DON, and MARILYN SEGAL, *Play Together/Grow Together*. White Plains, N.Y.: Mailman Family Press, 1983.

BEREITER, CARL, *Teaching Disadvantaged Children in the Preschool*. Englewood Cliffs, N.J.: Prentice-Hall, 1966.

BURNS, S.M., and C.J. BRAINERD, "Effects of Constructive and Dramatic Play on Perspective Taking in Very Young Children." *Developmental Psychology*, 15 (1979), 512-21.

CURTIS, SANDRA, *The Joy of Movement in Early Childhood*. New York: Teachers College Press, 1982.

DANSKY, J.L., "Make Believe: A Mediator of the Relationship Between Play and Associative Fluency," *Child Development*, 51 (1980), 576-79.

ENGELMANN, SIEGFRIED, *Direct Instruction*. Engelwood Cliffs, N.J.: Prentice Hall, 1980.

ENGSTROM, GEORGIANNA, ed., *Play: The Child Strives Toward Self-Realization*. Washington, D.C.: NAEYC Publications, 1971.

ERIKSON, ERIK H., *Childhood and Society*. New York: Norton, 1950.

FREUD, ANNA, *Normality and Pathology in Childhood: Assessments of Development*. New York: International Universities Press, 1968.

FEITELSON, D. and G.S. ROSS, "The Neglected Factor—Play," *Human Development*, 16 (1973), 202-23.

FREYBERG, J.T., "Increasing the Imaginative Play of Urban Disadvantaged Children Through Systematic Training," in *The Child's World of Make-Believe*, L.S. Singer, ed. New York: Academic Press, 1973.

GERHARDT, LYDIA A., *Moving and Knowing: The Young Child Orients Himself in Space*. Englewood Cliffs, N.J.: Prentice-Hall, 1973.

GOODNOW, JACQUELINE, *Children Drawing*. Cambridge, Mass.: Harvard University Press, 1977.

GRIFFING, PENELOPE, "Sociodramatic Play Among Young Black Children," in *Theory Into Practice*, 13, no. 4 (October 1974), pp. 257-66.

HURLOCK, ELIZABETH B., *Child Development*. New York: McGraw-Hill, 1972.

KELLOGG, RHODA, *Analyzing Children's Art*. Palo Alto, Cal.: Mayfield, 1970.

KROWN, SYLVIA. *Threes and Fours Go to School*. Englewood Cliffs, N.J.: NAEYC Publications, 1974.

MARSHALL, H.R., and S. HAHN, "Experimental Modification of Dramatic Play," *Journal of Personality and Social Psychology*, 5 (1967), pp. 119-22.

MILLAR, SUSANNA, *The Psychology of Play*. London: Penguin Books, 1973.

MOUSTAKAS, CLARK, *Psychotherapy with Children: The Living Relationship*. New York: Ballantine, 1974.

PARTEN, MILDRED B., "Social Play Among Preschool Children." in *Child's Play*, R.E. Herron and Brian Sutton-Smith, eds. New York: John Wiley and Sons, 1971, pp. 83-95.

PELLER, LILI E., "Libidinal Phases, Ego Development and Play." in *Psychoanalytic Study of the Child*, no. 9. New York: International Universities Press, 1959.

PIAGET, JEAN, *Play, Dreams, and Imitation in Childhood*. New York: Norton & Co., 1962.

ROSEN, C.E., "The Effects of Sociodramatic Plan on Problem-Solving Behavior Among Culturally Disadvantaged Preschool Children." *Child Development*, 45 (1974), 920-27.

SALTZ, E. and J. BRODIE, "Pretend Play Training in Childhood: A Review and Critique," in *The Play of Children: Current Theory and Research*, D.J. Pepler and K. Rubin, eds. Basel, Switzerland: Karger, 1982.

SINGER, JEROME L., *The Child's World of Make-Believe*. New York: Academic Press, 1973.

SMILANSKY, SARA, *The Effects of Sociodramatic Play on Disadvantaged Preschool Children*. New York: John Wiley & Sons, 1968.

SMILANSKY, SARA, JUDITH HAGAN, and HELEN LEWIS, *Clay in the Classroom: Helping Children Develop Cognitive and Affective Skills for Learning*. New York: Peter Lang, 1988.

SMILANSKY, SARA, and LEAH SHEFATYA, *Facilitating Play: A Medium for Promoting Cognitive, Socio-Emotional and Academic Development in Young Children*. Gaithersburg, M.D.: Psychosocial & Educational Publications, 1990.

UDWIN, O., "Imaginative Play Training as an Intervention Method With Institutionalized Preschool Children," *British Journal of Educational Psychology*, 53 (1983), 32-39.

WEIKART, DAVID, et al., *The Cognitively Oriented Curriculum: A Framework for Preschool Teachers*. Washington, D.C.: NAEYC Publications, 1970.

WOLFGANG, CHARLES H., *Helping Aggressive and Passive Preschoolers through Play*. Columbus, Ohio: Charles E. Merrill, 1977.

WOLFGANG, CHARLES H., BEA MACKENDER, and MARY E. WOLFGANG, *Growing and Learning Through Play*. Paoli, Pa.: Instructo/McGraw-Hill, 1981.

CHAPTER FOUR

ORGANIZING CLASSROOM SPACE AND PLAY MATERIALS

Since the young child will spend most of his day actively involved in the play-activity curriculum, the basic classroom space will be organized around interest areas: fluid-construction (arts/crafts), structured-construction (manipulatives), dramatic play (macrosymbolic play), restructuring-construction (carpentry). This classroom may appear to the uninitiated observer to be haphazard and disorderly, but in this apparent disorder are embedded the "structures" which facilitate learning through play. Studies indicate that the quality of program is related to well developed, organized, varied play materials. Poorly organized space results in low levels of play, increased aggression, and a very exhausted teacher at the end of the day (Phelps, 1989).

At first sight, a large U.S. department store or grocery market might appear chaotic to a visitor from a foreign country, but quickly he would learn the structures: how the materials were classified and arranged for easy access. Similar structures and organization must be established to run an open-play classroom.

CLASSIFICATION OF PLAY MATERIALS

Already we know the three types of play activities that will go on in our play-activity curriculum: sensorimotor play, symbolic play, and construction. Let's look at the materials for each type of play.

FLUID-CONSTRUCTION AND STRUCTURED-CONSTRUCTION

The materials used for construction play can be thought of as being on a continuum from fluids to structured.

TABLE 4.1   Constructional Materials Continuum

FLUIDS		STRUCTURED
Sand play	clay modeling	lego
finger-painting	drawing	Montessori Materials
Easel painting	blocks	Puzzles

The materials on the fluid side of the continuum are sensory materials, lack an internal form, and can be easily transformed. Children need to learn to control these materials, such as paints, before they can produce a symbolic product like a "doggie." Near the structured end of the continuum, the materials maintain their own internal form and have a narrower range of uses. Puzzles would be the most structured material, allowing only one predetermined product. As children move from the sensory-fluid materials to the more structured materials, their play becomes more work-like.

FLUID MATERIALS AND CHILDREN'S PERCEPTIONS

Centeredness and Reversibility

Piaget has demonstrated that dynamic fluid materials (water play, finger-painting, etc.) can present an intellectual challenge to the 3- to 5-year-old, who is in the stage of pre-operational thinking. Young children's thinking is described as centered and irreversible, and they are incapable of comprehending movement between states.

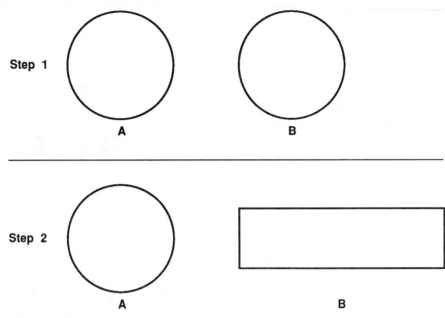

FIGURE 4.1 "Centering"

In order to demonstrate the centeredness in children's thinking, Piaget presented equal quantities of clay in the form of two balls to a child. After the child agreed that the two balls were equal, Piaget, as the child watched, rolled one ball into a sausage shape. Piaget found that the preschool age child would either declare that the sausage had more clay "because it is longer," or that the ball had more clay because "it is higher." A young child centers intuitively on the one dimension, either length or height. Unlike adults, he cannot simply mentally reverse the sequence of events to realize that nothing was added or taken away and, therefore, that the two portions of clay are still equal. The irreversibility of thought limits the child's understanding of time, space, and causality and the use of fluid materials.

States vs. Transformations

In order to explore children's ways of thinking related to transformation, Piaget presented a child with a pencil held in a vertical position above a table top. The pencil was permitted to fall to rest on the table in a horizontal position. The children were then requested to draw a picture of the movement of the pencil. Of the many children tested, at various ages, the preschoolers represented the pencil in the static vertical state and the static horizontal state, but it was not until the early elementary ages that children could understand the

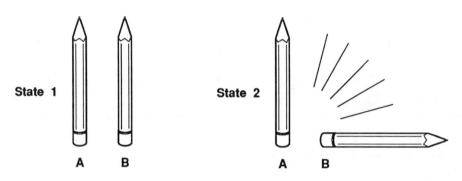

FIGURE 4.2 " Staves vs. Transformations"

transformation between states and draw the pencil in various descending stages. This inability to comprehend transformation is a characteristic of the young child and becomes particularly apparent when he is required to understand any dramatic change in his world. For example, a child younger than age six would have difficulty understanding the children's story of the *Ugly Duckling* in which the ugly duckling changes (transforms) into a beautiful swan (Brearley, 1969).

We can now see that the use of fluids, such as finger paints, water, or pouring juice at snack time, by a young child presents a major intellectual challenge. For a child to simply pour water from a larger container to a smaller container would involve a classic example of a transformation (change in states). For the child to understand when to stop pouring would require decentering (taking into consideration at least two variables) and how to coordinate the two containers and the flow of water.

HOW DO YOU PROVIDE A STRUCTURE FOR THE USE OF FLUIDS?

Materials classified as fluids are constantly transforming, making both cognitive and (since young children are often disciplined harshly for spills) emotional demands that require the child to apply control. Structured materials, puzzles, foam boards, Legos, and similar materials are more manageable and predictable. This is well demonstrated in the excellent insights of Maria Montessori (1969), who had the responsibility of teaching many "street" children whose world lacked predictability and structure in relation to time, space, and objects. She therefore created a classroom where every object had to be used in a structured manner.

This brings us to two important Montessori concepts: "control of error" and "degree of freedom." Maria Montessori wanted to create open, activity-

FIGURE 4.3   Water Play with Maximum Degrees of Freedom

based classrooms where children were free to choose from all materials provided, but she realized that it was upsetting to children when things drop, break, and spill. So, she designed the environment, including the toys, to minimize these occurrences. The equipment is built to be introduced "one concept at a time." Let's take the graduated cylinders. This equipment involves a large block of wood 4 in. square and 14 in. long. Cut out of the block are nine cylinders, each 1 1/2 in. thick, but from left to right the cylinders' depth increases gradually from 1/4 in. to 3 inches deep. Once removed from the block the cylinders can be put back only in one order, as with any puzzle; thus, the child cannot learn to do this task "wrong," and control of error is assured. Let's examine "water play" to see a demonstration of "error" and "freedom." In the Montessori classroom, water play would involve two 4-inch vinegar jars with handles, placed on an oval tray. One jar would be half full of colored water. Also on the tray would be a small sponge and paper towel. All of this is stored on a shelf at child height. The child takes the water play equipment by grasping handles at either end of the tray and carries it to a child-sized table, where he practices pouring from the full jar to the empty jar and back again. Thus there is little possibility that the child will drop, spill, or make an "error."

The Montessori goal of controlling for error is in direct contrast to a pure play preschool such as the Bank Street model or the British model, which include a large table, 6 inches deep 4 feet long 2 feet wide filled with water and equipped with funnels, measuring cups, hoses for siphoning water, and small suction basters. Sometimes the teacher even adds liquid soap. This water-play table gives the greatest "degree of freedom" to the children in their play.

We may take any fluid material and arrange it for the amount of *freedom* it grants to the child. A small plastic tub for use by one child at a time (4 in. deep by 12 in. square) with 2 inches of water and liquid soap could be seen as a halfway point between the Montessori water play and an open water table.

Play-curriculum purists would criticize the Montessori model as being too structured and stifling to children's creativity. However, the child-centered, play-based educator, with an understanding of control of error and degree of freedom can deliberately use this type of structure to achieve certain purposes with certain children. For example, if we have a shy, overcontrolled child who is fearful of water play, finger-painting, or easel paint, we may first borrow from the Montessori method and give the fearful child the vinegar jars of water to pour. Once the child practices control with these, we can move her or him along the "structuring" continuum by introducing the plastic tub with 2 in. of water and then, finally, assist the child to meet the challenge of the large, open water-play table. Thus, "structuring" by controlling for error may be used as an important tool in the open environment.

RE-STRUCTURING CONSTRUCTION

Carpentry, cutting-and-pasting, paper collage, and similar forms of construction involve processes whereby children take materials that do maintain their shapes and forms and, by cutting and sawing, restructure them to create unique products. This restructuring construction requires a child to have well-developed mental or object permanency in order that she can keep a mental image of a symbol that she would like to make, while at the same time solving the problems in restructuring (cutting, sawing, pasting, etc.) to produce a desired product.

SYMBOLIC TOYS

Another class of play materials is *symbolic objects,* or *toys.* This category includes the miniature (microsymbolic) toys designed to replicate people, animals, furniture, and other everyday items which children use in isolated dramatic play. It also includes macrosymbolic toys such as child-sized furniture, eating utensils, clothing, and role-play items. Both microsymbolic and macrosymbolic toys help young children carry out highly social, cooperative make-believe play.

The teacher who has developed an understanding of the fluid-to-structure continuum, restructuring of materials, and symbolic toys is prepared to design a well-balanced environment to support play. One cannot overstate the importance of the room arrangement; just as a well-organized airport provides for efficient movement of many people, so the organization of the classroom is a prerequisite for successful play.

STEPS AND PROCEDURES FOR ORGANIZING SPACE

The Floor Plan

Begin by actually drawing a plan or sketch of your classroom on a piece of graph or grid paper. Measure the classroom length and width, and draw it to scale making one square equal one foot in the actual classroom. Better still, write to Childcraft Education Corp., 20 Kilmer Road, Edison, New Jersey, 08818, and request *Early Childhood Planning Guide*. The guide provides the teacher with grid paper and pieces of silhouetted furniture, in scale, that can be arranged on the grid paper to represent your classroom—as in Figure 4.5.

Permanent Structures and Features

On your clean grid paper, mark windows, doorways, poles, partitions, and other permanent fixtures such as coat racks, storage cupboards, water fountains, and sinks found in your classroom. At this point it is important to include these permanent items in the floor plan drawing in order to work around them. (One classroom had a unusable fireplace that created a special problem for room design.) With a crayon, lightly color the "floor" area, giving different colors for *permanent* rugs, wood floors, and/or linoleum. Do this to scale.

Coat Racks and Children's Storage

Now, decide which door the children and parents will enter each morning. Do they exit this same door when going to the playground or is there a second door for this? If there is only one door, the coat lockers and children's storage bins (sometimes called "cubbies") must be placed inside this door for easy access. Depending on classroom space and the size of storage bins, children may have to share these spaces.

If there is a second door to exit for the playground, it might be best to place the "cubbies" along the wall near this door. In the morning there is one parent to one child, helping them to dress or undress, but when one or two teachers have all the "helping" to do, having an exit door near to the playground will create less "hassle" for the teachers. Another advantage of having a second exit door is that it requires parents to cross the classroom to get out, and this means parents and teachers are more likely to see and greet each other.

Scaled Furniture

Cut from black construction paper rectangles scaled to the "cubbies," and place the cubbie cutouts against the wall at whatever door you decide to use. (Note: The Childcraft guide provides all the furniture shapes you will need from this point on.) Do not glue permanently any of the cutout forms suggested!

You will need shapes representing your tables, nonpermanent shelves or partitions, and movable rugs. Shelving and partitions will be used to section off special play areas in the classroom.

Example Classroom Map

In the Sample Classroom Map (Figure 4.4) we have divided the classroom into zones A1, A2, B1, B2, C1, and C2. Note that zones A1 and A2 are floored with permanent linoleum. The fluid-construction area (two easels, sand/water table, two circular tables with six chairs each, and a hideaway storage area containing scissors, construction paper, glue, and similar items) and a nearby sink make up zone A1. Keep in mind that in this area activities of restructuring-construction (paper towel rolls cutting, paper cutting, etc.) also will take place.

Zone A2 contains the entrance door, parent message book with sign in/out form, parent bulletin board, mirror mounted on the wall near the door, and a science table with fish tank, gerbils, plants, etc. and two chairs (this is generally an "onlooker" activity, and the chairs delineate the number of children who can be at the table at once). Also, between the A1 and A2 zones is a long shelf containing adult storage underneath, and above, a water fountain and sink.

In section B2 are a variety of materials—structured-construction (puzzles, Lego, octons, etc.); fine-motor (dressing pads, lacing pads, etc.), and sensory materials (smelling bottles, sound boxes, color bars, etc.)—as well as two rectangular tables with chairs, two storage shelves, a nature table, a display bookshelf, and a soft couch for children to relax and "read." A tape-listening station (tape recorder with headphones) might be added near the couch. It would be ideal if a window were located behind the couch to give natural light to book reading.

We consider the computer to be a structured-construction item. And, since research indicates that children learn best by working in pairs, two chairs are placed in front of the computer.

FIGURE 4.4   Sample Classroom Map

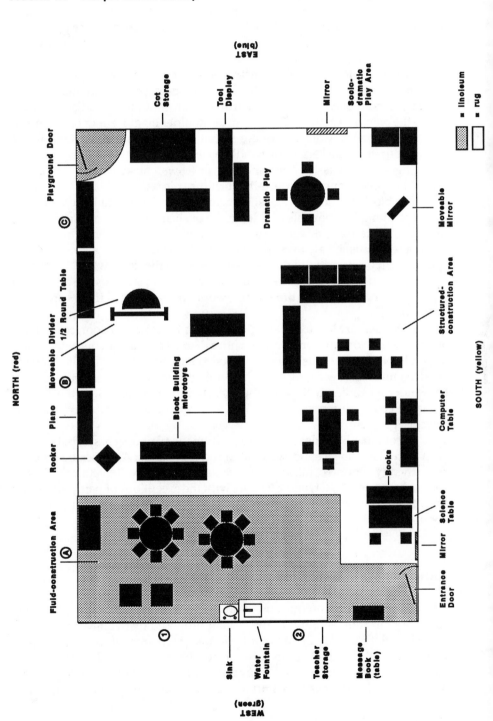

Notice that zone A1, A2, and B2 contain all of the seated activities and contain 27 child-sized chairs. We recommend that all structured-construction be done on tabletops, not the floor, because items with many piece get lost on the floor and at times trampled and broken. The tables help us "control for error."

Zone B-1 is for structured construction. It contains a microsymbolic play area and the circle area with the adult-sized rocker, piano, and audio center (tape and record player). Rhythm instruments are mounted on a display board above the piano, with the VCR-TV unit at shoulder height, either on the piano or mounted on the wall. Blocks are stored on all three shelves. On top are placed four fruit baskets with handles, containing aggressive toy animals (lions, tigers, etc.), passive domestic animals (cows, chickens, etc.), miniature-life rubber people and miniature-life furniture pieces.

The block and toy storage shelf nearest zone C1 would have wheels to enable it, along the movable divider, to be pushed back to increase the space for story/circle time, or for putting cots down for rest. A half-round table could also be pushed against the divider or the wall to create a potential unit space. The blocks and miniature toys are used on the floor, which is covered by a rug to cut down the noise when blocks fall; rug surfaces are also better for sitting on during circle time. A rug would be better used in this area than in any other.

In zone C1 are located coat lockers, the playground exit door, cot storage, and the woodworking bench, along with a display board with the woodworking tools. Notice that much space is given to the carpentry table, allowing the children much elbow room; and, since it is sectioned off, fewer children will be wandering aimlessly through this area. On good outdoor days the carpentry table could be moved outside, in view of the teachers, alleviating the sawdust problem.

All of zone B2 is devoted to sociodramatic play (macrosymbolic play), with its center being a child-sized table and four chairs. Also located here is a permanently mounted mirror (a movable mirror is available also). Notice, again, that zones B1, C1, and C2 have, with the exceptions of paint easels and sand table, all the activities in which children will be standing and moving about during their play.

Plan Enough Play Units

One of the most unique and interesting ways of determining good play space organization is found in the system proposed by Sybil Kritchevsky in her pamphlet *Planning Environments for Young Children.* In this system each play area within the classroom is considered a "sponge" that can absorb children into productive play. The evaluation for each play area is based upon how many children it can accommodate, and a scoring system is suggested:

A **simple unit** refers to play items that can be used successfully only by one child. This would include such items as a puzzle or an easel with paints and paper. The simple unit receives a score of **one**, and would thus have a small "play potential" and no number score.

A sand table with sand alone has limited play potential, but when miniature life toys and water are added, its complexity and capacity to accommodate children increases. When two or three materials are arranged together we have a **complex play unit** with a score of **four**. The number refers to the approximate number of children who might be accommodated (absorbed) by the play space. When more than three types of materials are placed together, we have a **super-complex unit**, with a score of **eight**. Usually the dress-up corner or the sociodramatic play corner, with items such as clothing, furniture, clay, and household items, is easily made into a super-complex unit.

Note that the simple unit has more "control of error," and as the units become more complex they begin to have maximum "degrees of freedom." The next time you visit a Montessori classroom notice that the entire room is designed with mostly simple units and only a few complex units. Rarely if ever will you find a super-complex unit. If we use Parten's definition of the stages through which young children progress socially, what we would find in the standard Montessori classroom is children performing socially in stages of unoccupied, onlooker behavior, with an abundance of solitary and parallel activity, and very limited associative play. True cooperative play would be very rare because of the lack of super-complex units. Therefore, our arrangement of space and objects can help determine whether the classroom might facilitate or retard development.

The final play unit, the potential unit, is an open table or space where material can be changed daily. Though the potential unit does not receive a score, each classroom should contain one or two of these in order to add variety.

Once the classroom is organized, the teacher can add up the number of play units and divide by the number of children who will be using the area. Ideally, there will be two-and-a-half potential play units for each child. The teacher should balance the number of simple, complex, and super-complex units based on the amount and types of play expected from each age group of children (see Figure 3.3, Developmental Play Capacities of Young Children) and on the amount of time that the children will spend in the classroom. For all-day programs, such as daycare, many more simple units might be added to enable children to isolate themselves and find privacy occasionally during the day. It is unrealistic to require egocentric young children to spend large amounts of time in highly socialized activity with other children.

If we add up the play potentials (Table 4.2) of our sample classroom we find that a score of 58 is obtained. When we divide that number by 2.5 play spaces desired for each child we get a rating of 22+ children that the sample classroom could hold effectively.

TABLE 4.2   Play Spaces or Units for Sample Classroom Map

PLAY POTENTIAL

ZONE A1

---

2 2-sided easels	
4 simple units	4
Sand/water table	
1 complex unit	4
2 tables with six chairs	
12 simple units	12

ZONE A2

---

2 seats at science table	
2 simple units	2

ZONE B1

Block/microsymbolic play	
1 super-complex unit	8

ZONE B2

---

12 chairs at structured-constuction tables	
12 simple units	10
Couch for book reading	
2 simple units	2
Computer with 2 chairs	2

ZONE C1

Carpentry table	
1 complex unit	4

ZONE C2

Sociodramatic play area	
1 super-complex unit	8
	-----
	58 divided by 2.5 per child = 22+

Label Activity Areas

Let's return to our sample classroom map (Figure 4.4). The large "sponges" or interest play areas to be put on the map and into our play environment are:

Fluid-Construction Area
Structured-Construction Area

Restructuring-Construction Area
Sociodramatic Play Area
Microsymbolic or Block and Miniature-Life Toy Area

STRUCTURED-CONSTRUCTION ORGANIZATION

The structured-construction area is full of manipulatives such as interlocking blocks; child-sized shelves face rectangular tables (two or three) with chairs. The shelving should create a "walled-in" effect, with the third side partially blocked (making a natural "door") and the fourth side left completely open. Every zone that is sectioned off, such as the manipulative area, should have two entrances to permit an easy flow of children in and out of the area. Having only one entrance forces children to enter and exit through the same narrow space, and this may lead to pushing and shoving.

Shelves and Containers

Well-constructed multipurpose shelves are sold by most good preschool supply catalogues with the three shelves divided into units.

TABLE 4.3   Basic Play Materials for Classroom of 15-20 Children

Beginning letter of catalog number indicates the company as follows:

    C=CHILDCRAFT Catalog: The Growing Years, 1988-89, Childcraft Education Corp., 20 Kilmer Road, P.O. Box 3081, Edison, New Jersey 08818-3081, (800)631-5652

    K=KAPLAN School Supply Corp., 1989-90, 1310 Lewisville-Clemmons Road, Lewisville, NC 27023-0609, (800)642-0610.

    H=HAMMETT Early Learning, 1988, P.O. Box 4316, Lynchburg, VA 24502, (800)446-0938.

    CP=Children's Playground, Inc., 2014 Massachusetts Ave., P.O. Box 1547, Cambridge, MA 02238, (617)497-1588.

    P=PYRAMID School Products, 6519 N. 54th St., Tampa, FL 33610, (813)621-6446.

    W=The Wright Group, 10949 Technology Place, San Diego, CA 92127, (800)523-2371.

    K=KOMPAN Playscapes, Inc., P.O. Box 3536, Windsor Locks, CT 06096, (203)623-4139.

CATALOG NO.	QUANTITY	DESCRIPTION	SUGGESTION
Zone A1			
Fluid-construction			
C13441	2	Sand and water table with cover	
C13680	2 sets	Water play kit	Buy locally
C151381	2 sets	Sand tools (20 pcs.)	Buy locally
C157792	1 set	Aluminum funnels and scoops	Buy real item

TABLE 4.3   Continued

C10942	2	Aluminum can and sifter	Buy real item
C154393	1	Fancy molds	Buy locally
C16600	2	Double adjustable easel	
C20693	3 sets	Non-spill paint storage pots	
C118844	2 sets	Plastic smock	
C18326	3 sets	Beginner paintbrushes	
		Tempera paint	
C16741	2 gal	blue	
C17020	2 gal	green	
C17038	2 gal	orange	
C17061	2 gal	red	
C16824	2 gal	yellow	
		Finger paint	
C18549	2 qt	blue	
C18549	2 qt	green	
C18556	2 qt	orange	
C18580	2 qt	red	
C18606	2 qt	yellow	
C17509	5 pkgs	Finger paint paper	
C120659	5 pkgs	Easel paper	Buy locally
C120675	5 packages	manila drawing paper	Buy locally
C139964	1	Paper holder/cutter	
C139824	1 roll	White paper roll	
C155838	2 sets	Standard crayons	Buy locally
C134932	2 sets	Finger crayons	
C119362	2 sets	Watercolor markers	Buy locally
P-RJ16	3	Marker stand	Make locally
C19927	2 gal	Glue	Buy locally
P-LC2300	2 doz	Roll-on glue	
C119388	2 boxes	Standard chalk	
C124966	2 boxes	Colored pencil set	Buy locally
C120428	3 sets	5-in. blunt scissors (right-handed)	
C97105	4	5-in. scissors (left-handed)	
P-AN919	2	Teacher's scissors	
P-AN725	4	Beginner's scissors	
P-WB4701	2	Scissor rack	
H71953D	1 set	Yarn with dispenser box	
C156745	1	Pencil sharpener	
C19992	5 sets	Primary pencils	
H24456D	2	Tape dispenser	Buy locally
H24404D	5 rolls	Tape	Buy locally
H24514D	10 rolls	Masking tape	Buy locally
H21271D	5	Beginner's ruler	
H20886D	2	Stapler	Buy locally
H20890D	1 box	Staplers	
H20859D	5	Paper punch	
H223456D	1	Rotary paper trimmer	Elective

(Note: thumb tacks, desk pins, plastic push-pins not recommended for ECE classroom—children swallow them.)

		Construction paper	Buy locally
C171363	1 pkg.	brown	

C119966	1 pkg.	blue	
C119974	1 pkg.	green	
C119982	1 pkg.	orange	
C119990	1 pkg.	black	
C120014	1 pkg.	red	
C120022	1 pkg.	violet	
C120030	1 pkg.	white	
C120048	1 pkg.	yellow	
C156935	2 pkgs.	Air-drying clay (25 lbs)	Buy locally
C156083	2 sets	Clay design kit	
C19919	2 sets	Clay hammers	
C156851	2	Airtight containers	Buy locally

Zone A2
Science Equipment

C49320	1	Easy-view magnifier
C68841	1	Thermometer
C153973	2	Classroom pet cage
C49437	1	Giant ant farm
C49577	2	Aquarium and kit
C46375	1	Magnastiks

Zone B1
Structured-Construction

		Blocks	
C14407	48	Half units	
C14415	192	Units	
C14423	96	Double units	
C14431	48	Quadruple units	
C14749	18	Pillars	
C14498	24	Large cylinders	
C14480	20	Small cylinders	
C14522	6	Circular curves	
C14514	8	Elliptical curves	
		Triangles	
C14472	8	Large	
C14464	16	Small	
C14613	6	Floor boards--11"	
C14647	12	Ramps (double triangle)	
C14704	2	Y switches	
C15966	1	Hollow blocks (1/2 set)	Elective

Microsymbolic toys

C14928	2 sets	Rubber zoo animals
C16410	2 sets	Rubber animals (farm)
C17160	1	Animal families
C168161	1 set	Zoo play-22 pieces
C153072	1 set	Police patrol (wheeled toys)
C153056	1 set	Fire patrol (wheeled toys)
C125120	1 set	Interstate road master (wheeled toys)
C151480	2 sets	Pliable people-black family
C21592	2 sets	Pliable people-white family
C22533	1 set	Hardwood doll furniture-35 pieces
C22988	1 set	Puppets (lp or hlm) (donkey, dolphin, rabbit, frog, pig, mouse, wolf, shark, elephant, alligator, hippo, giraffe)

TABLE 4.3   Continued

C22467	1	Puppet stand	Elective
Music			
C103184	1	Cassette tape recorder	Buy locally
C116897	15	Blank audio tape and/or	
C139634	1	Portable phonograph	
C159228	3	Extra phonograph needles	
C53769	1 set	Listening center	
P-YN19	1	VCR-TV combination	Elective
		Rhythm instruments	
C97022	1	Resonator bells	
C51359	2 sets	Maracas	Buy locally
C51243	4	Tambourines	
C51334	5	Castanets on stick	
C52902	5	Cymbal	
C52811	10 sets	Rhythm sticks	
C52852	3	Triangle	
C52787	5	Handle bells	
Zone B2			
Structured-Construction			
		Legos	
C12677	2 sets	Snap togethers	
C47837	2 sets	Interlocking cubes	
C171199	1 set	Frontier building blocks (300 pieces)	
C116046	1 set	Tinker toys (224 pieces)	
C46623	2 sets	Ring-a-majigs	
C47084	3 sets	Octons	
C66530	1	Jumbo hundred pegboard	
C68270	1	Patterns for jumbo	Make locally
		Hundred pegboard	
C139774	4	Stick pegboards	
C139766	1	Box of 1,000 pegs	Make locally
C150300	3	Parquetry	
C49056	1	Parquetry pattern cards	
C41764	2	Colorama	
C26310	1	Tactile domino blocks	
C111443	1	Double puzzle-numbers	
C68049	4	Color quantity math board	
C95430	2	Number pegboards (hlm)	
K1X15835	1	Fruit count	
K1X9090	1	Set and sequences-numbers	
K1X15834	1	Beg tape-measuring	
K1X8578	1	Jumbo domino set	
K1X2793	1	Jumbo animal dominoes	
C66977	1	Judy clock	Buy real item
	1	Apple IIGS Computer	Elective
	1	Epson dot matrix printer	Elective
		Software	
	1	Printshop	
	1	Stickiebears	

Sensorimotor

		Fine Motor	
K1X16612	1 set	dressing pads	
K1X9400	1	Lacing pads	
K1X0618	1	Lock board	Elective
H84357D	2	Etch-a-sketch	Buy locally
		Sensory	
K1X3198	1	Smelling bottles	
K1X1781	1	Sound boxes	
K1X3073	1	Color bars	
P-RJ27	1	Mystery sensori-box	
P-WB604	1	Bag of feelies	
P-LC656	1	Pictures and objects matching game	
P-LC1612	1	Jumbo touch and match	
P-RJ86	1	Hide and seek memory board	
P-LC382	1	Memory shapes	
P-LC929	1	Listen lotto 1	
P-LC930	1	Listen lotto 2	

Classroom library (read-aloud books)
Band, Mollie. *Ten, Nine, eight*. Greenwillow, 1983.
Burningham, John. *Mr. Gumpy's Outing*. Holt, 1971.
Carle, Eric. *The very Hungry Caterpillar*. Philomel, 1969, (1986). Cauley, Lorinda
Bryan. *Goldilocks and the Three Bears*. Putnam, 1981.
Gag, Wanda. *Millions of Cats*. Coward, 1928.
Hughes, Shirles. *Alfie Gets in First*. Lathrop, 1982.
Hutchins, Pat. *Titch*. Macmillan, 1971.
Keats, Ezra Jack. *The Snowy Day*. Viking, 1962.
Kitchen, Bert. *Animal Alphabet*. Dial, 1984.
Minarik, Else Holmelund. *Little Bear*, illustrated by Maurice Sendak. Harper, 1957.
Oxenbury, Helen. *The Helen Oxenbury Nursery Story Book*. Knopf, 1985.
Potter, Beatrix. *The Tale of Peter Rabbit*. Warne, 1902.
Rice, Eve. *Benny Bakes a Cake*. Greenwillow, 1981.
Spier, Peter. *Rain*. Doubleday, 1982.
Tolstoy, Alexei. *The Great Big Enormous Turnip*, illustrated by Helen Oxenbury.
Watts, 1968.
Wood, Audry. *The Napping House*, illustrated by Don Wood. Harcourt, 1984.

Shared Book Experience (highly recommended)

W-SB25XBB	1 set	Complete Set of 25 Big Books
W-SB101X	1 set	Complete Set all 6 Pack/stage one

Zone C-1
Restructuring-Construction

C122499	1	Carpentry table	
C65706	1 set	Tool set (2-7oz claw hammer, 12" back-type saw, 3" screwdriver, 4" screwdriver, pliers)	Buy locally

Zone C2
Sociodramatic Play

C29330	1 set	Kitchen furniture-complete set (refrigerator, sink, stove, dutch cabinet)

TABLE 4.3   Continued

C30221	2 sets	Miniature play food	
C20100	1 set	Aluminum cooking set (lp) (tea kettle with lid, 1 covered and 1 uncovered saucepan, frying pan, strainer and ladle)	
C29256	1 set	Aluminum luncheon (lp) (teapot, 4 cups and saucers, plates, covered sugar bowl and creamer)	
C28787	1 set	Kitchen utensils (lp)	
C28761	1 set	Aluminum flatware	
C21469	1	Cash register	Buy locally
C13453	1	Shopping cart	
C21725	2	Wood phone	Buy real item
C28431	1	Housecleaning set and stand (straight broom, wet mop, dust brush, pushbroom and dustpan)	
C29926	1	Iron and board	
C21394	2 sets	"Cast of characters" plastic hats	
	2 sets	Career costumes and accessories (police, fire chief, and doctors uniform)	
C165902	1	Truck #1 of costumes (black cape, mustache, bowtie, loincloth, turkey quill, head-dress, magician's wand, sheriff's badge, monster-teeth and bandana)	Locally make
C165910	1	Trunk #2 of costumes (metallic flapper band, ostrich plume, necklace, satin ribbon, red cape, witch's hat, devil's horns and tail, plus a crown)	Locally make
C28555	1	Doll bed	
or			
C28563	1	Doll cradle	
C29017	1	Mattress, pillow, and blanket for doll	Locally make
C172718	1	Baby doll-hispanic	Buy locally
C172726	2	Baby doll-black	Buy locally
C170845	3	Baby doll-white	Buy locally
C29082	1	Brentwood baby carriage	Elective
C28845	1	Baby doll highchair	
C157545	4	2-Position plexi-mirror (36-in. by 12-in.)	
C140954	1 set	8 Nonsexist career puzzles	
C805233	1 set	8 Nursery rhyme puzzles	
C76606	2	Wood puzzle rack	
General furniture			
C24935	1	Modular organizer shelves	
C25379	1	32-Tray hideaway cabinet	
C138339	1	Classroom cubbies with 25 white trays	
C23770	6	Toy shelves	
C25379	1	Hideaway cabinet	
C23838	1	Book mobile	
C141481	4	Bulletin board screen	
C24844	20	See-all storage tray	
C224851	20	See-all storage lid	

C94631	3	48" Round table	
C94540	2	48" Half-round table	
C93641	4	Rectangle tables (24" X 26")	
Cf701	10	Chair (11 1/2") (dark colors only)	
Cf702	10	Chair (13 1/2") (dark colors only)	
C24588	1	Adult rocker chair	
C23687	2	Rest cot	
K1X6812	1	Flannelboard	
H97372D	2	4-Drawer vertical file	
	4	Large waste paper cans	Buy locally

(Note: An adult teacher's desk not recommended in classroom.)

Playground
Gross Motor

C165381	5	Jumping balls	
C92676	3	Trikes (12")	
C171827	1	Wagon	
H83562d	2	Twinwheeler wheel barrow	
C183228	10	Balls (lp) (2)	
C153999	1	Air pump and needles	Buy locally
K1X2798	1	Bean bag toss game	
H95588D	1	Playground tower center (tire swing, slide pole, 12' single slide, platform, enclosed step)	Make locally

Or

CP131	1	Thornhill double tire ladder, plastic slide, platform, tire swing, fireman's pole, sandbox	Make locally

Or
CP-Children's Playground, Inc.

Page 30 of catalog	Components following basic items
Picture	

8	Suspension bridge		
16	Fireman's pole		
19	Chin-up bars (1 at 25', 1 at 36')		
21	18" wide plastic slide		
25	Hand-over-hand ladder		
27	Sandpulley, pail, sandchute		
30	Sandbox (minimum 8 in. X 8 in.), with canvas cover (use sand toys as suggested for indoor play)		
	Oval sidewalk, 4 ft. wide (for trikes)		Make locally
	Large galvanized water trough for lambs (12' X 2" X 5") (use water-play toys suggested for indoor play)		Buy locally
P-LCW610	4	Hand-on-the fence easel (include brushes, paints, cups)	
	3	Balance beams (2' x 4' x 8")	
K-M765	1	Outdoor playhouse	Make locally

Outdoors

		Picnic table	Make locally
	1	Adult porch swing	Buy locally
	3	Adult wooden bench	Buy locally
	1	Outdoor water fountain	

TABLE 4.3   Continued

	2	Large rubbish can with lid	Buy locally

(Note: Balls or any other equipment made of foam are not recommended because pieces of the foam are pulled off and eaten, and may present a suffocation hazard.)

Teacher's books

		Cooking and snacks
K1X130390	1	Super Snacks
K1X9444	1	Kids in the Kitchen
K1X7450	1	Cook and Learn
Science		
K1X9722	1	Bubbles, Rainbows, and Worms
K1X15596	1	Mudpies, Magnets

Recommended Computer Software

Language
"Animal Alphabet and Other Things" by Random House Software: Apple.
"Explore-a-Story" series by D.C. Heath and Company: Apple (128k).
Word Processing
"Kid Talk" by First Byte, Inc.: Macintosh, IIGS, Atari ST, Amiga.
"Muppet Slate" by Sunburst Communications: Apple.
Creativity
"Color Me" by Mindscape, Inc.: Apple, IBM, C64.
"The Print Shop" by Broderbund Software: Apple, Macintosh, IBM, C64, Atari, IIGS.
Cognitive
"Observation and Classification" by Hartley Courseware: Apple.
"Math and Me" by Davidson and Associates: Apple (124k), IBM, IIGS.
"Number Farm" by DLM: Apple, C64, IBM.
"Easy Street" by MindPlay: Apple, IBM, Macintosh, IIGS.
"Estimation" by Lawrence Hall of Science: Apple.
"Math Rabbit" by The Learning Company: Apple, IBM.
"1st Math" by Stone & Associates: IBM, Atari ST.
"Puppet On Stage" by Sunburst Communications: Apple, IBM, C64.
"KidsTime" by Great Wave Software: Macintosh.

Manipulatives should be on the shelf in containers which permit the child to take large quantities of, for example, Legos to a table and back again with little chance of "error" (spills or accidents). At the SYC we place the easiest manipulatives in a storage container on the top shelf, left corner; the manipulatives next in difficulty are placed in the container to the immediate right, and this easiest-to-more-difficult pattern continues across the first shelf until the shelf is full. Dropping down to the second shelf, the pattern continues; one finds the most difficult manipulatives on the bottom shelf, right corner. Facing these shelves we should be able to reach out and select the top left container and know that in it are the easiest manipulatives.

Color-coding shelves and containers helps children, teachers, and even strangers to the classroom to put everything in its place. Using colored plastic tape, 1/2 inch wide, let's suppose you assign red for north, blue for east, yellow for south, and green for west. Begin by declaring as "south" the classroom wall in which the morning entrance door is located. Mark the other walls on your classroom map as north, east, and west appropriately.

If the multipurpose shelves containing manipulatives in containers make up the west wall, use green tape for labeling, since green represents west. Starting with the top-shelf, far-left container, place on the front of the container one horizontal strip of tape and one vertical strip, each 1 in. long. Now, on the container to the right make again one horizontal strip, but this time two vertical strips. Continue moving to the right, using one horizontal strip and incrementing by one the number of vertical strips on each successive container. Now, on the edge of the shelf *underneath* each of the containers make parallel markings to match those on each container.

With the first shelf completed, drop down to the middle shelf, working from left to right, but this time make two horizontal strips in green (to denote that this is the second shelf), and one vertical; then, moving right, two horizontal strips, and two vertical strips, and continue across in this pattern, increasing the number of verticals as you move left to right. We hope you are ahead of us by now and realize that the third shelf will begin with the bottom left container having three horizontal strips and one vertical strip.

With the shelves thus organized, a 3-year-old can take a container of from the shelf and, when it's time to return them, simply look on the end of the container, turn to the green wall, match the markings on the container with those on the shelf, and place the toys in the correct spot. This gives him self-sufficiency, brings order to the classroom, and teaches him about using symbols for problem solving, and about spatial relationships, numbering, and concepts of color—all without direct teaching.

The containers on the same shelf should be similar in size and, if possible, of a clear plastic so that the child can see inside. To further label the objects, we glue onto the container a picture of the toy from its package—or, if necessary, we take a picture of the material. Both the color-coding strips and the picture should be painted over with clear varnish, so that they will not soil or come off. We do not recommend writing the names of the manipulative on the outside or using a numeral system before ages 5-6.

Tables

The structured-construction manipulatives, such as octagons, blocks, or ring toys, tend to be simple units which children bring to a table and use in isolated play. Two rectangular tables in this zone are suggested because children need more "private" tabletop space for manipulatives. Round tables may be used in the fluid area where children are crayoning, making paper collages, and doing other activities where they need to draw from a central supply of equipment. Also, circular tables permit greater sharing, and thus support parallel and cooperative play.

FIGURE 4.5   Lego Play as Structured-Construction

With very large rectangular tables it may become necessary to tape off the table-tops to mark private spaces in front of each chair. Another solution often found in the Montessori classroom is to use four to six very small tables (24 by 24 in.) in the manipulative area, each with two chairs facing each other from opposite sides.

Some teachers carry the color-coding scheme to the tables by painting them red, blue, yellow, and green, and training the children to take containers from a shelf with a green symbol to a green table. (This is an arbitrary decision which, we feel, further limits the child's "degrees of freedom.") As with structured construction, we do not recommend the use of manipulatives on the floor because the playthings may get stepped on by children passing through.

Table 4.4 matches chair and table sizes and suggests sizes for various ages. If you have children "family grouped," that is, with 3s and 4s, or 4s and 5s together, it would be wise to mix the sizes. But if you are doing homogeneous grouping it is easier to use the correct table selected from the chart

TABLE 4.4   Match Chair and Table Size

AGES	CHAIR HEIGHT	TABLE HEIGHT
2—3	10 in.	18 in.
4—5	12 in.	20 in.
5—6	14 in.	22 in.
6—8	16 in.	24 in. to 30 in.

above. If you err in purchasing sizes of chairs and tables it would be better to err with smaller chairs and higher tables, thus being always assured of plenty of knee room. Kidney-shaped and trapezoidal tables look "novel" but are very hard to live with and are generally not recommended. The exception is the purchase of two to four half-round tables that can be pushed individually flat against a wall in a small open area, and provide a space in which the child may work in privacy.

About Puzzles

Puzzles are expensive, come with pieces that are easy to lose, and call for control of error. They would eat up too much shelf space if we simply laid them out on shelves, so most puzzles of the same size are stacked in purchased puzzle racks. It is suggested that the puzzles be placed on the rack from top (easiest) to bottom (most difficult). Puzzles with small handles connected to pieces containing complete symbols (such as fruits or animals) are classified as simplest. You may need to watch the children for some time before determining how to order your collection of puzzles.

Here again, we use color coding. If the puzzles are stored on the top shelf of a "southern" shelf unit, we would use yellow tape, making one vertical strip on the top (or easiest) puzzle, and adding strips as we move down in difficulty. If more than five puzzles were on the rack we might use horizontals and verticals, much like the Roman numeral system.

If the puzzle does not have a puzzle base, but comes completely apart like an adult puzzle, it should be stored on a small plastic cafeteria tray, and stacked and coded according to the system described. The tray, of course, keeps all the pieces together and, if the tray is big enough, the puzzle can be assembled right on the tray at the table.

A word to the wise! For your own sanity, label the puzzle pieces. Take every one of your puzzles before school starts, after you have created the coding system, and turn each puzzle over, one at a time, on a table. With a magic marker of the same color as the front coding, make a like coding on the back at the top-left corner. Number all the loose pieces while the puzzle is still together from left to right, top to bottom. Do this with each puzzle, not repeating your numbers (use the alphabet symbols if necessary or a combination of letters and numbers). Once this is done, when you find a loose puzzle piece after cleaning up, you will not have to spend an exhausting half-hour trying to find where the "doggone" piece goes. There is nothing more useless or disturbing to the child than to have a puzzle with a piece missing.

FLUID-CONSTRUCTION AREA

The next play area to be placed on your classroom map is the fluid area, which will be located according to the water supply and type of flooring. If the northwest corner of the room has a sink, that corner becomes the hub for the fluid materials. If a sink or water supply is not in the room and one must go out the door to another room for water, the area near that door becomes the fluid area. Ideally, the floor surface needs to be one that can take getting wet. If there is a rug in this zone, it might be wise to have a large section cut away and the floor recovered with linoleum. If this cannot be done, large sheets of heavy plastic need to be placed under the easels, and sand and water tables.

Scream, shout, and get very authoritative (but professional) if the authorities for your building tell you that you may not put fluids in your classroom. Fluids are not a frivolity; they are essential equipment to a play-based program.

Water and Sand Play

A large (40 in. by 21 in. by 26 in.) sand or water table is basic equipment in the fluid zone. If space is limited and you cannot have two tables, it might be better to use the indoor table for dry sand that still has a watery-pouring quality, and move large water play tubs or wet sand play to the playground. Caution: Wet sand kept indoors goes sour quickly, so it must be changed often. Otherwise, you may return to your classroom after a long weekend to be met by a horrible odor.

The indoor dry sand table should sit on a piece of indoor-outdoor carpet (5 ft by 5 ft) to keep the sand from spreading throughout the classroom. A broom and dustpan should be mounted on the wall nearby. Also, trace the form of the broom and pan as they hang, to form a silhouette, and then paint the silhouette to correspond with the color-coded wall. Then, when the broom or pan "wanders off" both the teachers and children will know where its "home" is (another example of the use of the control-of-error concept).

Plastic smocks are recommended and are to be mounted nearby in a similar fashion. Limit the number of smocks to the number of children you feel can play at the water table at one time. Since this is a complex play unit, four or even more children can usually be accommodated here. Controlling the number of smocks per play unit permits us in a child-centered environment to say, "You need to wait until a smock is free before you can paint," which is more understandable to the children than, "You can't water-play now, there are too many children there!"

FIGURE 4.6   Fluid Construction with the Use of Clay

Water and Sand Playthings

A host of items can be used in the water table (except glass or metal, which rusts). Plastic is preferred. Here are a few suggested props: castoff teapots or coffee percolators, funnels, tubes, strainer, pitchers, squirt bottles, spoons, a piece of garden hose. A large liquid container may be cut in half to make a funnel and a water container. Punch holes in plastic cups or cans to create jets. Small boats, pieces of wood and cork, bubble pipes and straws, and liquid detergent are also items that might encourage microsymbolic play.

Sand Play

Sand is a relatively inexpensive material available in abundance in most communities. Order the prewashed type, as close to the color white as possible. The sand with a reddish tint contains a high concentration of iron and will stain children's clothing. Props for dry sand are very similar to those suggested for water play because of sand's pouring-flowing quality. Here are suggestions for wet sand props: spades, shovels, spoons, rubber or plastic buckets of varying sizes, small pie pans, old aluminum kitchen pots and pans, and large gelatin-molds (animal shapes preferred).

Although we have designated the table for sand and water play, the smaller plastic wash tubs can be allowed periodically on the table for fluids that are "potential play units," but these will be more restrictive than the large water table.

Clay, Modeling Clay, and Dough

Potter's clay is quite cheap and available at neighborhood art supply stores in 25- to 50-pound boxes encased in thick plastic bags. Move the bag of clay into 5-gallon plastic buckets or containers with lids that can be sealed airtight (closed diaper pails are excellent). This will help keep it moist. If it does get dry, add water and rework it. As with sand, to avoid clothing stains get clay that is not red.

To control for error have "clay boards" made (pieces of wood, approximately 14 inches square by 1 inch thick) and teach the children to sculpt on the boards. This not only defines ownership of space and clay, it facilitates cleanup.

Once the child is finished making a symbolic product in clay, the product can be kiln-fired. More likely, you will simply move this "treasure" to the windowsill, paint it with glue or spray it with clear varnish, and let it dry to harden. Children may, of course, paint their sculptures first, before a hardener is applied.

Homemade Dough

Made with flour and salt, sometimes with food coloring added, homemade dough provides a fun activity for most children. It has a more fluid quality than earthen pottery clay and is easier to squeeze and use for sensory play. The dough does not lend itself to three-dimensional products, but children produce two-dimensional figures by rolling, cutting, and shaping the material much like adults make Christmas cookies. Some tools for dough and clay are: rolling pins, small tin cans of various sizes, old butter knives, forks, and spoons, pie pans, plastic plates, lollipop sticks, wooden hammer, and gelatin or cookie cutters of various shapes. (But, realize that when we add molds or cookie cutters we take the "openness" away from the dough or clay, and rather than producing their own creative symbols, the children are limited to those shapes in the molds.)

Recipes

Simple Uncooked Dough

1 cup salt
1 cup flour
1/2 cup water
Knead the mixture. Add flour to reduce stickiness. Store, covered, in the refrigerator.

Cooked Play Dough

1 cup salt

1/2 cup cornstarch

2/3 cup water

Mix and cook until thickened, stirring constantly. Cool, then add vegetable coloring. Store in refrigerator.

Generally, play dough which is purchased is far inferior to both the earthen potter's clay and homemade dough. It is gummy, and would have to be purchased in very large quantities before there would be enough to work with; also, it dries out quickly. The only attractive feature of purchased plastic play dough is that it is easier to clean up. Save money and make your own—or get some good potter's clay.

Suggestion: Take a photo periodically of the child's best products so you may assess his symbolic development in this medium, and show it to parents during conferences. If this is too expensive, you, as the teacher, may wish to sketch it on paper, noting the date and any dialogue or information that the child has given you about this sculpturing, and file it in an art folder (which you maintain for each child).

Painting

Flat paper painting can be done either at an easel (where the paint drips) or at a table (where the paint tends to "pool up" and make holes in the paper). A double easel is a must for any early childhood classroom, and two doubles side by side are even better, if there is space. Keep in mind that painting is generally a simple unit, and the surrounding space, approximately 3 ft, belongs to this unit. To avoid accidents, pathways should not cut through this unit's space. If space is a severe problem two plywood boards (2 feet square) can be mounted directly to the wall with two large metal binder clips to hold the paper.

There are a couple of rules to remember in creating a painting center. The smaller the child the bigger the brush and the thicker the paint needed. A 3-year-old could enjoy a 2-inch brush, while the small, finer water-coloring brushes are for children in elementary school. The chubby 7 3/4-inch preschool paintbrushes are best for both easel and table painting. Deep paint pots are stored in their holes in the commercially purchased easels and help keep the long brushes from tilting over the paint pots. Lacking these, the teacher must wedge the paint pots into a sturdy box or a cardboard six-pack container with a handle. It is also helpful if the pots have some form of lid so the paints can be covered and not dry out over night. If lids are not available, cover each pot with plastic wrap. Remember, after three or four days the water in the paints will spoil and give off a bad odor.

Purchase primary colors and black and white powder paints. A small quantity of Ivory soap may be added for easier removal of spills from clothing. Some early childhood teachers give young 3-year-olds only black or dark color paints at first (true for crayons or magic markers as well) because they give greater contrast on white paper, which they feel helps the children develop an earlier ability to produce recognizable symbols with their paints.

We hope that the preschooler would soon have three to five colors available daily, as we reject that old kindergarten idea that painting with only one color each week will help a child learn his colors. Quite the reverse: children learn to classify colors by comparing a color with the colors that it is not.

Storage of paper, in containers just slightly larger than the paper size and accessible to the child, is critical for control of error. Newspaper, butcher paper (ask your butcher to purchase an extra roll of butcher paper with the next order), and thrown-away computer paper are fine media for beginners.

Another critical need is to cover windowsills or shelf tops with newspaper or plastic for laying paintings out to dry. Make sure you place the child's name and date on the top left corner of the back side before they begin to paint so you will know who it belongs to afterwards. There is nothing more embarrassing than two children fighting at the end of the day over a painting they both claim, in front of a mother who wants to hang the art on the "fridge." Drill a hole through a large primary school pencil and tie it onto a string (or tape the string to the pencil) and attach it to the side of the easel for ready access.

Also, it is advisable to create a form on small pieces of paper (about 2 1/2 in. by 2 in.) with space for the child's name, date of painting, and any explanation the child has given of his product. Some of the most advanced symbol paintings should be kept every two to three weeks so we may assess the child's development and discuss with parents in upcoming conferences.

Pencils, crayons, chalk, magic markers.

In selecting sizes, the same principle applies for pencils and crayons as for paintbrushes: the smaller the child the larger the marking tool. All of these media have very high interest for children, who will need space at child-sized tables with plenty of inexpensive paper at their elbows. Pencils, crayons, and similar media permit the child to do elaborate symbol drawings. These too should be labeled with name, date, and any description given by the child. In the thematic-project curriculum, discussed in another chapter, we see the teacher using these drawings for writing children's stories and making books. Again, samples of this work should be collected and stored in the child's artwork folder.

Paper Constructions and Junk Creations

Paper, as well as paints and crayons, can be a source of color and texture. A child might make a "picture" with green paper being the grass, cardboard the tree trunk, a "forest" background from a wallpaper design, and aluminum foil as an ice-covered pond. Added to this picture could be junk materials such as straws for telephone poles and old buttons for the wheels of a car. The child might glue, staple, or tape on many other fasteners and they should all be available in the fluid area.

Great care and creativity will be needed when the teacher arranges and stores these paper goods and junk materials if they are to be used by the children creatively and with a limited amount of "error." For example, after a group of children have used three balls of knitting yarn for a morning at the construction tables, the yarn will be a tangle of snags and knots, useless for further projects. To avoid this, put the yarn in a small, heavy cardboard box with a lid that folds tightly, put a hole in the lid the size of a nickel, and bring the end of the yarn out through the hole. Now when the children pull out a quantity of yarn the "ball" will not be bouncing off the table and rolling across the floor with three young children in pursuit.

In a child-centered play environment all of these materials—paper, yarn, junk, etc.—should be at the children's fingertips, permitting them to make their own creations. If the teacher announces, "Today we are going to make valentines," and sets up goals and objectives for the children, she or he has moved to method 2 (the project-centered curriculum), which we explore in another chapter.

Other Fluids

There are a host of other types of play using fluids, such as finger-painting, making stencil prints with different shapes, sand painting, string painting, etc., which can provide valuable experiences; but many of these require much teacher help and supervision.

MACROSYMBOLIC PLAY OR SOCIODRAMATIC PLAY AREA

If you have chosen the northwest corner of your classroom for fluids, place the sociodramatic play area (also known as macrosymbolic play area) in the directly opposite end of the classroom, the southeast corner. These are favored activities by children and locating the fluid and sociodramatic play at opposite ends of the room will tend to evenly distribute the children over all the classroom space. Also, this maximum distance away from the wet play area

FIGURE 4.7   Socio-dramatic Play Area

will more likely keep the dress-up clothing and similar materials dry and paint-free. Small alcoves are especially nice for socio-dramatic play; if available, you may choose to use an alcove even though it is not opposite the fluids.

Traditionally the sociodramatic play area includes a "domestic" play area with child-sized stove, refrigerator, sink, table, and chairs. There also may be a toy ironing board, washer and dryer, or microwave oven. Here are many similar items that may be included:

> shopping/push carts or baskets, miniature play food for each meal, a variety of kitchen utensils, aluminum luncheon sets, baking set, cook ware, plastic table setting with plates, cups, glasses and "silverware," play toaster, telephone, housekeeping cleaning stand with a real mop, broom, dustpan, and hand broom, hats of various occupations, dress-up clothing, a doctor set with uniform and kit, cash register and play money, and any other castoffs that might support role play of young children (high-heeled shoes, jewelry, or old clothes).

The key to making the sociodramatic play area effective is storing and organizing the materials so that the children know exactly where things belong. If we simply have boxes with any material thrown into them, children will not find what they want when they need it, and a low level of play will occur with a high likelihood of conflict and aggression. The color-coding system explained above may be used in the sociodramatic play area as well.

Miniature food and miniature pots and pans, for example, may be stored in separate containers. If we have a dozen miniature plastic fruits, and a similar number of vegetables, two separate containers can be used and each labeled with a picture of the food group. The children can be taught the difference as the miniatures are put away. For loose items that are solid but have uneven surfaces (such as a dustpan) we might cut a cardboard stencil of our horizontal-and-vertical-lines scheme and then, spray paint the cutout on the back of the items, in the color of the wall on which they will be stored.

The container should be marked with matching symbols. For things that will hang, such as large serving spoons and spatulas, mount a sheet of plywood on the wall, tacking headless nails on which the items will be hung. Draw around these items in silhouette form, and finally, paint them the appropriate color.

Finally, dress-up clothing can be organized on a plywood wallboard with standard hooks, or in child-sized cupboards, or in drawers. Sew the same, color-coded pieces of ribbon inside the neck of shirts and jackets or inside the waistband of skirts or pants. Then, above the hooks in the wallboard, on the door of the cupboards, or on the outside of drawers, a parallel ribbon sequence can be glued and then painted with varnish. When dress-up clothing needs to be put away children match the color ribbon sequences, first to the correct wall, and turn to the correct hook, cupboard door, or drawer.

In the sociodramatic play area a large, permanent full-length mirror is suggested and, when possible, a movable mirror that can help define the "housekeeping" area. Also, small movable partitions (2 ft by 3 ft) effectively section off the macrosymbolic play area, as well as the block area, as suggested below.

MICROSYMBOLIC PLAY AND THE BLOCK AREA

Micro play with miniature life toys in combination with large unit blocks is most easily done on the floor. This is the easiest area to organize: simply box it in by using shelving or the classroom walls on three sides, with the fourth side left open. One of the three sides might use a short shelf, creating a passageway for children to enter, since all play zones should have two openings to enter and exit.

Unit blocks will be stored together on multipurpose unit shelves. To indicate where each type of block goes, draw silhouettes of each type, color appropriately, and paste the silhouettes on the back of the appropriate shelves. If large wooden, wheeled toys, such as tractors or trailer trucks are used, place silhouettes of them on the back of the shelves where they belong; or, if the shelves are backless, directly on the shelves.

Generally, on top of the shelves we place containers for the micro toys: a container for rubber people figures, one for tame animals, one for wild animals, one for miniature furniture, etc. A large (6 inches by 1 foot) woven wood fruitbasket with a large oval handle makes an excellent container for such items, as do plastic containers. As in the manipulative area, these containers and shelves will be marked with the horizontal-vertical colored symbols system, with a picture of the items glued to the front.

TABLE 4.5   Stages In Block Building

Stage 1. Blocks are carried around, not used for construction.
Stage 2. Building begins. Children make mostly rows, either horizontal (on the floor) or vertical (stacking). There is much repetition in this early building pattern.
Stage 3. Bridging: two blocks with a space between, connected by a third block.
Stage 4. Enclosures: blocks placed in such a way that they enclose a space.
Stage 5. When facility with blocks is acquired, decorative patterns appear. Much symmetry can be observed. Buildings generally are not named.
Stage 6. Naming of structures for dramatic play begins. Before that, children may also have named their structures, but the names were not necessarily related to the function of the building.
Stage 7. Children's buildings often reproduce or symbolize actual structures they know, and there is a strong impulse toward dramatic play around the block structures.

(From Elizabeth S. Hirsch, ed., *The Block Book*. Washington, D.C.: National Association for the Education of Young Children, 1974. The book should be in the hands of every preschool-kindergarten teacher.)

Blocks are another of the most valuable play materials. Don't skimp! You will need plenty of blocks so children can play associatively and cooperatively as they build castles, forts, houses, and other structures. Before putting out a new set of blocks, wax them with a hardwood floor paste wax, and periodically have the children wash them with a mild soap and rewax them. Never permit blocks to be taken from this play zone, especially to the carpentry table area, as you can guess what will occur (see Table 4.5 for stages in block building).

Usually the children begin by building a structure and then bring out miniature life props that enable them to represent elaborate dramatic play sequences. Blocks with micro-props are conducive to play that leads to development of the highest social stages; therefore, we may call this area a super-complex unit.

Interest Centers for Onlooker and Isolated Activities

Interest areas which require less active involvement by the child but are nonetheless highly educational and entertaining, have traditionally been included in the play environment:

-Listening centers with music and story tapes
-Nature tables with plants and animals
-Book displays
-Computers

ROOM PLANNING

After you plan and arranges the play environment, you must "live" in the space to see if in fact the plan is working as desired. (The furniture pieces cut out for the classroom plan should be only taped or put down with "blue-tack" so they can be easily shifted around.) At the end of each school day you should make some mark on the classroom map to indicate where there were accidents, spills, or social conflicts between children. At the end of a week or two you may begin to see that these marks are all clustered in the same area, and will realize that this zone is not working and needs to be reorganized. Unfortunately, when spills, accidents, or social conflicts occur, teachers react many times by "laying on the rules" with young children, when a simple rearrangement of materials and equipment will very often eliminate the problems.

If excessive rules are needed regarding a certain piece of equipment, it might be best to simply remove it from the classroom. Possibly it might be used on the playground, porch, or hallway more successfully. Each time teachers' rules are added, the child-centeredness of the classroom diminishes. Therefore, many teachers make lists of all teacher-imposed rules and decide as a staff what actions can be taken in the form of reorganization so that these rules are not needed. Because we have authority in our classrooms, slowly and without realizing it, we can make our classrooms so overregulated that the children lose their freedom. Use a faculty meeting with all staff, after a long holiday or at the beginning of a new semester, to list all teacher-imposed rules and decide as a staff what reorganizing actions might obviate these rules.

Let's take a concrete example (or, more accurately, a brick example). One school playground backed onto a dangerously busy street, which was separated from the school by a brick wall 4 feet high and nearly 18 inches thick. The children "loved" to climb to the top of this brick wall and "look out" over the playground or watch the passing auto traffic. The rule "not climbing up on the fence" was understandably imposed. The rule required a teacher enforcer to be stationed near the fence.

After a "reevaluating of rules meeting" the staff decided that the children seemed to have a need to be free to "climb and look out." A father of a child in the classroom was a bricklayer and was invited to build, in the middle of the playground, a brick wall—4 1/2 ft high 18 in. wide 8 ft long. The children now use this new "safe wall." Also installed was a permanently mounted periscope containing mirrors with which a child could stand at ground level, in front of the wall, and see the "traffic" on the other side.

This minimizing of rules is central in an open, play-oriented school. At SYC our position is always to try to find a safe outlet for the intrinsic curiosity of the children—not to tell them what they may not do. Even good rules can often be creatively eliminated.

SUMMARY

Let's review what we've read about child centered teaching methods. If we now step into an open-play environment, such as in the store example, we can recognize the various forms of play going on: symbolic (micro or macro), fluid-construction, structured-construction and restructuring-construction. We could now organize a classroom for such play using the fluid-to-structured materials continuum, degree of freedom construct, and the simple, complex, and super-complex play units.

Activities

1. Go into two or three play-oriented classrooms, and make a map of the space and equipment on grid paper. Determine the play potential for the classroom and divide by the number of children normally using this space. What did you find? See if all play forms are abundantly represented or, if not, what is missing?
2. Interview a teacher in an open play preschool-kindergarten and ask her for 5 rules that she has in her room. Try to use the re-arrangement of space, and concepts of control of error to see if you could eliminate all these rules.
3. Using Parten's social development scale, observe four 3-year-old children playing and determine what levels of social development you observed. Do the same with four 4-year-olds and, finally, four 5-year-olds. Are there sex differences? In what category of play or materials did they demonstrate each of Parten's stages?
4. Do one 45-minute observation in each one of the four zones—fluids, structured-construction, sociodramatic play, and microsymbolic-blocks. Write what you saw using the constructs in the first four chapters.

References

BREARLEY, MOLLY, *The Teaching of Young Children: Some Applications of Piaget's Learning Theory*. New York: Schocken Books, 1969.

HIRSCH, E.S., ed., *The Block Book*. Washington, D.C.: NAEYC, 1974.

MATTERSON, E.M., *Play with a Purpose for Under-Sevens*. London: Penguin Books, 1970.

MONTESSORI, MARIA, *Dr. Montessori's Own Handbook*. New York: Schocken Books, 1965.

KRITCHEVSKY, SYBIL, et al., *Planning Environments for Young Children: Physical Space*. Washington, D.C.: NAEYC, 1969.

PHELPS, P., and others, "The Effectiveness of Playground Props on Levels of Aggression Among 4-year-old Children." Tallahassee, Fla.: Creative Preschool, (in process).

WOLFGANG, C.H., M.E. WOLFGANG, and B. MACKENDER, *Growing and Learning Through Play*. Paoli, Penna.: Instructo-McGraw Hill, 1981.

CHAPTER FIVE

PLAY-ACTIVITY LEARNING: GOALS AND TEACHING METHODS

The play-activity curriculum views developmental needs as unique to each child; thus, the child's self-initiated ideas and activities are most valued. The goals are related to developmental theory, and are long-term in nature. The play-activity curriculum aims to facilitate the growth of adaptive abilities.

One of the highly regarded play-activity models, also known as a developmental-interactionist model, is the Bank Street model. The general goals of the Bank Street model are to help children develop competence, interpersonal relatedness (to have affection for and get along with others), individuality (independence), and creativity (Biber, 1977). These are also the goals to which the School for Young Children's activity-play curriculum subscribes.

Specifically, the Bank Street model lists the following as its goals:

1. To serve the child's need to make an impact on the environment through direct physical contact and maneuver.

This suggests that the child must learn by being free to work and play in a well-designed classroom full of a rich variety of materials, with a teacher and same-age level peers.

2. To support the play move of incorporating experiences.

Cognitively

That learning from a play-activity curriculum is not an input-output process; rather, the sequence of learning is experiencing, playing through symbols or representation, new experience, and more elaborate play.

Emotionally

Through play the child can emotionally digest experiences such as separation, feelings of smallness, family conflicts and pressures, and similar age-appropriate concerns (Peller, 1959; Erikson, 1950).

> 3. To help the child develop impulse control and acquire patterns of positive social interaction (A. Freud, 1971).

The children will encounter clashes and conflict with other children and adults as a natural part of living with others, and can progress though the developmental phases of passivity, physical aggression and verbal aggression, to the level of maturity where they can master their emotions, learning to play and work with others through language and cooperation.

Note: See Bank Street goals for a more detailed explanation of developmental-interactive goals in *Promoting Cognitive Growth: A Developmental-Interaction Point of View* Barbara Biber and others. Washington, D.C.: NAEYC, 1977.

A child-centered method of teaching would be most appropriate for all of the above goals. To begin to use this method, recall the concepts developed previously:

> 1. The categories of play: sensorimotor, symbolic play (micro- macro- sociodramatic), and construction-fluids and construction-structured.
> 2. The level of Parten's social stages: unoccupied, onlooker, solitary, parallel, associative, and cooperative.
> 3. The level of symbolic activity (for example, can they role enact, interact with others, produce meaningful representations in art).

Using the above three concepts, what does a teacher do to facilitate play-activity? To answer this question, we have designed a Teacher Behavior Continuum (TBC), based on the idea that certain teacher behaviors (shown toward the left of this continuum) result in minimal teacher directiveness, while others (to the right) suggest an increase in the teacher's directiveness.

In a classroom where young children are actively moving about, interacting with peers and play materials, the major teacher action is "looking on," which means that the teacher is observing the actions of the children and, as she or he does so, is concerned with three questions dealing with the concepts

TABLE 5.1   Teacher Behavior Continuum (TBC)

OPEN					DIRECTIVE
-Visually looking					
	-nondirective statements				
		-questions -directive statements			
			-modeling		
				-physical intervention	

above: (1) What type of play is occurring? (2) What social level? and (3) What level of symbolic or representative activity?

The categories from which these questions can be answered appear in Table 5.2 as decisions to be made while "looking on."

TABLE 5.2   Decisionmaking While "Looking On"

LEVEL 1 PLAY FORM?	LEVEL 2 SOCIAL STAGE?	LEVEL 3 SYMBOLIC LEVEL?
Sensorimotor	1 unoccupied	1. Symbolic play
Symbolic	2 onlooker	dramatic play (micro)
Construction-fluids	3 solitary	a. imitates a role
Construction-structured	4 parallel	b. sustains theme
	5 associative	c. uses objects
	6 cooperative	gestures
		sociodramatic (macro)
		d. interact with others
		e. verbal exchange
		2. Construction-Fluids
		stages in
		finger-painting
		easel painting
		clay modelling
		drawing
		3. Construction-Structured
		stages in
		block building
		Legos
		puzzles
		Montessori materials
		form boards

From Table 5.2, we see that the answer to question 1, What form of play is occurring?, would be sensorimotor, symbolic (dramatic or sociodramatic), fluid construction, or structured construction.

The answer to question 2, What social level? would perhaps be "unoccupied" or "onlooker."

Goal-setting would come in when the teacher decides that the child needs help in moving to an advanced level of activity. For example, if the child was beginning sociodramatic play and socially was doing parallel play, the goal would be to intervene (through the use of nondirective statements, questions, directive statements, modeling, or physical intervention) to have the child move to "associative" and finally "cooperative" play. Question 3 asks, At what level is the child in symbolic or representative activity? Does he (1) imitate a role, (2) sustain a theme, (3) use gestures, (4) use objects, (5) interact with others, (6) have verbal exchanges? If, for example, you discover that the child is performing the first four activities but not the last two, you would use techniques to encourage interacting with others and verbal exchanges.

Let's consider an example of the "looking and evaluating" process:

Teaching Behavior   Explanation   Teacher Behavioral Continuum (Figure 5.1)

The teacher is seated on a chair near the "housekeeping" area. The children have placed the toy cash register on top of the toy ironing board and are playing "store."

The teacher has considered question 1, "What type of play," and has decided that Jane is doing symbolic play and attempting sociodramatic play.

LOOKING ON, question 1 decision - sociodramatic play

Jane is wearing a large straw woman's hat, full-length purple skirt, high-heeled shoes, and a plethora of beaded necklaces. She pushes her shopping cart about, plunking toy vegetables and canned goods into it. She seems to repeat these actions over and over without any further elaboration of the shopping theme.

Since two other shoppers are doing similar things nearby, the teacher answers question 2, "What social level?" with "parallel play" remembering that 3 1/2-year-old Jane has been doing this parallel activity for nearly two months. Her objective now is to see if she can move Jane to associative or cooperative play, and concomitantly to social levels 5 and 6.
As to the third question, what developmental level, she has decided that what is missing in this child's sociodramatic play is

"make-believe with others, and verbal exchange."

LOOKING ON, question 1—associative or cooperative play

question 2—developmental level -make-believe with others -verbal exchange

The teacher's first strategy is to use *non-directive statements*.

Teacher: "Oh, I see that Jane is a shopper today! She's collecting vegetables, and cans of soup!" Carol and James are also shoppers, and Mark, I see that you are the checkout teller and have set up a cash register ready to take shoppers' money."

NONDIRECTIVE STATEMENTS

(Jane, Carol, and James all stop for a moment, appear to be thinking, and move to Mark at the cash register, but their activity seems to stop there.)

(In the use of questions the teacher wants the children to reflect on what they are doing and what make-believe actions they may take next.)

Teacher: "Jane, What could you say to Mark? What happens next in your shopping trip?"

(Jane does not respond, but Mark does.)

Mark: "Pay me three dollars, Jane!"

Carol and James: "Hurry, up, Jane, pay Mark!"

QUESTIONS

(Jane does not respond, appears confused but interested.)

(In directive statements the teacher is suggesting verbal responses or physical action.)

Teacher: "Jane, open your purse, take out three dollars, and pay Mark."

(Jane opens her adult-sized purse, takes out a handful of "play dollars" and spreads the money on the ironing board-counter. She hands Mark a one-dollar bill.)

Mark (with great disgust): "Give me three, three. I said three dollars for your food."

(Jane hands Mark a five-dollar bill.)

Mark: "That's not right. You gave me five. Give me three."

Teacher: "Jane, what is on this dollar?" (The teacher has moved back to questioning.)

Jane: "One."

Teacher: "And this one?"

Jane: "One."

Teacher: "And this one?"

Jane: "One."

Teacher: "Now, count with me, Jane. One,
two, three. Now you count and give Mark
three dollars." (Using directive statements.)
Jane: "One, two, three. Here, here. I am
leaving." (She waltzes out of her "store"
taking her groceries with her.)

DIRECTIVE STATEMENTS

Modeling

(In modeling in sociodramatic play the
teacher may become a "player." Seeing that
the play is stalling, the teacher goes to the
kitchen table, gets seated and . . .)

Teacher: "I am hungry. Could I get something to eat, please?"

(The teacher has now become a "player"
and begins to model for the children.)

They all giggle. Carol sets the table for the
teacher with knife, fork, spoon, and soup
bowl. Jane goes to the stove, puts the vegetables in the pot, and stirs the pot on the
stove as it cooks.

MODELING
PHYSICAL INTERVENTION

The teacher's objectives, again, are to have Jane, along with a number of
the other children, move through associative to cooperative social play and to
use all elements of sociodramatic play. In the example above the teacher
moved from least directive to most directive on the TBC. The TBC behaviors
are listed to help the teacher gain an understanding of how to "fit into" the
ongoing activities of the children. The skilled teacher uses a minimal amount
of directiveness to best facilitate the children's play development. Once the
child is playing at the highest levels of play, such as sociodramatic play, the
teacher's role is to move out of the play and maintain a "visually looking"
stance. Following the Teacher Behavior Continuum the teacher intervenes,
first from outside the child's play, then moves inside by becoming a "player,"
and then moves outside again (Smilansky & Shefatya, 1990). It has also been
demonstrated that "shared" experiences, like visits to the doctor's office, trip
to the bakery, and similar field trips, where children get the opportunity with
the teacher to view and experience adults carrying out work roles can, when
the children return to the classroom, aid in facilitating play development
(Smilansky & Shefatya, 1990). The Table 5.3.1 shows another example of the
use of the TBC to support socio-dramatic play.

Construction-fluids play can also be facilitated using the three questions
and the TBC.

TABLE 5.3.1

THE TEACHER BEHAVIOR CONTINUUM WITH SYMBOLIC PLAY

VISUALLY LOOKING ON	NONDIRECTIVE STATEMENTS	QUESTIONS	DIRECTIVE STATEMENTS	PHYSICAL INTERVENTION
The adult does supportive looking to encourage children to play out a variety of fantasies which might potentially be frightening— the adult stands by to assist those children who get overexcited or lost in a fantasy.	The adult verbally mirrors the beginning play actions of the child. (Example: "I see you have the dishes and are ready to set the table.")	The adult uses questions to encourage children to play out and further develop fantasy themes. (Example: "Now that the table is set, what's going to happen next?")	The adult helps the children select, start or further develop their play themes by directly assigning roles. ("You're the mommy." "You're the doctor.") or by directly describing a new development in their play theme. (Example: "Now that you've finished setting the table, the doorbell rings and the mail carrier has a special delivery letter.")	The adult introduces a new prop to encourage further play or assumes a part and inserts him/herself into the play. (Example: You pick up the telephone and call the doctor.)

FLUID-CONSTRUCTION

While looking on, if the answer to question 1, What type of play is occurring, is construction-fluids, then intervention with the TBC is used as below:

Mike is standing before the easel dipping a
large brush into the paint pots, about to
apply the paint to the white paper.

Question 1 is answered as "construction-
fluids." Question 2 (social stage) is
answered as solitary. Because of the nature
of fluid materials, we will generally find

children in the "onlooker" and "solitary," modes while using them. Although double or triple paint easels will encourage parallel social play, fluid-construction, such as finger-painting, clay modeling, and crayoning, does not lend itself to associative play—with the exception of large mural paintings or similar art. Thus, because of easel painting's solitary nature, social facilitation will not be an immediate objective by Mike's teacher at this time.

Later, the teacher can answer question 3, What symbolic level?, by observing Mike's painting. Does it contain:

1. Random scribbling,
2. Controlled scribbling,
3. Face (or a recognized symbol)
4. Arms and legs (added detail to the symbol)
5. Body awareness (internal detail of the larger symbol)
6. Floating house (no base line)
7. House on bottom line (or paper)
8. Baseline supports house (symbol)
9. Two-dimensional drawing

As the teacher observes, Mike paints a small circle on top of a larger one, puts two eyes in the top circle, and a "tail" on the bottom. He announces, "Dog, dog!" Question 3 is answered: Mike's symbolic level has progressed to 3/4 (face and arms/legs). Mike has been painting to help him move to 5 (body awareness) or internal details of his "dog."

LOOKING ON question 1, type of play - fluid-construction question 2, social stage -isolated question 3 -"body awareness

"Teacher: "Oh, I see you have painted a dog. I see eyes, face, body, and a tail. (Verbal encoding of symbols.) You have worked hard on this, this morning!" (An encouragement statement; see chapter 6 on the difference between encouragement and praise.)

NONDIRECTIVE STATEMENT -encouragement

The teacher must be careful of describing what he thinks he sees in children's symbolic products, since this might be very different from what the child is trying to represent. It would be best to have the child tell what she has painted, with the teacher possibly recording it.

To return to Mike, the teacher might decide to escalate on the TBC with the use of questions.

Teacher: "Could you tell me about your painting, Mike?"

Mike: "Dog. My daddy's going to get me a dog for my birthday. Here is his tail."

Teacher: "What other things in you painting can you show me?"

If Mike does not respond, the teacher may move to directive statements.

QUESTIONS

Teacher: "Show me the tail. Show me the dog's head."

DIRECTIVE STATEMENTS

From a play-activity viewpoint we would not directly model "how to draw a dog" for Mike, because it is the child's role to construct from his own ideas. We may, though, model how to hold the brush more effectively, or crayon, or scissors. Also, we may guide the child to gain new knowledge about his interests. For example, the teacher might have a real dog brought to school, or read to the child well-illustrated books about dogs.

MODELING

Teacher: Mike, I see you pointing to the dog's collar (or bone, bowl, etc.).

NONDIRECTIVE STATEMENTS

Teacher: "Mike, show me in the picture the dog's collar.

The teacher might progress up a question taxonomy of (a) fact questions—What do you call this?, (b) convergent questions—How does this work?, (c) divergent questions—What do you think would have happen if . . . ?, and (d) evaluative questions (which do you think would be best? Why?. See the problem solving section to follow for a fuller explanation of higher order questioning.

QUESTIONS
-fact/labels
-convergent
-divergent
-evaluative

Teacher: "Show me where in the picture the dog lives. Point to (bone, bowl, etc.)."

DIRECTIVE STATEMENTS
After the story Mike is encouraged to return
to his painting. The teacher's objective is to
continue to give Mike encouragement with
easel painting, and if the theme "dog" continues to appear she would help him begin
a 4-year-old version of a research project on
dogs.

MODELING

Other representative artwork (fluids, finger-painting, clay sculpturing, drawing, etc.) can be facilitated by using the TBC in a manner similar to that described above. Table 5.3.2 shows another example of the use of the TBC to facilitate Fluid-Construction.

TABLE 5.3.2

THE TEACHER BEHAVIOR CONTINUUM WITH CONSTRUCTION

VISUALLY LOOKING ON	NONDIRECTIVE STATEMENTS	QUESTIONS	DIRECTIVE STATEMENTS	PHYSICAL INTERVENTION
The adult provides the materials and supportively looks on to encourage the child to freely and creatively use the materials.	1. The adult supports the child's efforts in using art media through such statements as, "You're working hard." 2. The adult verbally mirrors the concepts found in the child's construction. (Examples: "You're using blue." "You've made a circle." "You've added ears to your person.")	The adult uses questions to have the child verbally describe the concepts in his product. (Examples: "Can you tell me about your drawing?" "Is there a story in your drawing?" "What have you made with your clay?")	The adult helps the child to control materials or equipment with which he is having difficulty by using directive statements such as: "Keep the paint on the paper." "Brushes are used this way."	The adult helps the child develop his construction abilities by providing direct physical experiences, such as feeling a tree before drawing one or providing a model for the child's clay animal construction or having a pet visit the classroom.

About Fluid Materials

In Chapter 2 we describe fluids, mentioning that young children often have accidents with "spilling" of fluids and are corrected by adults, often with admonitions that stress "wrong" behavior. Thus, for some children fluid materials can be frightening, and they refuse to become involved. Or, the opposite may be true: fluids are a magnet to some children—but when they use them they become covered with them or will use the fluids aggressively, ripping the finger-paint paper or throwing water or paints at others. The teacher will therefore need to use "control of error" and "degrees of freedom" (described in Chapter 6) to mitigate such problems.

Water Play

When a child starts water play, we often see a "tooling up" period when she uses the materials in the form of sensorimotor play. Later, she might move to symbolic play as dramatic play (with floating pieces for "motorboats," for example). Later, the higher level of social play is seen and should be facilitated as symbolic play described above.

Finger-Painting Finger-painting is another fluid activity that has a high sensorimotor feel, and children will spend much time "tooling-up," becoming comfortable with the materials, before they begin recognizable symbols. For the child who uses finger paint aggressively, we may use cafeteria trays that have raised edges (control of error); or we may start with very large sheets of paper, gradually reducing these as the child learns to control and confine her movements. Thus, we are "structuring" the child gradually towards control. The opposite could be done with a child who is overly inhibited and can't stand to put his fingers into the paint. At first he is given a piece of paper, say 4 in. square; this is gradually expanded in size as he becomes freer and more expansive. Efforts should be made by the teacher to save finger paintings that contain recognizable symbols and are labelled by the child.

Some teachers permit and encourage children to finger-paint with food such as chocolate pudding on tops of clean tables, and to use cuts of potato, peppers, or carrots dipped into paint for stamping shapes onto paper. SYC rejects such frivolous use of food in view of the fact that many children of poor families go hungry. Also, we feel that young children should be learning social realities—that food is to eat, and toys and other materials are for playing. Also, permitting children to play with food may cause confusion, especially at home.

Clay or Play Dough

Clay and play dough are valuable fluids that lend themselves to producing three-dimensional products or symbols. Usually, like fluids, they are used in onlooker, solitary, or parallel social levels, rarely at the associative or cooperative levels. These three-dimensional materials will also pass through the symbolic stages of (1) push, pull, squeeze, (2) pat into pancake/roll into sausage, (3) squeeze pot as "bird" nest, (4) put eggs in bird nest, (5) construct elaborate symbol with two or three parts (such as a snowman, with arms, eyes, mouth, and buttons), (6) sculpt realistic symbols (which look like the real item with much detail). The teacher would facilitate this symbolic development with the use of the TBC in the painting example above; but, again, he or she would not model the symbol product for the child.

Keep in mind also that if we add cookie cutters of Christmas trees and animals, from a play-activity point of view we are imposing an external limit and would be restricting the child's own symbolic representation.

STRUCTURED-CONSTRUCTION

We have discussed what teacher actions may be taken if the "play" is symbolic, or with fluids. Now let's look at structured-construction.

With the more open structured-construction, such as play with unit blocks or Legos, the child will be able to create his own ideas in symbols (possibly a castle in blocks or a spaceship in Legos), and therefore we would use the TBC as in the painting example previously mentioned. Unlike the fluid materials, unit blocks (and to a lesser extent Legos) support a high level of social play. Children in groups cooperatively create elaborate block castles, communities, forts, etc. Also, with these two structured materials, children often add micro-toys to their end products (castles or forts) and then "jump off" into dramatic and sociodramatic play.

Puzzles, Form Boards, and Montessori Equipment

Puzzles, form boards, and Montessori equipment are true structured-construction materials; that is, they have built into their materials one symbol, form, or system which requires that the child complete it in a work-like manner in a limited way. Completing a four-piece puzzle of a dog requires the perceptual and fine motor skill of the child, but it doesn't permit the child creativity. Let us take puzzles and run through the use of the TBC (a process which would be nearly identical if we were using Montessori equipment or form boards).

Ellen is seated at a child-sized table with a six-piece puzzle she has selected. Pieces are scattered randomly on the tray. Ellen reaches out and places two pieces correctly together, but then her activity stalls.

It is obvious by now that she is doing structured-construction (question 1) social isolation (question 2) and the level of play is symbolic (question 3).

LOOKING ON
question 1-type of play
-structured-construction
question 2-social stage
-isolated
question 3-developmental
level
-symbolic; 6-piece puzzle

Teacher: "Oh, I see you have found two green pieces, one with a flat side, and put them together." (The teacher retreats to "looking on" to give the child time to think.) The child finds a third green piece and adds it to the other two, but then appears helpless to continue.

NONDIRECTIVE STATEMENTS

Teacher: "What is this piece a picture of?"
Child: "An eye."
Teacher: "Which one has the second eye?

QUESTIONS

(The child quickly finds the piece with the second eye and he now puts three more pieces together. But then tension seems to build up in the child, when he appears, again, not to make progress.)
Teacher: "Show me the corner piece that might go here."
(The child complies.)
"Now, a piece with flat sides here!"
(If the child continues to make no progress, the teacher escalates up the TBC to modeling).

DIRECTIVE STATEMENTS

In modeling the teacher physically takes over all or part of the puzzle and models (demonstrates) how to complete it. The teacher then encourages the child to take the puzzle apart again and try it himself. Montessori equipment requires modeling in this manner also.

MODELING

The teacher may also make the judgment (based on a level 3 decision of development) to take from the shelf a puzzle that the teacher is aware is slightly easier than the one the child is attempting, and physically place it in front of the child, encouraging the child to try it.

PHYSICAL INTERVENTION

To summarize the teacher's facilitation of learning with structured play materials: the teacher needs to make judgments as to what play is going on (level 1), at what social level the child is (level 2), and at what developmental level the child is (level 3). Then, with the construct of the TBC, the teacher gradually escalates the intrusion from minimal intervention (looking on) to maximum (modeling/physical intervention), if this is needed. The objective is to enable to child to freely engage in all forms of play: sensorimotor, symbolic, fluid-construction, and structured-construction. (Table 5.3.3 shows another way of using the TBC to support sensor-motor play.)

TABLE 5.3.3

THE TEACHER BEHAVIOR CONTINUUM WITH SENSORIMOTOR PLAY

VISUALLY LOOKING ON	NONDIRECTIVE STATEMENTS	QUESTIONS	DIRECTIVE STATEMENTS	PHYSICAL INTERVENTION
The adult engages in supportive looking to encourage the child in the use of equipment and is ready to provide help if needed.	1. The adult verbally mirrors the child's actions. (Examples: "You're walking with your hands out for balance." "You like to walk all the way to the end and then come back.") 2. The adult helps develop concepts by using such descriptive words as: fast, slow, long, short, over, under, between.	1. The adult uses questions to challenge the child to explore new ideas and skills. (Examples: "How many different ways could you go across the beam?" "What could you carry across the beam?")	1. The adult helps the child who is having some difficulty with a task by direct instruction. (Examples: "Place your foot here and your hand here." "You need to wait for Billy to finish before you begin.")	1. The adult physically moves the child's body while modeling the proper action. (Example: You physically help the child who cannot walk backwards on the balance beam as another child demonstrates how to do it.)

PROBLEM SOLVING ACTIVITY AS NON-PLAY

When the teacher is observing the free play activities in a well-designed play classroom, the first, Level 1, decision is to determine what type of play is going on. But there are occasions when play stops or is actually disrupted by a problem the child must solve. Such problems result from interacting with things or objects, or with people such as peers or adults. Two examples:

Problem Solving with Objects

Tommy and Chip are playing at a large water table drawing from a nearby "junk" box full of wood pieces, pieces of metal (nails and nuts), bottle caps, cardboard, styrofoam, and similar items. The two boys have taken junk pieces and made them into "boats." They are playing cooperatively, using a theme of tug boats, barges, and boats for transporting materials from one side of the water table to the other. Tommy needs one more "boat"; first, Chip passes him a nail from the box (which sinks), and then an old piece of clay (which sinks). They have a problem! The free play stops as they attempt to find a solution. They leave the water table and begin running around the playground, collecting any item they see that might become a "floating boat." Returning, they begin testing each item to see if it will float. They are now real 3 1/2-year-old scientists. But, what if the boys were not such good problem solvers, or the teacher wanted to help the children fully exploit this "teachable moment"? Again, the teacher would use the TBC to do this.

VISUALLY LOOKING ON
question 1, type of play
-problem solving
question 2, social level
-cooperative
question 3, cognitive process
-classifying (sink-float)

Non-directive Statements
Teacher: "Oh, I see that the nail sank. The piece of board floats. The bottle cap floats sometimes and sinks sometimes." (Verbally encoding the objects and actions.)

NONDIRECTIVE STATEMENTS
-verbal encoding

Questions:
Teacher: "What is it called when the styrofoam stays on top of the water? (Facts/labels.) What is it called when things drop to the bottom?" (Fact/labels.) What is this one that floats made out of? (Facts.) What would happen if I took the bottle cap

TABLE 5.4   Taxonomy of Questioning

4	Evaluative
3	Divergent
2	Convergent
1	Facts/labels

and put it upside down on the water—would it sink or float? (Convergent.) What would happen if I put the cap right side up on the water? (Convergent.) The ball of clay sank; what could you do with it to make it float like a boat? (Divergent; the children could squeeze clay into a boat shape, and place it gently on the water.) If you were going to make a real boat, what would be the best material to make it out of? (Evaluative.)

QUESTIONS
-facts/labels
-convergent
-divergent
-evaluative

What we see the teacher doing above is progressing up a taxonomy of questions from simple question of facts and labels, to a second level of convergent question, How does this work?, to a third level of divergent question (going beyond the facts available), and finally an evaluative question (making critical judgment based on previously acquired knowledge).

What is the child learning from this problem solving? Most problem solving by young children involves the following aspects:

Causality—How does one action make another occur? Example, the child puts his wet jacket on the warm radiator and at the end of the morning it is dry. The child wants to know why.
Time—Concepts related to before, after, next, later, what did we do or must we do first, then next, etc.
Space—Concepts of over, under, through, in/out, etc.
Classification—How things are alike or different, things that belong together.
Seriation—How things are ordered, such as biggest to smallest.
Number—One-to-one correspondence, such as one paper plate for each child's snack; or grouping, such as knife, fork, spoon, plate, and glass are grouped to make one place setting.

During level 3 decision making, in problem solving, the teacher does not ask what developmental symbol level the child is demonstrating, but what cognitive process or problem solving is occurring. Questions of facts/labels, convergence, divergence, and evaluation help children raise their thinking to the highest levels.

The teacher may feel that the boys are ready to fully explore the problem, and may use directive statements to carry their inquiry further.

Teacher: "Boys take the clay from the bottom of the water table and squeeze it into a pancake, and see if it will float." Later, "Now, squeeze it into a cup, and see if it will float." The teacher might go back to the TBC taxonomy of questions to help the boys think about the actions the teacher's directions have stimulated.

DIRECTIVE STATEMENTS

Modeling/Physical intervention

Finally, the teacher could take over the items and teach, through modeling, those concepts related to sink and float (space classification), or physically intervene by adding new props or even liquid soap, causing a totally new problem in the water play table.

MODELING/PHYSICAL INTERVENTION

In problem solving, we may now see that we have added a taxonomy of questioning (fact/labels, convergent, divergent, and evaluative). It takes a skilled and intuitive teacher to make a judgment as to just how much directive teaching is appropriate and necessary to sustain the children's learning activities. Generally, in the play-activity curriculum we use minimal directiveness, permitting the children to play, discover, and solve their own problems.

Problem Solving with Peers and Others

The following would be an example of the teacher's use of the TBC as she would help the child problem solve with a peer.

Martha and Jill are playing "doctor" in the sociodramatic play area, using true cooperative play and all elements of sociodramatic play. Jill is using the stethoscope to listen to the heart of her doll. She sets it down briefly to straighten her uniform; when she grabs for it again Martha has it. Both girls pull on the item, shouting at each other, "I want it, it's mine!" The play has stopped; there is a disequilibrium, or a clash between peers. How does that teacher help the children solve the problem?

VISUALLY LOOKING ON
-social disequilbrium

Looking on:
Teacher brings the children together so they are facing each other with the item in dispute between them. Teacher looks on, saying nothing, giving the children time to verbally mediate this themselves. After a reasonable period of time, the teacher escalates to nondirective statements.

VISUALLY LOOKING ON

Non-directive statements
Teacher: (The target child is Jill who has lost her stethoscope.) "You have lost you stethoscope, Jill." (verbally encoding the situation) If Jill speaks up and negotiating conversation occurs the teacher could stop with non- directive statements; if not she might escalate to questions.)

NON-DIRECTIVE STATEMENTS

Questions
Teacher: "Jill, what could you say to Martha." Then if necessary move to directive statements, and modeling.

QUESTIONS

Directive Statement/Modeling
Teacher: "Tell Martha, 'No,' (directive statement) 'I was using it and still need it.'" (modeling)

DIRECTIVE
STATEMENT/MODELING

The focus can now move from Jill to Martha and the same progression up the TBC may occur.
Nondirective
Teacher: "Martha, toys are hard to give up."

NONDIRECTIVE STATEMENTS

Questions
Teacher: "Are you listening to Jill? Do you need my help?"
Directive statement/modeling

QUESTIONS

Teacher: "Martha said no, she had it and still needs it. Give it back."

DIRECTIVE
STATEMENT/MODELING

Physical intervention
At this point, it might be necessary for the teacher to take the item back from Martha and return it to Jill, and then try to get the play started again. We are trying to teach Jill that she can defend herself with language, and Martha is learning to respond to language. If this incident or problem

degenerates into a behavior management situation, where verbal or physical aggression is involved, we may turn to Chapter 6, Discipline and Child Guidance, to see what further actions a teacher may take.

PHYSICAL INTERVENTION

To summarize this process, the teacher needs to make a judgment as to what play is going on (level 1), at what social level the child is, or problem solving (level 2), and what developmental level the child is demonstrating (level 3), and then the teacher, with the construct of the TBC, gradually escalates from minimum teacher intervention (looking on), to maximum (modeling/physical intervention). The object is to enable the child to engage freely in all forms of play: sensorimotor, symbolic, construction-fluids, and structured-construction. Also, with problem solving incidents the TBC may help the activity-based teacher to intervene with an awareness of the power being exerted or the amount of freedom the child is given to solve the problems herself.

The teacher having read all previous chapters, can now (1) define play, (2) understand the value of play for all aspects of development, (3) organize a play classroom, (4) use specific techniques for facilitating play and, (5) formally assist the developmental levels of this play activity. The teacher can, with the exception of evaluation and assessment (which are covered in Chapter 10), now teach in a play-activity curriculum.

Activities

1. Pick one child from each age group (3, 4, and 5) in a play-activity based classroom, and observe them over a period of days, until you are able to do a Child-Play Behavioral Rating Scale (to be found in Chapter 10) on them. What are their strong areas, based on the profile sheet? What goals would you set for them as a teacher, based on this scale?
2. Observe an experienced teacher facilitating play-activities, and on a checksheet with the behaviors on the TBC (visual looking, non-directive statements, etc.) put one tally mark each time the teacher demonstrates one of these general behaviors. In what play area did the teacher observation occur? What behavior was used most by this teacher? Was this directed toward one child or many children? Watch the teacher in a different play area. Did the behavior change? Why?
3. Observe an experienced teacher facilitating play-activities using Figure 5.6, Record of Teacher's Play Facilitation.
4. With the use of the Teacher Behavior Continuum (make a small one on a 3 x 5 card to keep in hand if need be), go to each of the interest areas (sociodramatic, fluids, structured, and sensorimotor play) and attempt to facilitate the activities of one child. What was the highest performance level demonstrated based on the three decisions needed to be made while "looking on" (Figure 5.4)? Have a friend observe you and create a tally score based on the TBC and then you do them.

5. Find three children using the water-table. Use the taxonomy of questions (Figure 5.5 facts, convergent, divergent, and evaluative) to help them problem solve around concepts of time, space, causality, classification, seriation, or number.

Suggested Readings   The following readings are ranked as (***) every preschool teacher must read, (**) very highly recommended, (*) highly recommended, ( ) recommended reading. Also, where appropriate, the book is marked very difficult reading or very easy reading for an undergraduate-level student.

(***)Axeline, Virginia, *Play Therapy* 6th ed. New York: Ballantine Books, 1971. Read for nondirective techniques of facilitating play.
( )Joyce, Joyce, and Marsha Weil, *Models of Teaching*. Englewood Cliffs, N.J.: Prentice Hall, 1986. Textbook, theoretical; difficult.
(*)Segal, Marilyn, and Don Adcock, *Just Pretending: Ways to Help Children Grow through Imaginative Play*. Englewood Cliffs, N.J.: Prentice Hall, 1981.
(**)Smilansky, S. and L. Shefatya, *Facilitating Play*, Gaithersburg, Md.: Psychosocial & Educational Publications, 1990.
(**)Wolfgang, Charles, and others, *Growing and Learning Through Play*. Poali, Pa.: Instructo-McGraw Hill, 1981. Easy-practical.

References

BIBER, BARBARA, and others, *Promoting Cognitive Growth: A Developmental Interactional Point of View*. Washington, D.C.: NAEYC, 1977.
ERIKSON, ERIK H., *Childhood and Society*. New York: Norton, 1950.
FREUD, ANNA, *Normality and Pathology in Childhood: Assessments of Development*. New York: International University Press, 1968.
LENSKI, LOIS, *Fireman Small*. New York: Oxford University Press, 1946.
PELLER, LILI F., "Libidinal Phases, Ego Development and Play," in *Psychoanalytic Study of the Child*, no. 9. New York: International Universities Press, 1959.
PETERSON, NANCY L., *Early Intervention for Handicapped and At-Risk Children*. Denver: Love Publishing Co., 1987, p. 398.
SMILANSKY, S. & L. SHEFATYA, *Facilitating Play*, Gaithersburg, Md.: Psychosocial & Educational Publications, 1990.

FIGURE 5.6   Record of Teacher's Play Facilitation

Child's Name_____ Birthdate___/___/___

Observer's Name_____Obs Date___/___/___

Observe a teacher in a play-activity classroom for a period of 15 minutes, and then complete as these actions occur.

Description of Observation Incident

_____
_____
_____

Check all appropriate boxes:
1. Play Form
   ( )a. Sensorimotor
   ( )b. Symbolic-micro
   ( )c. Symbolic-macro (sociodramatic)
   ( )d. Construction-Fluids
   ( )e. Construction-Structured
   ( )f. Problem solving (with objects) name _____
   ( )g. Problem solving (with peers) name

2. Social Stage
   ( )a. Unoccupied
   ( )b. Onlooker
   ( )c. Solitary
   ( )d. Parallel
   ( )f. Associative
   ( )g. Cooperative

3. Symbolic Level
   ( )a. Symbolic Play
     ( )1. imitates a role
     ( )2. sustains a theme
     ( )3. uses objects and gestures
     ( )4. interacts with others
     ( )5. verbal exchange
   ( )b. Construction-Fluids (describe stage)
     ( ) finger-painting _____
     ( ) easel painting _____
     ( ) clay _____

FIGURE 5.6   Continued

( ) drawing _____
( ) others _____
( )c. Construction-Structured
( ) unit blocks _____
( ) Legos _____
( ) puzzles_____
( ) others_____

Record (write) the teacher's play facilitation (based on TBC) Visually looking (what decision needed to be made?)

_____
_____
_____

Nondirective statements (list)

_____
_____
_____

Questions (list)

_____
_____
_____

Directive statements (list)

_____
_____
_____

Modeling/physical intervention (list)

_____
_____
_____

Give objective for future facilitation

_____
_____
_____
_____

CHAPTER SIX

NEW LEARNING THROUGH THEMATIC-PROJECT EXPERIENCES

When young children have new experiences, such a trip to the zoo, the visit of a pet to the classroom, or hearing new stories read to them, we find that the experience itself is not enough for young children to gain new knowledge or information (Smilansky & Shefatya, 1990). For real learning to take place these experiences require a teacher to focus children's attention on certain aspects and details, name and label new objects and processes, supply details of how things work, and ask and answer children's questions. The School for Young Children helps children gain this new knowledge through the use of thematic units and projects. Let's see how this might happen at the beginning of the first lesson of a new learning unit. (Refer to Figure 6.7 as we give a rundown of the teaching methods being employed.)

The teacher is seated on the piano stool with a class of 4-year-olds seated at her feet. She holds a book, a box-shaped object covered with a cloth is beside her, and there is a flannelboard in front of her. The children quickly become quiet because they know from past experience that they are in for a surprise. The teacher reads *The Tale of Peter Rabbit by Beatrix Potter*.

THEMATIC-PROJECT TEACHING   EXPLANATION   TBC/CONCEPT-LABEL

Reading the Story
Step 1—Say

"Once upon a time there were four little Rabbits, and their names were—Flopsy, Mopsy, Cotton-tail, and Peter. They lived with their Mother in a sand-bank, underneath the root of a very big fir tree. . . ."

Step 2-Show
(Teacher turns book so children can see the illustrations on each page of the book as she reads the words.)

The teacher begins with a story that serves as a **motivational experience** (*Nondirective statement*), giving the child new information. A three-step lesson strategy is being followed: Step 1—Say (reading the story), Step 2—Show (shows illustrations), and Step 3—Check.

Nondirective Statement
-motivational experience
Three-Step Lesson
-Step 1—Say
-Step 2—Show

(The teacher finishes reading *The Tale of Peter Rabbit.*

Step 3—Check
Which rabbits did not go to the garden? (facts/labels) Why? (convergent) Why did mother tell her children not to go into Mr. McGregor's garden? (convergent) Why did Mr. McGregor want to catch Peter? (convergent) How did Peter feel about the cat? (convergent) Why was the cat looking into the pond? (convergent) What do you think might have happened if the cat saw Peter? (divergent) Where do you think would be the best place to hide in the garden? (evaluative).

What are two reasons for Peter's becoming ill? (convergent) Why did mother give him chamomile tea? (convergent) What would your mother do when you got home after doing something that she told you not to do? (divergent) Who did the right thing, Mopsy or Peter? (evaluative).

The teacher has used a series of **questions** progressing up a taxonomy, helping the children think through the story content.

QUESTIONS
-Level 1 facts/labels
-Level 2 convergent
-Level 3 divergent
-Level 4 evaluative

Question Taxonomy

The thematic-project method of teaching follows a progression from (1) providing the child a learning experience either verbally (reading *The Tale of Peter Rabbit*) or motorically (petting and caring for a real rabbit or a visit to the zoo), to (2) helping the child to process new information through questioning; to (3) having the child represent this knowledge through play (see Chapter 5), in symbols (painting pictures about rabbits or doing sociodramatic play), and in signs (written or spoken words). These experiences cluster around a theme of study that now becomes "shared realities" or content (Smilansky & Shefatya, 1990) for classroom play.

The lesson generally follows a three-step format: Step 1, Say—provide the new experience for example, by reading the story, Step 2, Show—show the illustrations or represent the concept visually, and Step 3, Check—ask questions to further the child's understanding.

The Step-3 questioning facilitates an intellectual processing of the new information by following a taxonomy of four levels of increasing abstraction. The teacher generally begins with level 1, fact-label questions, which simply require factual recall. "What were the rabbits' names in this story?"(facts/labels) "Who went to Mr. McGregor's garden when he was told not to do so?" (facts/labels)

Then the teacher moves to level 2 convergent questions, which require that the child apply the facts and make simple deductions: "Why did Mother tell her children not to go into Mr. McGregor's garden?" (convergent) "Why did Mr. McGregor want to catch Peter?" (convergent) "How did Peter feel about the cat?" (convergent)

Level 3 divergent questions require that the child go beyond the facts given and speculate creatively about hypothetical events: "What do you think would have happened to Peter if Mr. McGregor had caught him?" (divergent) How do you think Peter could get his coat and shoes back?" (divergent)

At level 4, evaluative questioning, the child must make a value judgment among a number of competing choices. "Do you feel that Peter has learned a lesson from this, and will he be naughty again?" (evaluative) "Do you think it would be good for Peter to go back to the garden at night when Mr. McGregor is sleeping, to get his coat and shoes from the scarecrow? Why?" (evaluative)

To summarize, the child has an experience (hearing the tale of Peter Rabbit and seeing the story illustration), and then the teacher helps her process the new information by asking questions which progress from facts/labels to evaluative. Just what is the teacher trying to accomplish? Let's break down the lesson to answer that question.

THEMATIC-PROJECT TEACHING	EXPLANATION	TBC/CONCEPT-LABEL

Step 3—Check
Who were the friends of Peter in the garden? (fact/label question- classification)

Who were the enemies? (fact/label question-classification) When is a person a friend? (convergent question-causality) When is a person an enemy? (convergent question-causality) What would happen to Peter if Sparrow had not "implored him?" (divergent question-causality) When you are in trouble, without your parents, who can help you? (divergent question-causality) Was the mouse a friend or not? (evaluative question-classification)

We see the teacher using the Cognitive Content Area of Classification/Causality, and checking (three-step lesson) by asking questions from facts/labels, to convergent, to divergent, to evaluative.

QUESTIONS
-facts/labels
-convergent
-divergent
-evaluative
Cognitive Content Area (Explanation to follow)
-classification/causality
Three-step lesson
-Step 3—check

What were the vegetables in the garden? (fact/label questions-classification) What makes something a vegetable? (convergent-causality-classification)
What tools were in the garden? (fact/label-classification) What makes things tools? (convergent-causality-classification)

The underlying Cognitive Content Area is Classification, with the teacher using level 1 fact/label questions

QUESTIONS
-level 1 facts/label
Cognitive Content Area
-classification
Three-Step Lesson
-step 3—check

HOW THE MIND WORKS

In order to understand just what is being taught through this question related to classification, we need some understanding of how the child's mind works—how concepts are learned.

Let's imagine testing young children, such as Piaget (1958) has done in an attempt to understand how the mind works, by presenting to them a small box of glass marbles, three blue ones and seven white. The teacher states, "What if I move all of the blue marbles out of this box and put them in the other box—what will be left?" The young child normally says the white ones or three white ones, and they would be correct. The teacher now states, "OK, pretend that I have put all of the blue ones back into the box. Now, if I take out all of the glass marbles and move them over to this box, what will I have left?" Generally, the child younger than seven replies, "The blue ones." Or, he simply does not know.

Unlike young children, we adults have established in our minds an arrangement such as Figure 6.1 illustrates, an hierarchical classification system, whereby higher categories (marbles), can be subdivided into categories (wood, glass, plastic), and then these subcategories can be further subdivided (white and blue). To understand the marble test above, the child must understand that marbles can be white and blue, the lowest subcategory, and are also members of a higher category, glass, wood, or plastic. A marble can have an identity of first-order, white, and of second-order, wooden, at the same time. Marbles can also be thought of as belonging to a still higher class of objects called toys.

Children under age 7 generally do not yet have this hierarchy of categories established in their minds; therefore, they cannot do a classification task correctly. We have heard of the young child who has a dog at home, and then rides out into the country for the first time and sees a cow, and shouts, "Look, Daddy, doggie!" Or, the young child who opens the front door of his home to find an adult male and states, "Mommy, there is a daddy here." In both examples the child does not have the mental ladder of relationships to classify animals or people. Thus, a hierarchical classification system must be developed before children can understand concepts such as dog, daddy, marble, etc.

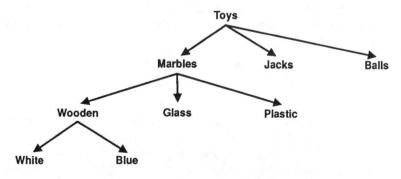

FIGURE 6.1   Classification Ladder: Inductive vs. Deductive Thinking

Inductive/Deductive Thinking

When a person senses an object (for example, hears a motor start outside the window) and then applies an identity label (a word) to that sound, we say that the person is thinking *inductively*. From a real object to a label—inductive. But, if I say an object of less density than water will float while one with greater density will sink, and *then* demonstrate this with nails, rocks, corks, and wood—then I am hoping your mind will work *deductively*. Rules and labels followed by sensory experience—deductive.

Transductive

When our mind moves up a hierarchical classification we are thinking inductively; when it moves down a classification system we are reasoning deductively. The young child who does not have this mental system jumps from one category to another arbitrarily: all men are daddies, all animals are doggies. We call this incorrect thinking "transductive thinking" (Phillips, 1969).

Let's take another example of transductive thinking by the young child. A 3- or 4-year-old picks up a piece of paper and waves it before his face like a fan, feeling the wind that is produced. The child reasons, "Moving paper causes wind." The child goes out into the playground, which contains tall, thin pine trees. A storm is approaching and the trees sway violently back and forth. The child feels the wind in his face, and transductively reasons, "Moving trees cause wind to blow" (Brearley, 1965). Most early childhood programs aim to give children educational experiences which will enable them to move from transductive thinking to inductive and deductive thinking. Therefore, many ECE curricula require children to classify and seriate, and work with concepts of time, causality, and number. Of course, the methods for doing so vary according to the philosophies on which the programs are based. From the developmentally appropriate-curriculum position, learning how to think more abstractly does not result from a simple input-output process of teaching, but would require children to be involved through play in direct and real experiences and activities.

Weikart Triangle

David Weikart (1970), drawing from the work of Piaget, used a triangle as a model to visually demonstrate the relationships between Piaget's representational stages of development and easily observable motoric to verbal levels of operation and corresponding classroom curriculum activities. Elements from each side of the triangle can be combined to create lessons at different levels of difficulty. Cognitive content areas, levels of representation,

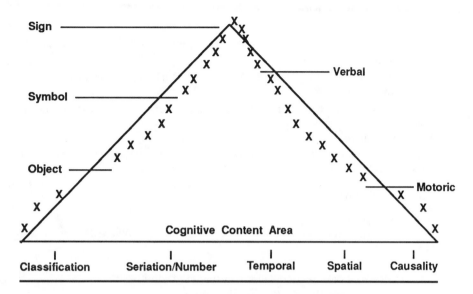

FIGURE 6.2   Weikart's Triangle of Cognitively Oriented Curriculum

and levels of operation, are terms which are heavily theoretical. These terms will be applied to the classroom situation in order to make them practical and meaningful. Other teaching techniques such as the questioning levels, and the say, show, check instruction methods will be applied to classroom activities centered around the tale of Peter Rabbit, and related to the triangular constructs of Cognitive Content Areas, Levels of Representation and Levels of Operation. The following discussion will be a practical application of what you can do with Piaget's theories on Monday morning.

COGNITIVE CONTENT AREAS

The Cognitive Content Areas (Figure 6.2) contain the subcategories of classification, seriation/number, temporal, spatial, and causality, which denote processes through which we try to understand our world. It is through the development of the Cognitive Content Areas that the young child will later be able to move to higher levels of thinking.

In our introductory look at the reading of Peter Rabbit we saw the teacher using questioning techniques, activities, and a three step teaching procedure of say, show, and check in order to help the children develop classification skills—using the concepts of tools, vegetables, etc.

An example of the use of the questions taxonomy as related to cognitive content areas:

TEMPORAL RELATIONS

1. Facts/labels

What happened first in this story? What happened next? Then, what? etc.

2. Convergent

What happened after Peter's coat button got stuck in the gooseberry net?

3. Divergent

If Mr. McGregor had not found Peter in the watering pail, how long do you think he would have stayed in there?

4. Evaluative

When do you think would be a good time for Peter to return to get his jacket and shoes—next day, nighttime, or next winter?

SPATIAL RELATIONS

1. Facts/labels

Where did Peter live? Where was the garden located? Where did Peter hide?

2. Convergent

Why did Mr. McGregor not climb through the window after Peter? Why did Peter not go under the gate like the old mouse?

3. Divergent

What would have happened if the window in the toolshed had been bigger?

4. Evaluative

If the watering pail had been empty of water would that have been a good place to hide?

SERIATION/NUMBER

1. Facts/labels

What happened first, second, next, last in the story?

2. Convergent

Who could place these pictures of the story in order? If Peter had time, how many carrots would he have taken home for his brothers and sisters?

3. Divergent

Who could name a smaller or larger animal, or enemy in the garden, that could have been about unseen and unheard?

4. Evaluative

If you were lost who do you think would be most helpful: a baby sister, your older brother, your teacher, a police officer? Who would be least helpful?

CLASSIFICATION

1. Facts/labels

What were the vegetables in the garden? What tools were in the garden?

2. Convergent

Why are a jacket and shoes not tools?

3. Divergent

What other tools might be in Mr. McGregor's tool shed?

4. Evaluative
If you were to make a garden, what would be the most important tool?

CAUSALITY

1. Facts/labels
What did Mother say before leaving?
2. Convergent
Why did Mother tell her children not to go into Mr. McGregor's garden?
3. Divergent
What are other rules that Peter should follow to be safe?
4. Evaluative
Should Mother have punished Peter when he returned home, or given him tea?

Through increasingly abstract levels of questioning, the teacher tries to challenge the children to think at higher levels in the Cognitive Content Areas. Let's return again to the Peter Rabbit lesson.

THEMATIC-PROJECT TEACHING

Step 1 Say, Step 2 Show
Teacher was prepared with flannelboard, pictures of friends, enemies, vegetables, and tools, and as the children called out the names in response to the teacher's classification questions (level of representation: symbols-pictures) the pictures were placed on the flannelboard.
Who were the friends of Peter? Who were the enemies?

The teacher shows to the children a 2 x 5 in. card with the word "friends" written on it (sign) in dark block letters. "Class, this word says, 'friends.'" "Say this word, class!" Children: "Friends" (as teacher runs hand under the word). "Yes, 'friends.' "Say it again, class!" "Friends." (All of these are fact/label questions.)

Step 3 Check
What group of pictures (symbolic representation) on this board are friends? (facts-

EXPLANATION

The teacher uses symbols to work in the cognitive content area of classification with low-level fact/label questions.

The teacher begins another lesson which will follow the strategies of Say: ("this word is 'friend'"); Show (MODELING -holds up card); Check. In the Say step of instruction the teacher introduces the highest level of Representation as Signs or written words which also includes beginning letter recognition.

labels-classification) Yes, I will put this word (sign representation) on top, here, and put all the friend pictures below it.
Now, this word says "vegetable," and I will put it up here. I will call on one of you to come up and move one vegetable picture underneath the word vegetable. Who can find the vegetable pictures?
(Teacher now repeats this sequence with enemies and tools.)

The teacher checks (MODELING). The cognitive content area of classification is being taught by combining the representation of symbols (pictures) with signs (written words), and this is carried out through fact/label questioning.

The teacher takes away all pictures, leaving the labels *friends, enemies, vegetables,* and *tools* on the flannelboard. "Now, Class, I'm going to give each of you a picture; don't show it to anyone. When I call your name, I want you to come up and put your picture (symbol) under *friends* (sign), *vegetable, fruits,* or *tools.*" (DIRECTIVE STATEMENT)
Each child does as directed, with the teacher reteaching if a child has difficulty. This has permitted the teacher to check each child's understanding. (classification)

This is a repeat of the third step, Check, in the three-step lesson of Say-Show-Check, and requires the children to Classify (Cognitive Content Area), by applying Symbols (pictures) to Signs, with the teacher using DIRECTIVE STATEMENTS ("put your picture under 'friend'").

LEVELS OF REPRESENTATION

After the child has heard the story he has new information; the teacher then helps him process that information by using questions related to the cognitive content areas. The next goal is to have the child learn to represent his ideas at increasingly abstract levels: first symbolically (pictures of friends, enemies, tools, and vegetables), then with signs (language —"friend," "enemies," etc.).

Symbols are representations, such as pictures, the objects which the child makes in construction (such as painting Peter Rabbit), or pretend play—being Peter in dramatic play. Signs, which are also representations, are spoken or written words—"rabbit." Developmentally, the child progresses through levels of representation as he matures and gains experience. These levels move from (1) real experiences such as feeding, petting, and caring for a real rabbit,

TABLE 6.1   Levels of Representation

LEVELS	TEACHING IMPLICATIONS	EXAMPLES
(3) sign	Words-The word itself evokes vivid and meaningful mental images (verbal and written).	1. The spoken word *rabbit*. 2. The written word *rabbit*.
(2) symbol	3.Pictures (realistic to abstract) 2.Clay models & drawings (child makes representation) 1.Motor encoding a)makes believe (uses objects) to represent other objects) b)imitation including onomatopoeia (child uses body to represent object or sound of object) c)Dramatic play (representation of familiar and/or common situations)	3.a)Child recognizes picture of rabbit when only feet are visible b)Child recognizes picture of rabbit among other pictures 2.a)Clay model of rabbit. b)Original drawing or tracing of rabbit; etc. 1.a)Box stands for rabbit. b)Child walks like rabbit. child says "quack,quack". c)Children play house.

(1) Real objects/experiences
The child has an experience with the object (a rabbit) being studied in order to make mental images of it. The order of presentation should be (1) experience with real object,then (2) symbolize it, and (3) apply signs (Weikart, 1970, p.5).

or hearing a story, to (2) representations by the child of his ideas about the story through symbols, and finally to (3) signs used by the child in speaking and writing about his own stories (Table 6.1).

In a thematic-project curriculum it is the teacher's role to encourage this representation, first in symbols and later in signs. Here is how this might be done with the rabbits theme.

Rabbits

Kinds of Direct Experience	Representation Symbolic level	Sign
child visits pet or rabbit	Paints rabbit, makes	word labels: rabbit

farm; seeing various kinds of rabbits	rabbits out of clay, 1 sew rabbits out of material	litter hutch rodent hare family
	enacts rabbit in socio-dramatic play	fur long ears
habitat	makes mural of rabbit information	bobbed tail burrowing
	makes diorama of different habitats where different rabbits live.	
care of rabbit (care for classroom rabbit) Is read: *Habits of Rabbits* *Rabbit-A Complete Pet Owner's Manual*		
	Makes graph of the number of pellets the rabbit eats each day, and graphs weekly weight of the rabbit.	
weighs rabbit weekly		

Thematic-Project Teaching	Explanation	TBC/Concept-Label
		(see Figure 6.7)

The teacher now quickly pulls the towel off the hidden box, opens a door, and takes out a young brown baby rabbit. "We have a new friend that has come to live with us in our classroom." The teacher has the children form a circle, permitting the rabbit to hop about, each child gently petting it.

The experience with a real rabbit is the culminative experience (Modeling) for tying up the lesson. Teaching still continues.

MODELING
-Culminating experience

A flood of observations are made by the children as they first have a sensory experience with the rabbit (level 1 operational-process-motoric) then encode this impression with words or language (level 2 operational-process-verbal), for example, he touches rabbit and says, "he is soft, nose is cold and wet, sharp claws"; looks at rabbit and says, "big teeth, long ears, brown and white."

The teacher is now working on the Levels
of Operation from the triangle construct, by
using NONDIRECTIVE STATEMENTS or
Verbally encoding (fur is soft) as the child
a Motoric experience (touches rabbit's fur).

NONDIRECTIVE STATEMENTS
-level of operation-motoric to verbal

A flood of questions now come from the
children: What is his name? Where will he
live? What will he eat? Is he a girl or boy?
Does he have brothers and sister? Where is
his mother?

The teacher does not attempt to answer
these questions at this time, but keeps them
in mind for later planning with the Web.

LEVELS OF OPERATION

The final side to the curriculum triangle is labeled Levels of Operation, the
two levels being motoric and verbal (Table 6.2). The operation can be thought
of as a process experience—the child feeling the rabbit and seeing the rabbit.
Or, cooking, tasting, and smelling ingredients such as salt, pepper, and sugar
would be another process experience.

How do we know the physical world? The answer is by its motor
meaning. The meaning of "cup" is the sensorimotor experience of one's
outstretched hand clasping a cylindrical object, bringing it to one's mouth,
and tilting one's head back. This sequence of behaviors (motoric operation) is
mentally stored as the "meaning of cup."

When the child is told "drink from a cup" (verbal level of operation) the
child truly understands the verbal label "cup." The child climbs under the table
(motoric operation), and the teacher says, "You are going 'under'." At times,
as in the "going under," while the teacher encodes, the child is working at both

TABLE 6.2   Level of Operation

MOTORIC	VERBAL
hear G bell then C bell	high vs. low
feeling the rabbit's fur	soft
feeling the rabbit's claws	sharp
(or polar concept with different senses)	
touching sand paper and	rough vs. smooth
silk cloth	
tasting a lemon and sugar	bitter vs. sweet
seeing two balls of differing sizes	large vs. small

levels of operation simultaneously (motoric and verbal), but generally the motoric experience must come first to give true meaning and understanding to the verbal.

To summarize, the Weikart triangle presents a construct for the teacher to use in carrying out lessons in the thematic-project curriculum. This triangle presents a model for the teacher to use in giving the children experiences of classifying, seriating, etc., representing those experiences with symbols and later signs, and acting or operating on those experiences, motorically and then verbally.

THEMATIC-PROJECT TEACHING

Above, we saw an introductory lesson on "rabbits," with the central motivation vehicle and source of new information being the classic children's book *The Tale of Peter Rabbit*. In the thematic-project curriculum, the skilled teacher tries to stimulate learning around a theme, such as rabbits, in order to: (1) keep children highly motivated to learn, (2) encourage them to represent their ideas in symbols (drawings, clay, etc.) and signs (written words), (3) help them gain knowledge about their world and the ability to think about that knowledge with increasingly high levels of mental operations, (4) expand their vocabularies, and finally, (5) help them acquire a true love of children's literature that will lead to developing a real readiness for reading. Children's literature is the hub around which the thematic-project curriculum is organized. The construct for organizing the curriculum is "webbing."

Webbing

The teacher, with co-teachers or aides, plans the learning unit with the use of a system called webbing. They begin by drawing a circle and writing in it the name of a motivational book, e.g., *The Tale of Peter Rabbit*. The story is read and the children and teacher discuss it. Then the teacher draws a second, larger circle around the first one, and sections off the circular space like a spider's web (see Figure 6.3). In each section is listed a very general topic relating in some way to the story (e.g., rabbits, friendship, gardens, rules, and safety). These broad, general topics are called strands.

The teacher then searches the library for children's books, music albums, or teacher resource books on these broad topics (see Table 6.3).

TABLE 6.3 Books

RABBITS

Aesop-*The Hare and the Tortoise*
Anders, Rebecca-*Whiskers the Rabbit*
Anderson, Lonzo and Adrienne Adams-*Two Hundred Rabbits*
Bate, Lucy-*Little Rabbit's Loose Tooth*
Brown, Margaret Wise-*Brer Rabbit; Home for a Bunny Brown; The Golden Egg Book;*
The Runaway Bunny; The Sleepy Book
Bruna, Dick -*Miffy at the Zoo*
Carroll, Ruth-*Alice in Wonderland*
Colby, Carroll-*Gabbit the Magic Rabbit*
Daniel, Kira -*Habits of Rabbits*
Delage, Ida-*Bunnyschool*
Dermine, Lucie -*The Rabbits Give a Party*
DeVault, Vere-*The Jack Rabbit*
Dunn, Judy-*The Little Rabbit*
Evers, Helen and Alf-*Fussbunny*
Fisher, Aileen -*Listen, Rabbit*
Friskey, Margaret -*Rackety That Very Special Rabbit*
Fritz, Jean-*How to Read a Rabbit*
Fritzch, Helga-*Rabbit-A Complete Pet Owner's Manuel*
Gag, Wanda-*The ABC Bunny*
Galdone, Paul-*The Hare and the Tortoise*
Grimm Fairy Tales-*The Hare's Bride*
Henrie, Fiona-*Rabbits*
Heyward, DuBose-*The Country Bunny and the Little Gold Shoes*
Howard, Matthew V., and Earl W. Moline-*Blink the Patchwork Bunny*
Jackson, Kathryn-*Tawny the Scrawny Lion*
Kaufman, Elizabeth Elias-*Bunnies and Rabbits*
Kohler, Julilly-*Collins and His Rabbits*
Lawson, Robert-*Rabbit Hill*
Memling, Carl-*Little Cottontail*
Moreman, Grace-*Walk Rabbit Walk*
Peters, Sharon-*Stop That Rabbit*
Potter, Beatrix-*The Tale of Peter Rabbit; The Tale of the Flopsy Bunnies; The Tale*
of Benjamin Bunny
Sadler, Marilyn-*The Very Bad Bunny*
Scarry, Richard-*I am a Bunny; Nicky Goes to the Doctor*
Schlachter, Rita-*Good Luck Bad Luck*
Tufts, Georgia-*The Rabbit Garden*
Weil, Lise-*The Candy Egg Bunny*
Werner, Jane Walt Disney's Bunny Book
Whithead, Pat-*What a Funny Bunny*
Williams, Margery-*The Velveteen Rabbit*
Wright, Betty Ren-*The Rabbit's Adventure*
Zolotow, Charlotte-*Mr. Rabbit and the Lovely Present*

GARDENS

Baker, Sam Sinclair-*Gardening*
Beller, Joel-*Garden Experiments*

TABLE 6.3   Continued

Chevelier, Christa-*Gardening-Stories*
Creative Educational Society-*Vegetable Gardening*
Cutler, Katherine N.-*Gardening*
Gibbons, Gail-*Tool Book*
Hudlow, Jean-*Vegetable Gardening*
Jobb, Jamie-*Gardening*
Keller, Beverly-*The Beetle Bush*
Kramer, Jack-*Plant Hobbies*
Kratz, Marilyn-*The Garden Book*
Kraus, Ruth-*The Carrot Seed*
Lesson, Robert-*Tools*
Lavine, Sigmund A. -*Vegetable Gardening*
Manley, Deborah-*Gardening*
Parker, Bertha Morris-*Gardening*
Parker, Bertha Morris-*The Plant World*
Poling, James-*Tools*
Robbins, Ken-*Tools*
Smith, Ken-*Garden Construction Know How*
Swenson, Allan A. -*Vegetable Gardening*
Vallin, Jean-*The Plant World*
Vasiliu, Mircea-*One Day in the Garden*

GARDEN ANIMALS

Berenstain, Stan-*Birds*
Blough, Glenn-*The Insect Parade*
Brandenbert, Aliki-*At Mary's Blooms*
Conklin, Gladys-*When Insects are Babies*
Cressey, James-*Max the Mouse*
Eastman, P.D.-*Are You My Mother?"*
Gans, Rona-*Birds Eat and Eat and Eat*
Ipcan, Dahlov-*Big City*
Koening, Marian-*The Mouse*
Kraus, Robert-*The Good Mousekeeper; Whose Mouse Are You?*
Lobel, Arnold-*Mouse Soup and Other Stories*
Pole, Lavine-*Spiders and Special Potter,*
Beatrix-*The Tailor of Gloucestor*
Raskin, Ellen-*Twenty-Two, Twenty-Three*
Wong, Herbert-*Where Can Red-Winged Blackbirds Live?*

HOMES

Burton, Virginia Lee-*The Little House*
Cutts, David-*The House That Jack Built*
Green, Robyn, Yvonne Pollock, & Scarffe Bronuen,-*When Goldilocks Went to the House of the Bears*
Heilbroner, Joan-*This is the House Where Jack Lives*
Hilbert, Margaret-*A House for Little Red*
Hutchins, Pat-*The House that Sailed Away*
Israel, Leo-*Our New Home in the City*
Palmer, Helen-*Why I Built the Boogle House*

Parkeks, Brenda & Smith, Judith-*The Three Little Pigs (retold by)*
Roffery, Maureen-*Door to Door*

FAMILY

Berenstain, Stan and Jan-*The Berenstain Bears and the Weekend at Grandma's*
Berger, Terry-*Big Sister, Little Brother*
Blaine, Marge-*The Terrible Thing That Happened at Our House*
Borack, Barbara-*Grandpa*
Brindwell, Norman-*A Tiny Family; Clifford's Family*
Byars, Betsy-*Go and Hush the Baby*
Fehr, Howard F.-*This is My Family*
Flack, Marjorie-*Wait for Williams*
Galdon, Paul-*The Three Bears*
Hazel, Beth, & Dr. Jerome C. Harste-*My Icky Picky Sister*
Hoban, Russell-*The Little Brute Family*
Hogan, Paula Z.-*Will Dad Ever Move Back?*
Hutchins, Pat-*Don't Forget the Bacon*
Keats, Ezra Jack-*Pete's Chair*
Knoche, Norma R. & Mary Voell Jones-*What Do Mothers Do?*
Lindman, Maj-*Flicka, Ricka, Dicka Bake a Cake*
Low, Alice-*Grandmas and Grandpas*
Mayer, Mercer-*Just Grandma and Me; Just Grandpa and Me; Just Me and My Dad*
Melser, June & Joy Cowley-*Grandpa, Grandpa*
Myers, Bernice-*My Mother is Lost*
Relf, Patricia-*That New Baby*
Simon, Norma-*All Kinds of Families*
Stecher, Miriam B. & Alice S. Kandell-*Daddy and Ben Together*
Swetnam, Evelyn-*The day You Were Born*
Wittram, H.R.-*My Little Brother*
Zolotow, Charlotte-*The Quarreling Book*

FRIENDS

Aesop-*The Lion and the Mouse*
Aliki-*We Are Best Friends*
Anderson, Janet-*A Hug for a New Friend*
Anglund, John Walsh-*A Friend is Someone Who Likes You*
Arneson, D.J.-*A Friend Indeed*
Baker, Laura Nelson-*The Friendly Beasts*
Barkin, Carol-*Are We Still Best Friends?*
Battles, Edith-*One to Teeter-Totter*
Behrens, June-*Together*
Berenstain, Stan-*The Berenstain Bears and the Trouble with Friends*
Berger, Terry-*A Friend Can Help*
Bonsall, Crosby-*It's Mine...A Greedy Book; The Case of the Hungry Strangers*
Bornstern, Ruth-*Little Gorilla*
Bourque, Nina-*The Best Trade of All*
Carruth, Jane-*Making New Friends*
Cavanna, Betty-*Jean and Johnny*
Cohen, Miriam-*Best Friends; So What; Will I Have a Friend?*
Conta, Marcia Maher-*Feelings Between Friends*
Curry, Nancy-*My Friend is Mrs. Jones*
Deering, Janet-*Eddie's Moving Day*

TABLE 6.3   Continued

Delton, Judy-*Two Good Friends*
DeRegniers, Beatrice Schenk-*May I Bring a Friend?*
DeWitt, Jamie-*Jamie's Turn*
Fremlin, Robert-*Three Friends*
Gans, Margaret-*Pam and Pam*
Gehm, Katherine-*Happiness is Smiling*
Gould, Deborah-*Brenden's Best-Timed Friend*
Graham, John-*I Love You Mouse*
Harmey, Barbara-*I Used to Be Older*
Heide, Florence Parry, & Sylvia Van Clief-*That's What Friends Are For*
Hilbert, Margaret-*Not I, Not I*
Hoff, Syd-*Danny and the Dinosaur; Who Will Be My Friends?*
Holland, Joyce-*Porter, the Pouting Pigeon*
Hughes, Shirley-*Alfie Gives a Hand*
Ichikawa, Satomi-*Friends*
Johnson, Gladys O.-*Jimmie, the Youngest Errand Boy*
Krasilovksy, Phyllis-*The Shy Little Girl*
Lavelle, Shiela-*My Best Friend*
Lobel, Arnold-*Frog and Toad All Year; Frog and Toad Together*
Masterson, Audry Nelson-*The Day the Gypsies Came to Town*
Mazer, Norma Fox-*B, My Name Is Bunny*
Minarik, Elsa-*Little Bear's Friend*
Moncure, Jane Belk-*Julie's New Home*
Oxenbury, Helen-*Friends*
Park, Barbara-*Buddies*
Peterson, Mike-*The Biggest Giraffe*
Rey, H.A.-*Cecily G. and the 9 Monkeys*
Robins, Joan-*Addie Meets Max*
Simon, Shirley-*Best Friend*
Slote, Alfred-*My Robot Buddy*
Steig, William-*Amos and Boris*
Tabot, Winifred-*Dennys Friend Rags*
Waber, Bernard-*Lovable Lyle*
White, E.B.-*Charlotte's Web*

SAFETY AND RULES

Ady, Sharon-*We didn't Mean To*
Alexander, Martha-*No Ducks in Our Bathtub*
Bendick, Jeanne-*Accident Prevention*
Berenstain, Stan-*The Bike Lesson*
Berry, Joy Wilt-*Accidents*
Grossman, Jill-*Bicycle Songs of Safety*
Hader, B. & Elmer Hader-*Stop, Look, and Listen*
Kessler, Leonard-*Last One in is a Rotten Egg*
Leaf, Munro-*Safety Can Be Fun*
Marron, Carol A.-*Mother Told Me So*
Talanda, Susan-*Dad Told Me Not To*

BEATRIX POTTER

Crouch, Marcus-*Beatrix Potter*
Mayer, Ann Margaret-*The Two Worlds of Beatrix Potter*
Potter, Beatrix-*The Classic Tale of Peter Rabbit and Other Cherished Stories*

TEACHER RESOURCE BOOKS

Carlson, Nancy-*Bunnies and Their Hobbies*
Hodgson, Harriet-*Toyworks Simple Toys to Make and Enjoy for Ages 3-7*
Lionni, Leo-*Let's Make Rabbits*
Warren, Jean-*1-2-3 Games No—Lose-Group Games for Young Children*
Wilmes, Liz, and Dick Wilmes-*Circle Time for Holidays and Seasons Book*

AV MATERIALS

RECORDS:

Learning Basic Skills Through Music—Educational Activities, Inc.
Learning Basic Skills Through Music Vocabulary—Educational Activities, Inc.
The Tale of Peter Rabbit in Story and Song
Little Grey Rabbit Goes to Sea
Little Grey Rabbit's Christmas
The Rabbit and the Cat

FILMSTRIPS:

Bunnies' Easter Surprise
Dinosaurs Beware
I'm No Fool With Safety
Many Kinds of Pets
Rackety Rabbit and the Runaway Easter Egg
Watch Out—Learning Tree

VIDEOS:

Playground Safety: As Simple as A,B,C
Primary Safety: Bus Safety
Primary Safety: On the Way to School
Primary Safety: School and Playground
School Bus Safety and Courtesy

Note: A special thanks to Dr. Carolyn Schluck and her students, Doris Jean Whitten, Sue McDaniel, Krissy Gentry, and Tina L. Easterwood, for the Peter Rabbit web and list of rabbit books.

After reading through the available children's books and again reflecting on the children's discussion of the first lesson, the teacher adds a third circle, filling it in with subtopics related to the second-strand broad topics:

STRANDS

A	B	C	D
Rabbits	Friendship	Family	Rules &
-kinds	-types	-care of	Safety
-care of	-who is a friend	-roles	-class
-enemies	importance	-members	-school
-protection	-qualities	-feelings	-home
	-feelings	experiences	-community
E	F	G	H
Beatrix Potter	Homes	Garden Animals	Gardens
-author	-materials used	-birds	-plants
-life of	-animals	-mice	-plant cycle
-illustrator	-people	-spiders	-vegetables
-other stories	-kinds	-ladybugs	-seeds
	-designs	-enemies	-tools
		-life cycles	-parts
		-characteristics	

FIGURE 6.3   Peter Rabbit Web

Under the heading of each strand above, we see the subheadings which have been indicated by the interest of the children and by the resource materials. The web, with its parallel list of books, is an outline of the course of study, backed by information sources. The web narrows down the content while at the same time graphing an interrelationship between the headings and strands.

The teacher may design many learning activities using the Cognitive Content Area constructs:

Strand A-Rabbits, kinds of rabbits (classification), care of (seriating steps in caring for rabbit), habitat (causality-white rabbits in snowy places, brown ones in fields, etc.), life cycle (seriating stages of growth), enemies (classification-from the land, from air), protection (causality-camouflage, speed, quietness).

Strand B-Friendship, types of friends for rabbits (classification)—forest rangers, children, who can be one (causality), importance/qualities (seriate actions one might take to make friends), feelings (classification).

(Progressing in a similar manner with the remaining strands.)

TEACHER BEHAVIORAL CONTINUUM—THEMATIC-PROJECT TEACHING

With an understanding of the web for organizing content knowledge, the triangle construction as representational level, Cognitive Content Areas, operational level, and finally, the taxonomy of questioning, we may now apply these constructs to the process of thematic-project teaching. We may visually represent the use of these constructs with the Teacher Behavioral Continuum (TBC)—Thematic-Project Teaching.

Step 1, Say

We begin teaching new information with directive statements, such as "This is a ___." Or, we may begin with reading a book—which may also serve as a motivational experience. If the child is already motorically involved (petting the rabbit) we may verbally encode concepts for the child (levels of operation).

Step 2 Show

Next, we show the child a model of the concept at any of the three levels of representation: a real object, symbolic representation of the object (e.g., a picture), or a sign (spoken or written word, such as "rabbit").

Step 3, Check

Checking to determine if the child understands the concept is done by asking questions, which progress up the taxonomy from facts/labels, to

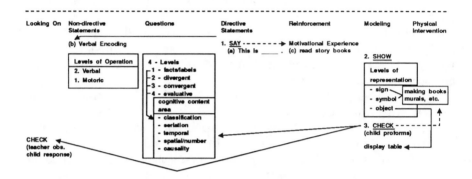

FIGURE 6.4   Teacher Behavior Continuum——Thematic-Project Teaching

convergent, to divergent, and finally, to evaluative. The questions relate to one of the Cognitive Content Areas (classification, seriation, temporal, spatial/number, causality). Checking can also be done by having the child motorically enact the concept (hop like a rabbit). The child might also be checked for learning by observing her level of representation as seen in her paintings, drawings, etc. Read again the introductory example of *The Tale of Peter Rabbit* to see where these teaching concepts would be applied.

A culminating experience, such as all the children having the opportunity to touch and observe a real rabbit, might occur after a daily lesson; or an art show or skit for parents might be presented at the end of the learning unit.

Let's take another example. The "garden" strand leads to the making of the children's own "Mr. McGregor's garden" in the corner of their playground (or on the windowsill). They have classified seeds, used spatial concepts in planting their seeds, and used temporal and number concepts in measuring and graphing the plants as they grew. They have also made a book related to gardens/vegetables using, of course, symbols and signs. The "Culminating" experience might be making vegetable soup with the vegetables they have grown, and eating it for lunch.

LESSON PLANS

A lesson plan (Figure 6.5) provides an outline to guide the teacher through content and method presentation and processes.

1. Lesson Plan

The top items, teacher's name, date lesson presented, theme name, and strand name are self explanatory. The lesson number keeps the lessons in

FIGURE 6.5   Lesson Plans

Theme Name _____

Strand Name _____

Lesson Number _____(letter) _____(no.)

Teacher's Name _____

Date Taught _____

To Group: (circle) A B C D

II. Goals:
      1. _____
      2. _____
      3. _____
      4. _____
      5. _____

III. Key Vocabulary

_____

IV. Materials Needed
      1. Teacher _____
      2. Child _____

V. A. Motivational Experience (adv. org.)

_____

    B. Procedures
      1. _____
      2. _____
      3. _____
      4. _____
      5. _____
      6. _____
    C. Follow-up Lesson
      Go to: _____

VI. Methods of Evaluation
      1. _____
      2. _____
      3. _____

sequence. Many plans will be made under the headings of each strand. Circling the group (A,B,C,D) records which students have been taught this lesson.

2. Goals

Goals are statements as to what the children should gain from their study of a particular strand. Implicit in these goals will be the Cognitive Content Areas, levels of representation, and levels of operation. We may also see goals related to level of thinking(facts/labels, convergent, divergent, and evaluative).

> Example: Children will gain an the ability to classify (Content Area) kinds of rabbits (Strand A) and their native habitat, and represent this though creating a diorama (symbolic representation) for snow, dessert, and forest rabbits.
> Example: children will be able to care for (Strand A) the rabbit (Motoric operation) and graph the number (Content Area- seriation/number) of pellets eaten and rabbit's weight. (Levels of representation-symbol and sign)
> Example: Children will be able to classify (Content Area) vegetables (Strand H) a root (in soil), head (on soil), and veining (above soil) by making plant shapes (Level of representation-symbolic) and placing them correctly in a Garden picture. (Page 3 in Rabbit Book to follow)

3. Key Vocabulary

The Key Vocabulary contains the new words that the child will learn, and will come from the Strands, Cognitive Content Areas, and Operation Level experiences.

4. Materials Needed

As the teacher prepares to give the lesson, it is critical to have all needed materials at hand. A glance at the Materials Needed list can quickly reveal if anything is lacking. At times the materials list is divided into Teacher materials and Child materials (to be used by the children).

5. Methods of Evaluation

Did the children understand the concepts taught? The Evaluation methods listed here are general ones which might come at the end of the unit, but the evaluation should take place throughout the lesson. The Child Play Behavioral Rating Scale (Figure 12.3) and Social Observational System (Figure 12.7) or written observations could be use to assess the children's knowledge or representational ability. See Chapter 12 on methods of assessment and evaluation.

Strategies

The subheadings under Strategies are: "A. Motivational Experiences," "B. Steps," "C. Evaluation," and "D. Culminating Activity."

Motivational Experience

The opening of a lesson should seize the children's attention. It also models what will be learned: "We will read Peter Rabbit and learn many new things about rabbits and their surroundings." The children now know where they will go in the journey (lesson) with the teacher. Although storybooks will often be used for motivational beginnings, other methods, such as audiovisual aids, could be used.

Steps

An outline is written to help the teacher follow the three-step lesson (say, show, check), and apply various aspects from the TBC (Figure 6.7), such as modeling, directive statements, questions (facts/labels, convergent, divergent, and evaluative), nondirective statements and looking on.

Evaluation

Evaluating the children's learning should be done throughout the lesson.

Symbols to Signs

In the thematic-project process the child acquires new information and then represents his understanding first in play symbols—(paintings, clay, sociodramatic play, etc.) and with the use of written words. Symbolic development has been described in the play-activity curriculum. Painting and similar symbolic projects will move from random scribbling, to controlled scribbling, to the circle, etc. We may use the Child Play Behavioral Rating Scale

(Figure 12.3) to assess where the child is in symbolic development. The projects that the teacher will set up and encourage the child to complete will involve all forms of expressive media, e.g., sociodramatic play; mini-life toys; murals; string painting; sewing; wire sculpturing; pasting, cutting, tearing; puppet making; collage; and carpentry.

The bridging to signs requires that the teacher take the child's dictation after he has completed one of his theme-related symbolic projects. For example, the child has cut from white corduroy materials a rabbit shape, and glued it onto a sheet of cardboard. He brings this to the teacher and asks, "Could you write 'Peter Rabbit' on my picture?" The child is beginning to bridge from symbols (pictures he has drawn) to signs (words he wants written) in such paintings or drawings, which during the kindergarten year can be bound as "books."

Reading Readiness

It might be surprising to the beginning teacher to see that the child is actually writing before he can read. This is because we are following the Piagetian-Weikart construct for the developmental progression of representational ability. When is the child ready for formal reading instruction? Marie Clay has devised a *Concepts About Print Test* (1979) that is given in a one-teacher-to-one-child situation using a small child's book called *Sand*. With the use of the *Sand* book the child is tested for his understanding of the print traditions which indicate readiness for formal reading instruction. The concepts about print test asks, does the child know:

1. the front of the book?
2. the difference between illustrations (symbols) and print (signs)?
3. print (not the picture) tells the story?
4. what a letter is?
5. what a word is?
6. the first letter of a word
7. the function of the space
8. use of punctuation (periods, question marks, quotation, or "talk," marks)

This individualized test is standardized and used by the thematic-project teachers to determine when children are ready for more formal instruction.

Culminating Activity

The culminating activity should require the child to use the new information gained, and should involve an element of fun. Another example for use with the Peter Rabbit unit would be having the children enact the story. A culminating experience for a cooking-science lesson would be to "eat the bread" that they made. Others are: making murals or books, and producing plays.

CLASSROOM DISPLAY TABLE AND MURALS

In most thematic-project classrooms what is being studied is apparent as soon as you walk through the door! Displays of art or "construction" work are prominent, usually forming a classroom mural. This mural would use children's creations to demonstrate what they have learned. A mural on the Peter Rabbit unit, for example, might have on the left side a fir tree with a hole underneath Peter's home. This home "under the ground" would have a table with a fireplace in the background, and a bed for Peter when he is ill. There could be a road leading to Mr. McGregor's garden, with gates, toolshed, various vegetables grown, the blueberry netting, the water can, the scarecrow with Peter's coat and shoes on it, and the various animals to be found in the garden (cat, mice, and sparrow). Of course, Mr. McGregor would be there, too.

Located near the front door of the thematic-project classroom one usually finds attractively covered tables and boxes which create a display area for those items which children bring in to share, such as books about rabbits, a "lucky" rabbit's foot, mounted pictures of various types of rabbits, etc. These items are all shared at circle time, and are on display for children and parents to inspect.

TRADITIONAL SUBJECT AREAS

Subject areas such as science, math, music, and reading are not taught separately in the thematic-project curriculum. Each of these subject areas is integrated into the webbing. The learning unit would contain music related to rabbits, science related to garden planting, and math as children seriate and use numbers to make graphs and charts.

SUMMARY

A series of constructs has been provided for implementing the thematic-project curriculum. One of the primary teaching techniques is questioning, using the four-level taxonomy (facts/labels, convergent, divergent, and evaluative). With these types of questions, the students will develop knowledge that can be subcategorized as classification, seriation/number, temporal, spatial, and causality (Weikart's triangle). Once the children have acquired new information or knowledge, they will attempt to represent it, first through play (symbols) and finally through the written word (sign). The general content to be studied can be organized using the webbing process, with the central factor being children's literature and real-life experiences.

Activities

1. Read a high-quality children's book to a group of young children, and when finished question them using the question taxonomy, starting with lower-level questions and working your way up to greater abstraction. Repeat this with a new book, but this time select one of the Cognitive Content Areas from the Weikart Curriculum Triangle, questioning the children with the taxonomy related to one of these content areas.
2. Locate yourself at an outdoor water table with a group of young children who are playing intently with the water. See if you can verbally encode their learning as they motorically interact with the water.
3. Make a webbing for these topics, selecting a book for the center of the web: bears, circus, musical instruments, dinosaurs, space rockets, the seashore, and the zoo.
4. Find the *Concept of Print Test* by Marie Clay and give the *Sand* test to three children ages 4, 5, and 6.

References

BREARLEY, M., *The Teaching of Young Children*. New York: Schocken Books, 1971.

BRIGGS, C. and C. ELKIND, "Characteristics of Early Readers" in *Perceptual and Motor Skills*, 44, 1977.

CAZDEN, C. B., *Classroom Discourse: The Language of Teaching and Learning*. Portsmouth, N.H.: Heinemann, 1988.

CLAY, M., *The Early Detection of Reading Difficulties: A Diagnostic Survey with Recovery Procedures*. Exeter, N.H.: Heinemann, 1979.

COCKRAN-SMITH, M., *The Making of a Reader*. Norwood, N.J.: Ablex, 1984.

COHEN, D. H., "The Effect of Literature on Vocabulary and Reading Achievement" in *Elementary English*, 45 (2), 1968.

DURKIN, D., *Children Who Read Early: Two Longitudinal Studies*. New York: Teachers College Press, 1966.

ELLEY, W.B., "Vocabulary Acquisition from Listening to Stories," in *Educational Leadership*, 36 (2), 1978.

FERREIRO, E., and A. TEBEROSKY, *Literacy Before Schooling*. Exeter, N.H.: Heinemann, 1979.

GLAZER, J. L., "Reading Aloud to Young Children," in *Learning to Love Literature*, L.L. Lamme, ed. Urbanna, Ill.: National Council of Teachers of English, 1981.

HERRELL, A., "A Child and an Adult Interact with a Book: The Effects on Language and Literacy in Kindergarten." unpublished dissertation, Tallahassee, Fla.: Florida State University, 1989.

HOLDAWAY, D., *The Foundations of Literacy*. Sydney: Ashton Scholastic, 1979.

MARTINEZ, M., and N. ROSER, "Read It Again: The Value of Repeated Readings During Storytime." in *Reading Teacher*, 38 (8), 1985.

PHILLIPS, J.L., *The Origins of Intellect: Piaget's Theory*. San Francisco: W.H. Freeman, 1969.

PIAGET, J. and B. INHELDER, *The Growth of Logical Thinking: From Childhood to Adolescence*. New York: Basic Books, 1958.

SMILANSKY, S. and L. SHEFATYA, *Facilitating Play: A Medium for Promoting Cognitive, Socio-Emotional and Academic Development in Young Children*. Gaithersburg, Md.: Psychosocial & Educational Publications, 1990.

WEIKART, D. and others, *The Cognitively Oriented Curriculum: A Framework for Preschool Teachers*. Washington, D.C.: NAEYC Publication, 1970.

CHAPTER SEVEN

PLAYGROUND AND OUTDOOR SPACE

The father of early education, Fredrich Froebel, called his early school for young children the Kindergarten, or children's garden, because in fact it was located during large amounts of the day in a garden. Our garden or playground, as we now call it is a space that historically has been given little to no thought. Critics have called them asphalt deserts! Some adults consider that playgrounds are places where children are taken out for a 15-minute period to "run off steam" before getting back to the important learning inside.

We must be careful that such attitudes and traditions do not guide our design and use of outdoor space for young children. It is our position that the outdoor space is just as important as indoor space, and in some aspects we can do many things outdoors that could never be accomplished indoors. Primarily, the outdoor space will be organized around the play-activity curriculum constructs, but with the addition of much more equipment and materials to support fundamental movement patterns in sensorimotor play.

The arrangement of outdoor space is based on the classification of play as symbolic, fluid-construction, structured-construction, and restructuring-construction, with greater space and equipment for sensorimotor play, and applying the unit-play potential measure of simple, complex, and super-complex units (Krichevsky, 1969). Outdoor equipment, once built, is difficult to rearrange because many pieces of equipment (climbing towers, decks, and poles, for instance) are permanently cemented down; thus, it is critical to plan carefully. Grid paper, as used for our indoor diagram, can be used also for the outdoor plan, with one square equal to one square foot.

Some state laws stipulate a minimum amount of square footage of "usable, safe, and sanitary outdoor play area" per child in any group using the play area at one time. The SYC playground is built on 2,400 sq ft and, based on Florida's requirements, would be able to hold 50+ children. This means that at least two classes of 20 to 25 children could be on the playground at one time.

A number of variables must be considered when arranging your equipment to support play:

-slope and water runoff
-sun and shade
-ground surfaces (concrete, P-gravel, sand, grass, etc.)
-visual supervision
-storage of props

Before beginning your plans, consider the use of drainage pipes to permit water to drain quickly, and retaining walls, which will stop erosion. Children love to climb banks and slopes, but their feet soon kill the grass and erosion occurs. These slopes can add to the variety of surfaces in a playground, and if they can be terraced properly, can be considered a climbing or running area. If you are inexperienced in such matters, check with a landscape expert or a construction specialist: one of your student's parents might have this expertise and a parent-teacher playground planning committee could be formed.

SAMPLE PLAYGROUND

To explain the dos and don'ts of playground building we will use the sample playground (Figure 7.1), which is 40 by 60 feet and has been divided into six zones (A1, A2, B1, B2, C1, and C2). Every school's outdoor space will present unique problems—harsh sun in Phoenix, fire ants and insects in Orlando, etc., so the teacher or playground committee may want to read in depth such excellent books as *Children's Play and Playgrounds* (see booklist at the end of the chapter).

Zone A1—Upper Body Exercise

The northeastern zone (A1) of our playground map contains a large maple tree, an adult park bench, a three-tire pyramid, an L-shaped frame made

FIGURE 7.1   Sample Playground

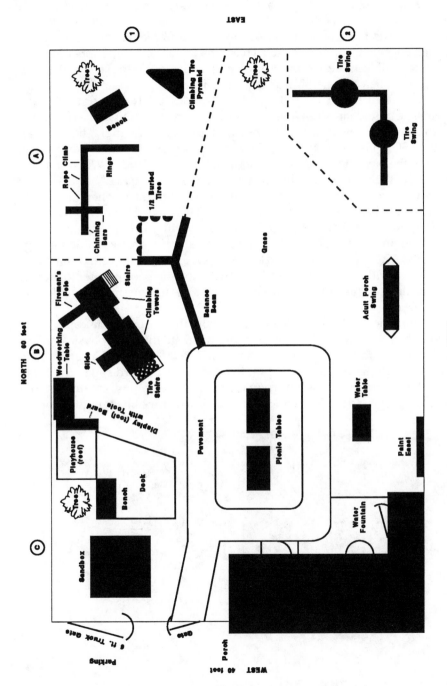

out of treated 6 in. x 8 in. x 8 ft wood beams held up by three uprights at each corner, 6 ft off the ground surface for hanging ropes, ladders, and rings. The surface can be sand, but P-gravel is best because it never hardens up, and it moves when children fall on it. The drawback to P-gravel is that since it does move it needs to be 14 to 18 in. deep and well-framed in by wood beams (dotted lines on the map). We do not recommend the new chip rubber surfaces for young children because they put chips in their mouths to chew, which may get stuck in their throats, similar to foam balls.

The adult bench (B) is located well under the tree in order to take advantage of its shade (remember that we will have the sun in the east in the morning and setting in the west, on our map, in late evening). The first step on the TBC is visual looking and the two benches (A and B), the adult swing (C), and the picnic table (D) will be located with this in mind. When children challenge themselves on this equipment they will quickly check these teacher's observation points, make eye contact with the teacher and "know that a teacher is watching" to keep them safe. This shaded bench is also a good place to snuggle with children and read stories with them.

Hanging from the east side of the L-shaped frame are two chinning rings on chains. The rings are mounted at the height that the tallest child can reach. One or two wide but small tires (drilled with holes to permit water to escape) can lay about in the area to be used as step-stools for the smaller children to reach the rings.

From the north side of the L-frame hang three 1 in. cotton ropes and a rope ladder with wooden steps. In order to create different physical motor problems, one rope has knots tied every 6 in. and the second 12 in. apart, with the end touching the ground left untied and free. The third rope's knots are also 12 in. apart, but the bottom end is buried in the ground, creating a fixed rope. The rope ladder is made up of two similar ropes hanging free at the

FIGURE 7.2   Zone A-1: Upper Body Exercise

bottom, and running through 1 1/2 in. thick wooden dowels, creating steps. The steps are at graduated distances, one 6 in. apart, the next 8 in., the next 12 in., the next 18 in., and the last 24 in. On the crossbeam above each ladder is mounted a small "dinner bell" with a thick string hanging from the clapper. This is a reinforcer: The children climb to the bell, grab the clapper rope, and pull to ring the bell. For young 3-year-olds the clapper string can be lengthened.

On the west support beam are mounted three galvanized bars 1 in. thick, in a cross arrangement, for chinning. The lowest bar of the three should be at the height of the full reach of your smallest child, and the highest at the full reach of the tallest child. The third bar should be placed equidistant from the two. This climbing apparatus should be 5 ft to 6 ft from the fence or bench.

The last item in this zone is a tire pyramid three tires high. The inside space of the pyramid provides a "secret" place for the young child to be alone at times. All tires need to be drilled with holes to permit drainage. Although some people feel that tires are unattractive, they make excellent climbing surfaces for children. SYC discourages metal climbing frames or any metal outdoor equipment. In hot climates the metal surfaces burn children, and in freezing climates the children unfortunately put their tongues on them. A climbing frame should permit a child to fall freely, not hitting any bar. An upright or a half-globe shape will permit unobstructed falling. (Holes should be 1 1/2 times the size of the child's body.) The square multibar honeycombed apparatus strikes the child in the face and neck as he falls through it; it is the most frightening piece of equipment seen on the playground for children of any age.

The play potentials can be counted as:

3 ropes/1 ladder	4 simple units	4
1 bench	2 simple units	2
3 chinning bars	3 simple units	2
1 tire pyramid	1 complex unit	4
		----------
		total 12

Zone A2—Swinging

In zone A2 is located an L-shaped support beam for two swivel tire swings (purchase good quality swivels with greased fittings). We discourage back and forth swings, which often strike and injure children. Also, from a programmatic point of view, young children historically had their parents or a servant to push them, and we would not want to use teacher time this way.

The tire swings, on the other hand, require cooperation of two or more children, and create a natural need for cooperation if everyone is to ride. Much is learned on a tire swing by very active, assertive children. P-gravel or sand is a good surface, boxed in by beams on all sides. The beams should be at least 12 in. above ground level, which will section this zone off. If a child is running, he will need to stop or slow down to step over the beam, and will thus be less likely to run through the swing area. The upright support beams need to be 10 ft apart with the crossbeam located 6 to 8 ft above the ground, depending on the age of the children. The fence and terracing beam should be well back from the swing so that a child would not fall on them, if he should fall off the swing at its highest point.

Play Potential

2 tire swings	2 complex units	8
		----------
		total 8

Zone B1—Climbing Towers, Balance Beams, Carpentry Table

Located in Zone B1 are, first, two climbing towers (platforms) standing no more than 3 ft above ground level. Each tower should have two entrance/exits with an upright board ladder at the southeast end of the small tower. If ladders are not upright, and placed at an angle, falling children will hit each rung of the ladder with their chins; upright ladders permit them to fall free.

The other exit, on the north side of the small tower, is a fireman's pole. Also, at the stepoff point a predrilled tire should be mounted on the outside in such a manner that if the child does fall backwards his head would hit the rubber tire, not the wood platform. The pole should be positioned 18 in. away from the tire, requiring the child to reach out and providing much clearance.

On the large tower we have a two-tier upright ladder for entering or exiting, and the second exit is a 3 ft wide slide providing a steep slope into a sand pit. Notice that this slide, which has a great deal of surface area, is facing northwest, away from the sun, and is also shaded by the tower. When children commit themselves to going down the slide we want them to slide quickly, not to stop halfway with other children behind them. We warn against narrow, freestanding metal slide-ladder combinations. These slides are among the top three most dangerous pieces of play (Frost, 1979). The children become "drunk" and competitive, like rats in a maze—sliding, running quickly to get back in line, climbing quickly, and pushing those in front of them off at the top, where there is no platform. Wide slides combined with platforms create greater choice and complexity.

We suggest that this area be framed in by groundbeams 6 to 8 in. high. (Note: Be careful where you purchase sand because in some areas of the country the sand might contain industrial toxic waste. Or get the seller to provide in writing that the sand has been tested and is free of harmful materials.) The towers may be walled in on one or two sides (north side will section it off from the sliding areas) making clubhouses under each tower. If a floor is not put in children will play with sand under these towers. Ask experts in your area about the best wood to use in the platforms where children will be seated. Some treated wood gives off a chemical which can be absorbed by children's bodies, and some soft wood, when weathered, dries out producing lots of splinters.

The landscaping beams that section this zone off on the southeast corner can be used for balance beams by also including upright half-buried tires as "steppingstones." You may want to raise one end of the beam to create a balance uphill problem, but keep all beams close to the ground.

At the northwest corner of this zone we have placed a carpentry table against the fence on a small deck with a tool display board. The display board should have locks on silhouettes of the tools so control of error with these potentially dangerous tools can be maintained. Ideally, if the display board had doors that could be locked, these tools would not need to be taken in each evening.

Play Potential

2 towers	2 complex units	8
slide	1 simple unit	1
fireman's pole	1 simple unit	1
carpentry table	1 complex unit	4
balance beams	3 simple units	3
2 clubhouses	2 complex units	8
		----------
		total 25

Zone B2—Open Grass, Porch Swing

Nearly 80% of Zone B2 is made up of the tricycle sidewalk- oval, and an open space with grass. This can be considered "potential" space, and boards, wooden barrels, and boxes can be placed here permitting the children to build their own structures. (See *Moving and Knowing* by Lydia A. Gerhardt for a thorough understanding of such materials.) The wooden adult porch swing supported by two uprights and one cross beam is another seated area for teachers to observe and have children join them. Leave plenty of space behind the swing and the fence.

Play Potential

open grassy area with props	2 complex units	8
2 swings	2 complex units	4
		----------
		total 16

Zone C1—Sandbox, Deck, Playhouse, Large Blocks

Zone C1 contains the entrance gate with a sidewalk that takes visitors from the parking area to the front of the school, and the trike sidewalk-oval. We would suggest a 6 ft fence with a 6 ft gate, the latch mounted as high as possible to permit easy access by adults and prevent children from opening the gate and slipping out of the playground unnoticed. The 6 ft fence with a lockable gate gives the playground greater security at night and on weekends from vandals. We like the primary entrance and exit to the classroom for school parents to be inside the playground fenced-in area, giving us double protection if the child should go out the school door unnoticed. If there are back doors that do not open onto the fenced-in area, teachers should discourage its use by parents and children.

There is a second gate on the west side, a 5 ft locked gate, which can be opened to permit a truck to back in and deliver sand. We would strongly suggest the outdoor sand box be located in the shade in hot climates, in the sun in cold climates, where a sand truck can back up to it, and never under the edges of roofs from which water drips off. Many sandboxes in playgrounds are sandless from a lack of time or strength or money to get 6 tons of prewashed sand wheelbarrowed in; sand is inexpensive, but labor for wheelbarrowing is not. And one can always depend on sand to disappear every fourth month, stolen by sand fairies to be found on the floor of the parents' cars or on the bed where the child takes off his jeans.

The sandbox should be covered by a strong canvas tarp or wooden top which can be folded back, to prevent animals from fouling it at night. Prop storage should be nearby. In our example, props are kept in a large wooden box with wheels, stored in the shed in Zone C2, which can be brought out by pulling an attached rope or pushing by the children across the tricycle sidewalk. The tree in this zone provides all day shade to the sandbox, the adult park bench (A), the deck, and the playhouse, which are all areas were children tend to be seated or to use large muscles less.

The deck is raised 1 ft above the level of the tricycle sidewalk, thus preventing the tricycles from being ridden on the deck. Three sides of the deck are further sectioned off by a low rope fence. On the south end of the deck are large wooden blocks with an auto-steering wheel mounted nearby. Also included are baskets of cars and trucks and miniature life toys and furniture. Children may use the blocks for structured-construction or dramatic play, or props can be brought over from the playhouse for sociodramatic play with the large blocks.

A playhouse is found on the north side of the deck, walled off with lattice on three sides and covered with a roof. Mounted inside are shelves, an old porcelain sink, and a host of domestic props which are of limited value and are permanently stored under the shelving.

Play Potential

sandbox	super-complex	8
large blocks	complex	4
props	complex	4
playhouse	super-complex	8
bench	2 simple units	2
		total 26

Zone C2—Storage Shed, Water Table, Paint Easel

In the final zone, C2, we find a water fountain with a faucet for attaching a hose. Concrete leads to the tricycle sidewalk, and, without any step, into the storage shed. When the door to the storage shed is open, then tricycles, wagons, and balls can be brought out by the children. Once the equipment is out, the door is hooked open so children can drive the tricycles into the shed and make it a playhouse. Teachers planning to use this storage shed must organize it together, deciding where to paint marks on the floor where tricycles will be parked, labeling storage boxes, and painting silhouettes where equipment will hang. If this is not done, children will not know where to return the equipment, and things will just be thrown inside by the children and tired teachers at the end of the day. This will destroy equipment, cause conflicts with other staff who must use the equipment, and limit play because the props just won't get out of the shed.

On the south side of the zone is a double painting easel mounted on the fence. Under the easel is a wood-framed trench containing P-gravel (2 ft deep), so that the easel can be hosed down and colored water contained in the trench. Nearby is a water table, the ground surface covered with grass. A circular sidewalk, wide enough for two tricycles, channels the wheeled toys around the painting space. In the center of the tricycle oval are two picnic tables, one containing structured construction materials, and the second for pasting, cutting, and other restructuring-construction. These tables can also be used for snacktime.

Play Potentials

double paint easel	2 simple units	2
water table	1 complex unit	4
storage shed as play-house	1 complex unit	4
3 tricycles	3 simple units	3
1 wheelbarrow	1 simple unit	1
1 wagon	1 simple unit	1
1 picnic table (st-con)	1 complex unit or 4 simple units	4
1 picnic table (re-con)	4 simple units	4
		total 23

Adding the play potentials, we get 110 units on the playground; add 15 more units for other simple unit props from the storage shed (e.g., hoppity-hops) and we have 125 units. Dividing by the 2 1/2 play units required for each child, we have now designed a playground to hold 50 children at one time. Notice also that we have sociodramtic play, structured-construction, restructuring-construction, fluids, and many sensorimotor play items for a balanced play-activity environment.

It is also important to point out that we have four observation points from which the teachers will be able to keep watch over and facilitate the play activity of the children: the bench (A) under the tree in zone C1, which would also be an excellent spot for the teacher to be located first thing in the morning and at the end of day to greet parents arriving and departing, as well as to supervise the sand, deck, and play areas. The teacher on bench (B) in zone A1 would monitor that zone plus the towers and large structures. The teacher on the porch swing (C) would monitor the swings, the large grassy areas, and part of the tricycle oval. Finally, the teacher standing or seated at the picnic table (D) would monitor the water table, paint easels, storage shed and water fountain, and also would greet parents.

PORCHES AND ENCLOSURES

In climates with extreme heat or cold, or heavy precipitation, a porch with roof is an important addition to the school space. When children are confined indoors for many days, the movement to a protective nearly-outdoor space with fresh air, where they can use "outdoor" voices and larger motor behavior, seems to help children to relax. If this space is limited in size the teachers may rotate the play daily between various play classifications.

The storage shed and large structures have been located in corners so they do not create "dead" areas in which children cannot be observed. Locations of teacher observation points must be clear to staff and children, thus facilitating visual supervision.

Finally, storage is an important consideration. Outdoor playgrounds should not consist only of statically arranged permanent equipment, but must also have props so that children can play imaginatively.

With a well-organized outdoor space the teacher can now use the observation system or do a play-behavioral rating to see how children are performing outside, and then set goals for play facilitation, using the Teacher Behavior Continuum.

The sample playground is one way of organizing space and equipment, and has permitted us to demonstrate way in which variables (shade, surfaces, etc.) may be used. Every outdoor space will be unique with its own problems and strengths. For more reading in this area, consult the references which follow. With these constructs, the teacher is well on the way to organizing a playground, but more reading might be needed to handle unique situations.

Activities
1. Locate and visit a playground designed for children younger than age 6. Score the play potentials using the Kritchevsky system. Select the play-ground facilities which scored highest and lowest in this system, return to each for 1/2 hour, and keep a running tally of the aggressive or con-flict incidents for each playground, and compare them. What differ-ences did you find? Why? Now, use Parten's stages, observe each child, and place a tally mark under each social stage in which each

child is performing. Does this playground support higher social play? What would you recommend?

2. Visit three preschool playgrounds where children are active and teachers are supervising. Draw a map of the space, and then with a magic marker, for a 15 minute period, draw a line on your map to record the moving events of the teacher. What space in the playground is being monitored and facilitated? What equipment or materials are in this space? What space is not visited by the teacher? What equipment is in this space?

3. Visit a preschool playground. List all the equipment and materials under the play classifications (symbolic, construction, etc.) and determine what is underrepresented. How would you change it? How does the sun help or hinder the activities in the playground? How would you change it? What are the surfaces under each type of climbing equipment? Would each surface create any danger to children if they should fall on it?

4. Interview an experienced teacher of young children, and ask him or her what children are expected to get from a playground experience. Ask what his or her role is, and why the school has the equipment they have.

5. Find an inadequate playground used by young children and, using grid paper and symbols, organize this space as if you had limited funds using the constructs introduced above.

6. Select five catalogues selling playground equipment for young children. Pick out from each catalogue one piece of equipment that you like which is not on the sample playground and one that you feel is definitely inappropriate, and show these to two experienced teachers of young children. Ask them to evaluate the ten items.

References

Florida Administrative Code, Chapter 10M-12, *Child Day Care Standards*. State of Florida, Tallahassee, Fla: Department of Health and Rehabilitative Services, 1986.

FROST, JOE L. and BARRY L. KLEIN, *Children's Play and Playgrounds*. Boston: Allyn and Bacon, 1979.

GERHARDT, LYDIA A., *Moving and Knowing: The Young Child Orients Himself in Space.* Englewood Cliffs, N.J.: Prentice-Hall, 1973.

KRITCHEVSKY, SYBIL, and others, *Planning Environments for Young Children: Physical Space.* Washington, D.C.: NAEYC, 1969.

CHAPTER EIGHT

DISCIPLINE AND CHILD GUIDANCE

Remember our preschool child Linda, who sucks her first two fingers constantly, eats crayons which produce a "rainbow of colored teeth," masturbates repeatedly, spends most of her time daydreaming, rarely bathes at home, and demands lap-time cuddling late on a hot Monday morning? And Oliver, whose vicious bites produce bluish sets of teeth marks on the arms of a hapless passerby? And Kathy, who, after we make a minor request of her, "Come inside out of the rain," shouts, "I hate you—I hate you Mrs. Anderson. You're the meanest teacher in this whole school. No one likes you!"

These three children are typical of some of those we face as early preschool/kindergarten. How shall we view these types of behavior and what actions should be taken? In Chapter 1 we describe these children and the concept of "product vs. process" love.

In discussing methods and techniques of discipline and child guidance, we take the position that all children, especially at the preschool age, need to feel loved and accepted by adults and by the other children in their classroom. All children need to be able to use language to be understood and to get the wider world to respond to their needs—simple needs, such as to use a toy or materials, to keep a toy once they have it, to get their fair share of snack, to get help in toileting, to get a "hug" from the teacher, to be a co-player with other children in the classroom, and so on.

If children feel unloved, unaccepted, and helpless in the classroom, possibly these feelings developed before they started school because of poor early care or unfortunate life experiences. These children act out in negative ways: excessive daydreaming, physical aggression such as biting, or verbal aggression such as swearing or "I hate you Mrs. Anderson!"

Rudolf Dreikurs, the psychiatrist who developed a practical program for dealing with misbehaving children, would say that they are motivated by one of four forces: attention-getting, power, revenge, or helplessness. He might propose that introverted Linda feels "helpless and unworthy" in her world, and simply wants to be left alone. Oliver, with his biting and physical aggression, might be considered a child who feels so hurt by the world that he simply wants to get even.

Kathy, on the other hand, might be motivated by "power": she wants to do what she wants to do, when she wants to do it! A simple request to leave the sandbox to come out of the rain threatens her overwhelming need for power and she strikes out by physically refusing to come in, and by being verbally aggressive when the teacher carries her in.

"Acting out" may also take the form of a constant quest for attention and approval. "Look at this, Ms. Anderson." "Do this for me, Ms. Anderson." Other attention-getters perform a host of naughty actions like spitting out food at snacktime, making bizarre noises at rest time, or disrupting story times. Basic to all these children may be feelings of inadequacy in their world. They may, perhaps unconsciously, decide that if they cannot be accepted as the best "good" student or friend, they will become in our classroom the "best" bad child.

WHY DO CHILDREN MISBEHAVE?

A simple, but we believe accurate, answer to this question is that children misbehave because of past experiences and negative learning. Erik Erikson's theory proposes that what we are like today as adults or as young children is the result of early socio-emotional stages. These stages, theoretically, have two pushing and pulling forces which later affect our personalities. Young preschoolers, ages 3, 4, and 5, have passed through the stages of Trust vs. Mistrust (birth to age 1) and Autonomy vs. Shame and Doubt (age 1 to 3), and would be currently struggling with feelings related to Initiative vs Guilt.

INITIATIVE VS. GUILT

We may speculate that the misbehaving young children are those who have an overdeveloped sense of mistrust; that is, they are not sure that their needs will be met or that those who care for them are dependable. The same children possibly could have a strong residue of shame and doubt about their own actions and lack the independence or belief that they can master the world. The acting out behaviors or misbehaviors are an attempt to get individual attention, or power, and to "make up" for early inadequacy. Some children will have been so hurt by their world that they may be vengeful, or may have retreated helplessly from the world about them.

Our goal in attempting to help misbehaving children is to reestablish their basic trust in their caregivers or teachers, and to create many opportunities for them to have power over their world. We would resist actions and statements that would heighten a child's sense of guilt.

SETTING LIMITS

When students act out in a manner that requires us as teachers to set limits for them, there is a high degree of risk that we might damage our relationships with those children. We can hear an angry mother or teacher shouting, "Get your feet off that table immediately—I mean now!" Such harsh commands, possibly even justified, breed hostility and anger in children. The problem for the teacher of young children is how to set limits or "get those feet off the table" in a manner that not only shows respect for the child, but also enables the teacher to take care of the "table" or classroom.

Actions taken by a teacher toward a student who is misbehaving are based on "degrees of power." Minimum-power actions alert the child to the teacher's desire for a change in behavior with the hope that time and the suggestion of a wide range of acceptable alternative behaviors will bring the desired change. Maximum teacher power is exerted when a teacher demands a specific action within an immediate time period, specifying a punishment that will swiftly follow noncompliance. The problems with using power behaviors toward students stem from the danger of "overshooting" the amount of power used—or from using too little power in a serious misbehavior situation.

At SYC we wish to grant the student the initial autonomy to self-correct his or her actions, using as little coercive power as necessary. But if the student fails to take advantage of the opportunity to self-correct, we gradually, in a purposeful way, increase our power actions in order to get the behavior necessary to maintain good classroom discipline. The general method we use involves escalation and de-escalation of power, as exemplified (at a teen-age level) below:

(The teen has just turned 16 and is going out with the car on his first date.)
Teenager: What time should I be home?

Mother: You are old enough now to drive and be responsible. You know what is reasonable. (minimum power)
(Teenager returns home at 3 A.M.)
Mother: "What are you doing? This is unacceptable and this needs to change. What is a reasonable hour that we can both agree upon? Let's make a contract! (escalating power)
(Teenager returns at 3 A.M., again.)
Mother: "I need you to be home with the car by 12 midnight, if not, this...will occur." (escalation of power; if need be, the car is taken from the teen)

If we continued to follow the plight of the teenager above, we might see the mother begin to give back (de-escalate) some power in the form of freedom to make decisions, once the teen had begun to show responsible behavior by obeying the rules.

In the case of the mother setting limits above, we saw three positions taken toward her child's misbehavior. The first was a trusting Relationship-Listening (RL) position. The mother started out with the belief that the child could be trusted and was rational about evaluating his own actions (how late to stay out); thus, she gave him nearly total decision-making power. The second position, although simplistic in our example, was one of Confronting-Contracting (CC). The mother insisted that the son agree to a contract with her to specify his curfew. Finally, because of continued misbehavior, she took a third stance, moving to a Rules-Reward-and Punishment (RRP) position.

The RRP position recognizes that the child has demonstrated a lack of ability to rationally reflect on his own actions, and to correct himself in a reasonable manner. Note that the "locus of control" shifts in each of the three positions. The child holds the locus of control in the Relationship-Listening position; there is a shared locus of control in the Confronting- Contracting position; and an external locus of control by the adult exists in the Rules-Reward-and-Punishment stance, where external rewards and sanctions are used to get a desired behavior from the child. It has also been suggested that if the teen began to show responsible behavior, the mother could de-escalate her power, moving from an RRP stance to CC. Still later, with continued success, she could move to a RL position of interacting with her son.

In the classroom application of limit setting, we propose a "gear shifting" process of escalation (or de-escalation) of power as used in the example above. The use of power by the teacher can be thought of as moving along a Teacher Behavior Continuum from minimum to maximum power (see Table 8.1). The power interactions on the continuum would move from Relationship-Listening techniques of (1) looking on and (2) non-directive statements, to the Confronting-Contracting techniques of (3) questions, and finally to the Rules-Reward-and-Punishment techniques of (4) directive statements, and (5) physical intervention.

TABLE 8.1   Teacher Behavior Continuum

CHILD POWER		TEACHER POWER
RELATIONSHIP-LISTENING		
Nonverbal Cueing visual cueing tactile cueing **Nondirective statement** "I-" message active listening door-openers		
CONFRONTING-CONTRACTING		
	Questions *Three levels Facts: "What did you do?" (broken-record) Convergent: "What was the rule?" (broken-record) Divergent: "How will you change?" Contracting	
RULES, REWARD, AND PUNISHMENT		
		Directive Statements tell what to do state logical consequence preparatory command **Physical Intervention** timeout chair/space mirroring lap-time body to toy, play, work

RELATIONSHIP-LISTENING

Nonverbal Cueing

Obeying rules requires students to listen to inner messages of *no* and to make quick decisions to control their actions or seek what they want in an acceptable way. The younger the child, the less permanent this memory of *no* seems to be. The young child tends to become carried away with enthusiasm when working or playing with peers and can easily miss those inner messages.

When we make our presence known to the child this memory often quickly returns and behavior changes.

"Nonverbal cueing" is a minimum-power technique through which the teacher simply moves toward the student and emphatically, but in a nonaggressive manner, makes his presence known. This is the first step in setting limits for an individual child. The teacher's presence radiates a zone of safety and control for children. The students feel that within this adult observation zone their rights will be protected.

The effectiveness of "looking on" can be seen when teachers and students are traveling on the bus during field trips, when they are sitting in the auditorium during school assemblies, when they are on the playground, etc. Now, there are some children whose sense modality is not visual, and the teacher may need to touch such children's shoulders or tactilely cue them in a nonpunitive way to get their attention.

Spheres of Communication

It is helpful to think of the attention of the teacher, when nonverbally or verbally cueing, as creating a "sphere of communication" or "bubble" in which teacher and children will feel varying degrees of warmth and acceptance. The first sphere is created when we deal directly with one child who gets our total attention as we listen to and communicate with her. In this sphere, one teacher and one child appear to be in a relationship "bubble" cut off from other actions going on around them. Communication flows from child to teacher and back again, with encouragement for the child to express his or her thoughts, ideas, and feelings. This is much like the infant-mother relationship.

The second sphere is a small-group relationship where we have one teacher and three to six other children communicating. The child feels less intimacy and communication with the teacher than in the one-to-one sphere, but still feels included. The communication flows between children and teachers, and usually they must keep to a shared topic. This is much like the family relationships, with mother, father, child, and siblings.

The third sphere of communication involves the teacher with the entire classroom of children. All children must stop their actions and focus on the teacher as she or he speaks or lectures to them. The teacher attention is diffused to all, and thus minimal intimacy is felt by the child. The communication goes in one direction, teacher to child, as in formal classroom relationships.

Studies have demonstrated that large numbers of school age children receive communication only in the third sphere for days and weeks at a time. For weeks, then, some of these children are never spoken to by any child, teacher, or school staff member in an intimate way. We have to be especially careful when dealing with children in schools for young children and even more so in daycare centers, that they do not become cut off from intimate communication with adults and peers. We need to balance the daily schedule so that they can have large blocks of time in the first and second spheres, where they can express their ideas and feelings and can experience close relationships with others.

"Bringing them Back Alive"

On a bus trip, a teacher with a group of young children should sit on the last seat of the bus, while a "room parent" or aide sits in the middle of the bus on an aisle seat. If the teacher is seated in the first seat of the bus, trouble is on its way! The children can see her but she can't see them. "Trouble" is generally not the result of calculated rebellion, but of the restlessness of young children who are flooded with enthusiasm but unable to move around. The same is true in the cafeteria or auditorium, or on the bleachers at sporting events— where teachers should distribute themselves throughout the body of students.

"Showing the Flag"

Where teachers should be placed to supervise playgrounds or similar situations depends upon where the students and where other teachers are: positions of supervisors shift to maintain a fairly even distribution of teachers among students. Teachers gradually circulate, making their presence known—"showing the flag."

"Dining at the Ritz"

Group snack or other meal periods should be valued times for first and second sphere communication. Rather than teachers disappearing on coffee breaks, they need to be seated at tables with children, conversing. Sharing food and conversation, or "dining at the Ritz," is a common adult behavior and can be very beneficial to young children.

Nondirective Statements

We often assume that the student is old enough and has been taught the rules often enough that he *should* know the rules and be following them. However, human behavior, especially for younger children, is regressive: developmentally, children seem to take three steps forward and two back. There will be times when the child is emotionally "flooded" (possibly by events at home, by being angry with others, or from gnawing feelings of inadequacy) so that this emotional flooding washes away the memory of *no* or the "rule." Before escalating use of teacher power we need to give the student time to self-correct. Nondirective statements are a minimum intrusion to "awaken" the memory of the prohibition without the child's feeling guilty or fearful of punishment.

The two techniques under nondirective statements are "I-messages" and "active listening" (Gordon, 1974). These techniques are used by the teacher to help "flooded" children reflect on their actions. When students do not respond to the first steps of cueing (looking on) we advance to the nondirective "I-message." First, we ask ourselves as teachers, "What is the misbehavior?" Second, "What direct and concrete effect is the misbehavior having on us as teachers? Is it stopping us from teaching? Is it damaging property for which we are responsible?" Finally, "How do we feel about it? Are we angry, frustrated, fearful, . . . or what?"

Let's take an example. A young child is standing at an easel and begins to flip paint with his brush, first at the paper and then at other children passing by. The teacher moves toward the child, cues visually, and touches his shoulder. He doesn't stop. She says: "When paint is thrown it makes our floor and clothing messy, and I have to clean it up—and that makes me angry!"

Notice that this "I-message" does not contain a "you" accusation for the student ("You are throwing paints...!"). What the teacher is doing is bringing to the child's awareness the problem *she* is facing as a result of the student's actions. Since the problem is hers, she uses "I" rather than "you." "You" messages should be avoided because they suggest guilt on the student's part and can only be destructive, worsening the child's feelings about himself—making him feel less capable of being a worthy student.

Let's look at this from another perspective. When a teacher communicates or transacts with students, that teacher unknowingly uses one of her own **ego states** of *parent, adult,* or *child*. For example, when a student has spilled a pot of paint, the teacher, pointing to the large, red pool on the floor, may say:

Teacher

How disgusting! What a mess you have made again.	Parent
or	
What is needed to clean this up?	Adult
or	
Oh, what am I going to do, another mess for me.	Child

The parent-like communication from the teacher implies guilt and failure. The childlike statement from the teacher shows that he or she feels helpless, vulnerable, and inadequate to deal with the student's actions. The adult-like statements keep to an assessment of the facts, and a statement of a problem to be solved. The "I-message" is the most refined of the adult statements teachers can use toward students who are misbehaving. It raises student consciousness about the effect of their actions and permits time for them to act positively.

When we transact with an "I-message" we dramatically increase the likelihood of getting a self-correcting behavior, but this does not always happen. Sometimes students are emotionally flooded with anger or resentment and they respond to us or transact back from one of their "ego states." For example, if the teacher uses an "I" statement as follows:

"When paints are thrown, I am afraid. . . ."

Student states:	Teacher	Student

I don't care!	Parent	Parent
Oh, I did not know that.	Adult	Adult
Let me wipe this up.		
Tommy did it, not me!	Child	Child

The student's use of the above adult-like statement shows rational thinking and understanding, while the student's parent-like statement (I don't care!) is definite and hostile, and the child-like statement (Tommy did it . . . !) is "whining" and makes excuses. When we hear parent and child statements coming from students, we know that they still do not have their adult ego state or rational thinking in gear. Such responses may even include hostile language such as swearing as the beginning attempt of the child to communicate. We respond with active listening.

Active listening is a process of summarizing what we think the child is saying to us by "saying it back to him" in nondirective terms:

Student: "I don't care!" (shouting)
Teacher: "You're angry when you're asked to stop."
Student: "It is my turn to paint. I didn't get my turn!"
Teacher: "You are worried that someone will take your turn away from you."

Active listening is a helpful technique whenever children are emotion-flooded and cannot rationally discuss or reflect on their own actions. It is a nonpunitive way of responding to verbal aggression, hostility, and even swearing. It simply helps to elicit and clarify communication from the child, and to demonstrate that the teacher is listening and is offering a caring, one-to-one relationship to that child.

A third set of techniques called "door openers" can be placed under the relationship-listening stance. Door openers are simply questions asked of children to get them to talk about what might be upsetting them: "Carol, I can tell by your face that you are very unhappy this morning. Would you like to talk about it?" Once the child begins to talk, teachers suppress the tendency to lecture them, give suggestions, etc.

CONFRONTING-CONTRACTING

Questions

Our goal is to use the minimum amount of power toward a misbehaving child to get the child to self-correct. If need be, we escalate our power. After we have used nondirective statements with no results for a reasonable period of time, we then increase power through questions. The questioning of the misbehavior is to have the child think out what he is doing and consider ways of changing behavior.

The questions strategy involves three levels of questions which require an increasing degree of abstract thinking by the child. First, "fact" questions are asked; then "convergent" questions; and finally "divergent" questions.

Fact Questions

Simply ask for the facts. We ask a misbehaving child, "What are you doing?" This forces the child to consciously reflect upon and acknowledge her actions. Young children, when flooded with emotion do not necessarily reflect upon their behavior. When they say, "I don't know!" they really may not know consciously what they did do. Our *What* question and confrontation is used to guide them to think about their previous actions. Many children will respond to us with "fogging" to divert us to a side issue: "Tommy did it first!" or "I didn't get my turn!" We simply ignore these "fogging" statements and continue (like a "broken record") with, "What did you do?"

After a reasonable period of time, if the child cannot or will not state what he did, we simply tell him, "Jim, this is what you did. You kicked down the block arrangement." This is not said in a hostile way by the teacher but in a controlled, purposeful manner so that the behaviors that are unwanted can be identified.

Convergent Questions

Next, we ask the *what-rule* convergent question: "Jim, what is the rule about blocks?" If we receive no reply, the *what-rule* question is repeated; we ignore any "fogging" statements made by the child. We want the child to consciously bring to memory and state the rule that has been previously taught to him or her. If this does not come from the child we would clearly state the rule. "Jim, our rule here is that we do not knock others' blocks down."

The process of questioning requires us to suppress any wish we might have to moralize, lecture, or preach to the child, since such statements might heighten the child's feelings of naughtiness or guilt—which, according to Erikson's theory, are part of the pulling-pushing force (initiative vs. guilt) for the child ages 3 to 7.

Divergent Questions

After a verbal summary of the child's actions and a statement—by either the misbehaving child or the teacher—of a pertinent rule, we now "push" for a contract: "How will you change?" or, "If this happens again, what will you do?" The fact questions had the child reflect on the past event; now, the divergent questions require the child to think about how he or she will behave in the future, and this will become the basis for a contract. Teachers working with school-age children would be able to have the students actually write out an agreement, which would then be signed by both parties. For the young child, however, a verbal agreement with a handshake would be more appropriate.

To summarize, questioning is used to get the children to consciously reflect upon and to verbally summarize errant behavior, and to then state applicable rules they have learned. The teacher suppresses any desire to preach, moralize, or express opinions about the child's actions, simply using *what* questions—in a repeated, "broken record" manner, if necessary. Finally, the teacher pushes for a contract.

RULES, REWARD, AND PUNISHMENT

Directive Statements

The next step on the Teacher Behavioral Continuum is the use of directive statements. At this point we have accepted the position that the child cannot or will not verbally summarize his actions, and it has become imperative to bring about a behavioral change. We therefore tell the child what we want him to do in specific terms: "Keep the paint on the paper!" In making such a statement we need to have a child in the first sphere of communication, look him directly in the eye, say his name, gesture, touch her in a nonhostile manner, and state what change is necessary.

We always attempt to tell the child what *to* do, not what *not* to do. "Keep the paint on the paper!" will more likely get results than will "Don't throw paint!" The latter is highly likely to encourage the child to react to the verb "throw" by doing so! Again, if the child does not comply, we may have to sound like "broken records" and keep repeating the directive statement.

After a number of repetitions of the directive statements have proved fruitless, we may escalate to a more powerful position and state a "logical consequence": "If I see you throw the paints again, it will tell me that you do not know the painting rules and I will have to ask you to play in another area." This is not a threat of punishment, but an expression of "logical consequence." Let's look at the difference.

Both punishments and "logical consequences" are actions taken in response to the breaking of a rule. They differ in these ways (Dreikurs, 1972):

LOGICAL CONSEQUENCES	PUNISHMENT
A learning process.	A judicial proceeding.
Teacher plays the role of an educator.	Teacher plays the role of police, judge, and jailer.
Distinguishes between the deed and doer.	Denotes sin.
Expresses the reality of the social order.	Expresses the power of authority.
Are intrinsically related to misbehavior.	Has an arbitrary connection to misbehavior.
Is appropriate in a democratic setting	Belongs only in an autocratic setting

If a child is "spanked" or put in time-out for throwing paint, we have punishment because the sanction has little relationship to the misbehavior. On the other hand, we are using logical consequences when we state, "Throwing paint wastes it and there will not be enough for others. If that occurs again you will have used up your share and will have to leave the paint area until you learn the rules."

As adults, when we are driving a car and come to a stoplight we usually stop. Why? Is it because we are afraid of getting a ticket and fine? If so, we are operating from a lower moral position—from fear of punishment. On the other hand, if we obey the stoplight because we wish to promote a safe system of traffic regulation, we are operating from a higher moral position: groups of people need certain rules in order to function effectively and safely. We obey rules not from fear, but from a desire to promote the general welfare. The SYC position is that we do not want children to obey rules out of fear—but because they have been made aware of how their actions affect others. It is in school that children have the time and opportunity to grow morally.

If the child acts positively as a result of our directive statements we may use encouragement, which is not to be confused with praise.

Encouragement vs. Praise

"Jim, look what you have done! You have worked all morning with your group of Bob, Carol, and Alice, and you have built a castle with the blocks. You must feel proud that you're now able to work with friends." This is an encouragement statement, and is quite different from praise, such as, "What a beautiful castle, I am so proud of you!" Praise statements take a moral position, make value judgments on those less powerful, and focus on actions and end products; "encouragement" statements are made to help the child become aware of how she is growing and becoming more effective, so that these strides in themselves are reinforcing. The idea is that the "process is more important than the product."

Here are other examples of encouragement vs. praise.

ENCOURAGEMENT	PRAISE
How nice that you could figure that out for yourself!	Aren't you wonderful to be . . .
Your skills are growing.	I'm so proud of you for . . .
You're working hard on that painting.	You're my favorite student.
	What a beautiful painting.

As positive changes in the child's behavior become apparent, we may use encouragement statements to help her become aware of her own progress, valuing her efforts rather than a product.

If the misbehavior continues after using the above-described escalation of power techniques, the situation would seem to call for an additional escalation to physical intervention. But before this action we always give a preparatory command as the last step under directive statements. The preparatory command is usually stated as a contingency followed by a logical consequence. "Tommy, if the blocks are knocked down again, it's telling me that you still have not learned the rule on using blocks, and I will need to take you from the block area to play somewhere else." If the child again knocks down the blocks, we will tell him to move to another area and, if he refuses, will follow through with the logical consequences before escalating to physical intervention.

Physical Intervention

Physical Intervention, that is picking up or bringing a child by the arm or hand to a new area, is seen as a strong use of power on the TBC continuum. This should not be done with anger or in any hostile manner, but simply as a routine. If the child complies and moves off as requested the intervention is completed; but many children may respond with physical defiance, such as screaming or kicking. We as teachers should not be surprised by such aggression; but how do we understand and deal with it?

After a misbehavior many children expect that their bodies will be hit or dealt with in a rough physical manner. They expect to be hurt! They feel mistrust and possibly shame or guilt for their actions. We as teachers must recognize that children's actions toward us are not necessarily directed to us personally. The child has learned responses long before she arrived in our classroom. Our goal in working with a violent or hostile child is to *refuse to return* this hostility and to reestablish feelings of trust and safety in the child. We state clearly as we physically intervene, "I'm not going to let you hurt others (or destroy others' work), I'm not going to let you hurt me, and I'm not going to let others hurt you! And, I am not going to hurt you." We repeat these safety statements several times. If the child can accept this verbal assurance and complies with our request the intervention is over, but if he continues to defy us we have two choices: move the child to a chair or personal space, or use mirroring techniques.

Relax-chair or Personal Space

When a child has a temper tantrum or loses emotional control, we say he is "flooding." Flooding means that the child is overwhelmed with guilt and fear, and cannot rationally think or process information or stimuli. Using a relax-chair, not to be confused with a time-out chair, or personal space (a corner of the room or floor space), is a way of excluding stimuli and giving the child some personal time to "defuse" and get himself under control. We simply give the child space to relax. When the "emotional storm" or "flooding" has subsided we may approach the child to have him begin to rethink the actions he has taken. In doing this we work our way through the TBC using nondirective statements and questions.

(The child is seated quietly on a chair.)

Teacher: I can see that you have had an angry morning. (active listening) When blocks are kicked over and thrown, I am afraid that children will get hurt, and that frightens me as the teacher.

(If the child begins to talk, the teacher could for a period of time continue with active listening, permitting him to "talk it out." If no discussion comes from the child, the teacher may escalate to questions.)

Tommy, I want to talk to you about what happened this morning. What did you do? (fact question) What was the rule? (convergent question) What will you do next time? (divergent) (Pushes for a contract.)

As the example shows, the use of the relax-chair or personal space is not for punishment, but to permit the child to gain self-control and to be reapproached for rational discussion. Once the contract is made the child is free to move back into the full space of the classroom. If the child will not talk or respond to the techniques shown above, it means that he is still full of anger and needs more time in a personal space—perhaps as much as an entire morning. We simply say, "We must talk about the things that happened this morning. You can tell me when you're ready, or I will check back with you later."

Mirroring

A second technique to be used with the flooded young child is called mirroring. Bring the child before a large upright mirror so that she can see herself, her own actions, and you. Again, we would want to repeat the safety statements, "I'm not going to let you hurt others (or destroy others' work). I'm not going to let you hurt me, I'm not going to let others hurt you, and I will not hurt you." We would also, through directive statements, say to the child, "Look at your face, its tells me that you're really angry; look at my hand, I am holding you so that you can be safe, but my hands are not hurting you. You are safe!"

The image in the mirror helps us not only to limit the amount of stimuli the "flooded" child is receiving but also helps the child to see herself and her actions. The mirror gives another perspective. We may need to do many mirror interactions with a mistrusting child until she begins to believe that she can "even be naughty" and we will not hurt her. In this way, the world of the young child can become a safe place where this child can become attached to and trust in us as teachers.

Lap-time

A young child awakens early in the morning, dresses quickly, eats quickly, is driven by a rushed parent through heavy street traffic, and comes through the school door at 7:45 in the morning. The child enters our classroom like a bowling ball, pounding from one play area to another, knocking over equipment and clashing with other children. This child needs "lap-time."

Children live hypothetically in three worlds: one, an inner world full of thought and feeling; another, a body world where the they can physically feel power in running and climbing, or enjoy the warmth of a bathtub; and, a third,

FIGURE 8.1   Some Children Need Lap-time

the "outer" world where they produce, create, and work with others. You and I as adults freely move back and forth among these three worlds. When we are tired we pull up our favorite chair and magazine, kick off our shoes, and retreat to an inner world; at other times we enjoy playing and using our bodies vigorously, and at still others, going into the outer world, working with others. The young child, however, can get "stuck" in one of these worlds, unable to retreat "inside" to relax.

The "bowling ball" child entering our classroom in the morning may be "stuck" in the body world. Therefore, we may say, "James, I see that you need some lap-time this morning! Come sit with me for a few minutes as I show you this book." On our laps we can feel James relaxing into the inner world. Once relaxed, he can go out into the classroom and become productive. For the child who lacks trust in his world and repeatedly "floods," large amounts of "lap-time" may help to reestablish trust in others and in himself. So, physical intervention is not only physically removing children as a logical consequence, but also requiring them to come to our laps to cuddle and relax before they "flood" or emotionally explode.

Diversion

The third way of handling a misbehaving child is the widely used method of diversion. We divert the child from the potential problem area or activity to a different activity that he might work in successfully. Our prescription for diversion is "from the body, to the toy; from the toy, to play; and from play to work," following the normal development of play observed in young children (A. Freud, 1968). How does this work? We see the child buzzing aimlessly about the room. He is into everything but doing nothing productively. The teacher moves to the child using directive statements and physical intervention: "I see you going around and around the room. Come with me and I will show you where you can go around and around."

Taking the child to an area or corner that can be sectioned off, the teacher gives him some small miniature cars and encourages him to sit on the floor and "make the cars go 'round and 'round." The teacher has moved the child who might be stuck in the "body world" to the toy. The child's first use of the wheeled toys might be aggressive, but the vigorous activity in defined space permits the child some release of possibly pent-up tension or emotions. Later, the teacher might say, "Oh, now your cars need a road and a garage; see if you can use these blocks to make them!" The child has now been moved from the toy to play. In the play level other children can join him in his activity and, if this works out, we have helped the child though play to be a cooperative "worker" with others.

AGGRESSION

Aggression can be simply defined as energy misdirected. Our way of handling that aggression is diversion (from body to toy, etc.) Other suggestions for channeling aggression are work with clay, vigorous play with make-believe animals, and hammers on the carpentry table (see Figure 8.2).

Biting

Encourage the biting child to transfer his "bite" to microsymbolic toys such as alligator puppets or miniature animals (tiger/lions) with teeth (body to toy). At first the themes of this miniature toy play will be violent and aggressive: The tiger or alligator puppet eats up "the world." We then intervene with the techniques on the TBC to attempt to have the child move out of violent themes to more positive themes. We may ask such questions as, "Could your alligator puppet keep the people safe today? Does your tiger have any baby tigers that they could keep safe today? (toy to play) Once the child is using positive themes we may encourage other children to join him to produce true sociodramatic play (play to being a cooperative worker with others).

Spitting

Spitting is aggression with the mouth; therefore, we may follow the suggestion made above for biting. Also, we find many "spitters" who are afraid

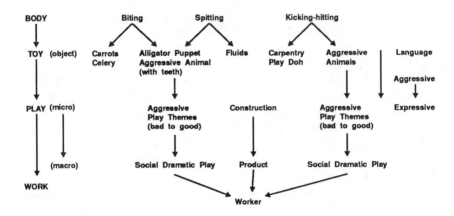

FIGURE 8.2   Channeling Aggression

of fluid play materials, so we might gradually and deliberately introduce the aggressive child to finger-paints, easel paints, clay or water, etc. (body to toy). The painting may at first be actually an aggressive use of the material, such as rubbing right through the paper in finger painting; but after a while the child should become comfortable with these materials, and when that happens we intervene, attempting to have the child make symbolic products with these materials (toy to play). Borrowing from Anna Freud, we believe that the child can move from play to work through the ability

> (a) to control, inhibit, or modify the impulses to use given materials aggressively and destructively (not to throw, to take apart, to mess, to hoard), and to use them positively and constructively instead (to build, to play, to learn, and——in communal life——to share);
>
> (b) to carry out preconceived plans with a minimum regard for the lack of immediate pleasure yield, intervening frustrations, etc., and the maximum regard for the pleasure in the ultimate outcome." (A. Freud, 1965, p. 82)

Kicking-hitting

The same pathway would be followed for dealing with children who are kicking or hitting. Figure 8.2 suggests that we would introduce carpentry and/or clay to facilitate construction play, or aggressive animals (body to toy), for symbolic play. The materials would be used aggressively (ripping the clay apart), and then the child would gradually move to construction or dramatic play themes (toy to play), and finally to products or sociodramatic play with other peers (play to work).

Some teachers use punching bags, toy guns, inflatable dolls, and similar hitting or aggressive items to give children opportunities to vent aggression.

However, the trouble with punching bags and similar play items is that they are a "dead end," limited to aggressive use. In other words, we may move the child from the body to the punching bag, but we cannot move the child's hitting of the bag into more positive forms of play, in which others may join.

SOCIAL ENGINEERING

Case History

During the first year of school Carol and Janey were the closest of friends; in fact, their relationship was so exclusive that they rarely permitted other children to play with them. Then, during summer vacation the friendship broke off. In the new pre-kindergarten class Janey kept attempting to renew the friendship—but Carol had joined with a small group of other children, a clique, and would not permit Janey into the "special" group. Janey soon became a classroom discipline problem.

One morning the clique, led by Carol, was being especially mean to Janey, taunting her and calling her names. The teacher witnessed this and decided to use some social engineering. "Janey, today we are going to make Thanksgiving cookies and I am going to give you the job of being the boss of cookie making. Pick three friends and come to the mixing table and we will go to work." The teacher refrained from directly instructing the girls, but positioned herself behind "the leader," Janey, coaching her periodically and dividing jobs among other cooperating students.

Now, Carol and her little clique no longer found what they were doing as interesting as what the girls making cookies were doing, so they wandered over and said to the teacher, "Mrs. Anderson, can we make cookies, too?" Mrs. Anderson responded, "I am not the boss of the cookie making. Janey is. You will need to ask her." They did, and after three or four long seconds of thought, Janey said yes.

The teacher continued to coach from the sidelines, making sure that Janey maintained her power in the cookie making process, and the result was that the clique and Janey had a great time working together and later passing out the cookies to the other members of the class. The teacher, through social engineering, had endowed the powerless student with power—made her special. This experience, along with a few other similar incidents, helped Janey to find new friends and become a cooperative worker with peers rather than going down the "black hole" of being labeled a discipline problem.

Social engineering occurs when we as teachers set up fun tasks to be completed, deliberately putting together certain students with a misbehaving student who lacks power and social skills, coaching him from the sidelines to help him gain social skills. This could involve such activities as painting a mural, making Christmas tree decorations, being a member of a class play, etc.

The teacher's role in dealing with young children who seem to have special problems is to help them find positive solutions.

Another form of social engineering is modeling reality solutions for children who have social conflicts or emotional concerns. Since the child has limited language capacities, the teacher must turn to symbolic expression, such as modeling with puppet play, flannelboards, or children's literature. The teacher can enact scenes of mother-child separation, arguments between children over possessions, and other daily incidents which cause children difficulty.

In enacting with puppets, for example, a mother-child separation, the teacher dubs one of the puppets "mother" and the other ones "child" and "teacher." The teacher makes the puppets play out an incident in which the "child" cries, "No, no, Mommy, don't go! I want you to stay!" The "mother" responds that she will stay for a few minutes, but then must leave. "Mother" also gives the child her "handkerchief" to keep, and assures him that she will return.

After the "mother" leaves, the "teacher" states, "You look very unhappy. You're sad because your mother had to leave, but she will come back. I'm here to help you." The puppet drama continues until "mother" returns and they are reunited.

Such dynamic enactment (or, more likely, reenactment of actual incidents) allows the child to participate vicariously and perhaps discover a solution to a dilemma. Reenactment through the use of puppets or flannelboard characters allows the teacher to dramatize immediate classroom situations. Children's literature dealing with death, divorce, fear of the dark, nightmares, making friends, and other topics that children may have difficulty with, presents some solutions and may encourage children to verbalize solutions of their own (see booklist).

The key to modeling reality solutions is to enable the child, without his reaching a too-high level of anxiety, to verbalize his concerns and to see certain ideas for resolving problems. While there are many incidents such as death and divorce which are not easily resolved, such symbolization can help the child gain a greater emotional and cognitive understanding of these happenings.

TABLE 8.2   Literature with Special Meaning for Young Children

---

SIBLING RELATIONSHIPS

CONTA, MARCIA MAHER, and MAUREEN REARDON, *Feelings Between Brothers and Sisters*, photography by Jules M. Rosenthal. Milwaukee, Wis.: Advanced Learning Concepts, Inc., 1974. A variety of brother and sister relationships is presented. Age 4-7.
HOBAN, RUSSELL, *Best Friends for Frances*, ill. by Lillian Hoban. New York: Harper and Row, 1969. Frances learns to be friends with her sister. Ages 5-7.
HUTCHINS, PAT, *Titch*. New York: Macmillan, 1971. Titch is the littlest, and always has smallest things. In the end, he has the little seed, which is most important. Ages 3-5.

PARENT-CHILD RELATIONSHIPS

DEREGNIERS, BEATRICE SCHENK, *The Little Girl and Her Mother*, ill. by Esther Gilman. New York: Vanguard Press, 1963. The little girl imitates her mother, then realizes that there are things she can do that Mother is too big for, and that some day she will grow up to be like her mother. Ages 4-6.

KUMIN, MAXINE W., *The Beach Before Breakfast*, ill. by Leonard Weisgard. New York: Putnam, 1964. Family members enjoy the beach together. Ages 4-6.

LEXAU, JOAN, *Everyday, a Dragon*, ill. by Ben Shecter. New York: Harper and Row, 1967. Father and child play dragon. Ages 5-8.

ZOLOTOW, CHARLOTTE, *A Father Like That*, ill. by Ben Shecter. New York: Harper and Row, 1971. The boy lives with his mother, and he tells her what his father would be like. His mother replies that the boy can grow up to be a father like that. Ages 4-7.

RELATIONSHIPS WITH GRANDPARENTS

BUCKLEY, HELEN E., *Grandfather and I*, ill. by Paul Galdone. New York: Lothrop, 1959. A boy and his grandfather enjoy things without being rushed. Ages 3-7.

BORAK, BARBARA, *Grandpa*, ill. by Ben Shecter. New York: Harper and Row, 1967. A girl tells all the things she and her grandpa do. Ages 4-8.

LENSKI, LOIS, *Debbie and her Grandma*. New York: Walck, 1967. Debbie visits Grandma by herself. Ages 3-6.

MINARIK, ELSE HOLMELUND, *Little Bear's Visit*, ill. by Maurice Sendak. New York: Harper and Row, 1961. Little Bear spends the day with his grandparents and tires himself out. Ages 3-6.

A NEW BABY

BERGER, TERRY, *A New Baby*, photography by Heinz Kluetmeier. Milwaukee, Wisc.: Raintree Editions, 1974.

GREENFIELD, ELOISE, *She Come Bringing Me That Little Baby Girl*, ill. by John Steptoe. Philadelphia: Lippincott, 1974. A black boy is confronted with a baby sister when his mother returns from the hospital. He feels resentment, then begins to like her when he holds her. Ages 3-6.

HOLLAND, VIKI, *We Are Having a Baby*. New York: Charles Scribner's Sons, 1972. A little girl tells the story of the arrival of her brother, including the funny feeling in her stomach which causes her to lose her appetite for lunch. Photographs illustrate the story. Ages 3-6.

STEIN, SARA BONNETT, *That New Baby*, photography by Dick Frank. Chicago: Walker and Co., 1974. The family is black, and the two older children show rivalry in a variety of ways. Age 2-8.

SIBLING RIVALRY

ALEXANDER, MARTHA, *Nobody Asked Me if I Wanted a Baby Sister*. New York: Dial Press, 1971. Little boy tries to give away his baby sister. She begins to cry, and it is discovered that he is the only one who can quiet her. He decides to keep her. Ages 3-6.

HOBAN, RUSSELL, *A Baby Sister for Frances*, ill. by Lillian Hoban. New York: Harper and Row, 1964. Frances becomes annoyed with this baby sister and runs away, under the kitchen table. She returns. Ages 3-7.

HOBAN, RUSSELL, *A Birthday for Frances*, ill. by Lillian Hoban. New York: Harper and Row, 1968. It is Gloria's birthday, and Frances buys her sister a candy bar that she almost eats herself. Ages 3-7.

TABLE 8.2   Continued

KEATS, EZRA JACK, *Peter's Chair*, New York: Harper and Row, 1967. Peter's father paints all his old furniture pink for his baby sister. He runs away with his little blue chair, but finds that he no longer fits in it. He comes home and helps his father paint. Ages 3-5.

WELLS, ROSEMARY, *Noisy Nora*. New York: Dial Press, 1973. Nora is a noisy little mouse who wants some attention. She finally gets it by running away to the broom closet. Ages 3-7.

ZOLOTOW, CHARLOTTE, *If it Weren't for You*, ill. by Ben Shecter. New York: Harper and Row, 1966. Older brother tells all the things he cannot do because of the younger one, but the story ends with him realizing that without the younger brother, he would be alone with the grownups. Ages 5-7.

FRIENDSHIP

COHEN, MIRIAM, *Best Friends*, ill. by Lillian Hoban. New York: Collier Books, 1971. A child goes to a nursery school worried about having a best friend. Ages 4-6.

Will I Have a Friend? ill. by Lillian Hoban, New York: Macmillan, 1967. Deals with making friends at school. Ages 3-6.

LOBELL, ARNOLD, *Frog and Toad Are Friends*. New York: Harper and Row, 1970. Stories about the friendship of Frog and Toad. An easy-to-read book. Ages 5-8.

UDRY, JANICE MAY, *Let's Be Enemies*, ill. by Maurice Sendak. New York: Harper and Row, 1960. Two friends are angry with each other and become enemies. They resolve their conflict and go skating together. Ages 4-7.

ANGER

PRESTON, EDNA MITCHELL, *The Temper Tantrum Book*, ill. by Rainey Bennett. New York: Viking Press, 1969. A variety of young animals tell why they get angry. Ages 3-6.

SENDAK, MAURICE, *Where the Wild Things Are*. New York: Harper and Row, 1963. Max is angry with his mother and fantasies that he is king of the wild things. Ages 3 and up.

SIMON, NORMA, *I Was so Mad!* ill. by Dora Leder. Chicago: Albert Whitman and Co., 1974. A variety of children explain what makes them angry, leaving the impression that it is all right to feel that way. Ages 4 and up.

BEDTIME FEARS AND MONSTERS

BROWN, MARGARET WISE, *Goodnight Moon*. ill. by Clement Hurd. New York: Harper and Row, 1942. Ages 3-6.

FENNER, CAROL, *Tigers in the Cellar*. New York: Harcourt, Brace, 1963. A little girl believes there are tigers in the cellar. She has a dream in which the tigers are friendly and fear goes away. Ages 4-7.

HOBAN, RUSSELL, *Bedtime for Frances*, ill. by Garth Williams. New York: Harper and Row, 1960. Frances is a little bear who has a difficult time going to sleep. With help from her parents, she finally goes to sleep. Ages 3-6.

KAUFFMAN, LOIS, *What's That Noise?* ill. by Allan Eitzen. New York: Lothrop, Lee & Shepard Co., 1965. A boy can't sleep because of a noise in the night. He and his father try to find out what it is. Finally, the boy goes to bed with his father and finds that the noise is his father snoring. Ages 4-8.

SENDAK, MAURICE, *In the Night Kitchen*. New York: Harper and Row., 1970. Mickey dreams of being in the night kitchen. Ages 5-8.

TANIUCHI, KOTA, *Up on a Hilltop*. New York: Franklin Watts, 1971. Boy sees a train, then dreams about one. Ages 4-8.

VIORST, JUDITH. *My Mama Says There Aren't Any Zombies, Ghosts, Vampires, Creatures, Demons, Monsters, Friends, Goblins, or Things*, ill. by Kay Chorao. New York: Atheneum, 1973. A little boy reaffirms his trust in mother's opinion that monsters don't really exist. Ages 4-7.

TOTAL FAMILY RELATIONS

EHRLICH, AMY, *Zeek, Silver Moon*, ill. by Robert Andrews Parker. New York: Dial, 1972. Ages 4-8.

KRAUS, ROBERT, *Whose Mouse Are You?* ill. by Jose Aruego. London: Macmillan, 1970. A young mouse explores his feelings concerning his relationships with each member of his family. Ages 4-7.

SCOTT, ANN HERBERT, *Sam*, ill. by Symeion Shimin. New York: McGraw-Hill, 1967. Sam is excluded by each member of his family and finally cries in frustration. His family realizes what they have done, and his mother finds a way for him to help her. Ages 3-7.

DEATH

BROWN, MARGARET WISE, *The Dead Bird*, ill. by Remy Charlip. New York: Young Scot Books, 1971. Children find a dead bird and bury it. Ages 3 and up.

VIORST, JUDITH, *The Tenth Good Thing About Barney*, ill. by E. Bleguad. New York: Atheneum, 1971. A cat dies. Ages 5-8.

HOSPITAL FEARS

REY, M., and H.A. REY, *Curious George Goes to the Hospital*, Boston: Houghton-Mifflin, 1966. George the monkey goes to the hospital and enjoys it. Ages 4-7.

ROCKWELL, HARLOW, *My Doctor*. New York: Macmillan, 1973. The woman doctor and all her instruments are described. Ages 3-6.

ROCKWELL, HARLOW, *My Dentist*. New York: Macmillan, 1975. The dentist and all his instruments are described. Ages 3-6.

SHAY, A., *What Happens When You Go to the Hospital*. Chicago: Reilly Lee, 1969. Photo essay of the hospital experience. Ages 3-6.

STEIN, SARA BONNETT, *A Hospital Story*, photography by Dick Frank. Chicago: Walker and Co., 1974. Ages 3-6.

ACCOMPLISHMENT

KRAUSS, RUTH, *The Carrot Seed*, ill. by Crockett Johnson. New York: Harper and Row, 1945. Story of planting a seed and watching it grow. Ages 5-7.

FEELINGS

BARRETT, JUDI, *I Hate to Take a Bath*, ill. by Charles B. Slackman. Englewood Cliffs, N.J.: Four Winds Press, 1975. Children give reasons why they hate to take a bath, then what they like to do in a bath if they have to take one. Ages 3-8.

TABLE 8.2   Continued

BUCKLEY, HELEN E., *Michael Is Brave*, ill. by Emily McCully. New York: Lothrop, Lee & Shepard, 1971. Michael is afraid to climb the ladder of the slide. His teacher asks him to help a girl who is frightened at the top. As he helps her, he overcomes his own fear. Ages 4-8.
DUNN, PHOEBE, and TRIS DUNN, *Feelings*, words by Judy Dunn. Minnesota: Creative Educational Society, 1971. A variety of feelings are described and photographed. Ages 4-8.
IWASKI, CHIRRIO, *Staying Home Alone on a Rainy Day*, New York: McGraw-Hill, 1968. Allison is staying home by herself and is afraid. Ages 5-8.

THE SPECIAL TOY (TRANSITIONAL OBJECT)

BROWN, MYRA, *First Night Away from Home*, ill. by Dorothy Marino. New York: Franklin Watts, 1960. A boy stays overnight with a friend but can't go to sleep. His mother brings his favorite stuffed animal. Ages 4-8.
FREEMAN, DON, *Corduroy*. New York: Viking, 1968. A bear in a store is purchased by a girl who makes a home for him. Ages 4-8.
PINCUS, HARRIET, *Minna and Pippin*. New York: Farrar, Straus, 1972. Story of a little girl and her doll. Ages 3-7.
SKORPEN, LIESEL MOAK, *Charles*. New York: Harper and Row, 1971. Story of a boy and his bear. Ages 3-7.

LOVE

JEWEL, NANCY, *Snuggle Bunny*, ill. by Mary Chalmers. New York: Harper and Row, 1972. A bunny wants to snuggle. It finally finds an old man and they snuggle all winter. Ages 4-7.

SEX ROLES

LEVY, ELIZABETH, *Nice Little Girls*, Ill. by Mordecai Gerstein. New York: Delacorte, 1974. Jackie changes some of the sex-role stereotypes in her classroom. Ages 5-8.
ZOLOTOW, CHARLOTTE, *William's Doll*, Ill. by William Pene Dubois, New York: Harper and Row, 1972. William wants a doll. Only his grandmother doesn't laugh at him, and she gets him one. Ages 4-7.

LOSS AND RECOVERY

BROWN, MARGARET WISE, *The Runaway Bunny*, ill. by C. Hurd. New York: Harper and Row, 1942. A young bunny tells his mother all the places he will run to. She reassures him that if he did, she would be there as well. Ages 2-7.
FLACK, MARJORIE, *The Story of Ping*, ill. by Kurt Wiese. New York: Viking, 1933. A duck becomes separated from its family on the Yangtse River and, after a series of adventures, finds them again. Ages 5 and up.
KRAUSS, R., *The Bundle Book*, ill. by H. Stone. New York: Harper and Row, 1951. A mother tries to guess what kind of bundle is in the bed. The child pops out in the end, and they give each other a hug. Ages 3-5.
LIONNI, LEO, *Little Blue and Little Yellow*. New York: Obolensky, 1959. Two friends, Blue and Yellow, mix together to become green while they are playing. They separate and become individuals again. Ages 3-8.

MCCLOSKEY, ROBERT, *Blueberries for Sal.* New York: Viking, 1948. While picking blueberries, a little girl, her mother, little bear, and mother bear get mixed up. Mothers and children are reunited and return home. Ages 4-8.

POTTER, BEATRIX, *The Tale of Peter Rabbit.* New York: Warne, 1902. Peter ventures into forbidden territory and is quite glad to return home. Ages 2-7.

TARIASHIMA, T., *Umbrella.* New York: Viking, 1966. A 3-year-old girl's awareness of growing up as she goes to preschool in her new boots and umbrella. Ages 3-6.

THE MOST-WANTED TWOSOME OR THREESOME

The children who are our Johnny and Janey No-Goods are those children who have acquired reputations that keep them buried in holes of isolation. When this happens the student heightens his or her level of misbehavior, thinking, "If I can't be the best good star, I will be the best bad star!"

Although we may not admit it, such children actually frighten us as teachers. We are afraid that we are failing them, and we lie awake at night worrying. One way to help these children would be to change the attitudes of the teachers and all other adults in the school who have contact with Johnny so they will stop "shunning" him or ignoring him, and will begin actively, verbally accepting him. Not just an in-classroom process can accomplish this—a schoolwide campaign is needed. How to proceed?

The classroom teacher, director or principal, counselor, or any other adult takes a photo of Johnny and pastes it onto cardboard paper. Under the paper is written all the factual information that can be obtained on Johnny: pets, their names and species, brothers or sisters, parents' names, hobbies or talents, out-of-school activities, etc. The card is then passed around at a faculty meeting of all the working adults, including the janitor, cafeteria workers, playground supervisors, and teachers.

With this information, every adult is to pretend that Johnny is a "new boy" in school; thus, he is given a clean slate. Each time the adults pass him in the hall or have any minor contact with him they meet him eye to eye, say hello, use his name, touch him in a friendly manner if possible and, if there is time, inquire about his interests. Thus, we "give him the time of day." Imagine what effect this can have on a Johnny who day in and day out has felt disliked by all teachers and adults in his school. At first this may seem to some teachers unnatural, but if all adults in the school can maintain this friendliness for two or more weeks, we will begin to find that Johnny No-Good is not really a little devil, and that real friendships can and do follow. In turn it throws Johnny completely out of kilter. People are actually acting *nice* to him! How could this be? A change of behavior on his part will be almost inevitable as he begins to feel worthy and accepted and gains a sense of belonging.

The "Most-Wanted List" refers to those one or two children who are the greatest discipline problems to the entire school. Our position is that they do not feel wanted by the school and that is why they misbehave; so, we focus on them as individuals in need of our affection and acceptance. The adults in the school must change towards *them* if we want them to change toward the school and in our classrooms.

CONFLICT OVER POSSESSIONS

The class has just gone out to the playground. Kate has found a shovel in the sandbox and is just about to fill a bucket. Mark, seated nearby, has a bucket but no shovel. His solution: reach out and take Kate's shovel. How should we handle such incidents which are seen again and again in the early childhood classroom? Though many teachers may not be aware of it, incidents such as these present some of the most important "teachable moments" in daily classroom life!

Our goal is to have Kate use language to retrieve the shovel, and for Mark to realize that others have rights and that he needs to respond to language. Here the TBC can be used to gain a perspective on the use of power in mediating conflicts.

Looking On

We begin by bringing the children together either at a private corner of the sandbox, or by simply holding one of each child's hands and bringing them face to face. Now we "look on," allowing some time to the children to settle their argument without any more teacher intervention. Our target is Kate, because she has the immediate problem—she lost her shovel! Kate can respond in a number of nonproductive ways: by being passive—just leaving or surrendering the toy; by being physically aggressive—striking out at Mark; or by being verbally aggressive (calling Mark names, swearing, etc.). However, we want social conflict to be resolved through impulse control and expressive language (see Figure 8.3); so, if Kate does not assert herself we move up the TBC to nondirective statements: "Kate, I can see by your face that you are unhappy; you have lost your shovel." We have verbally encoded both Kate's feelings (much like active listening), and the problem needing to be solved, without being directive.

If there is no reaction from Kate, we escalate to the question strategy: "Kate, what could you say to Mark?" We then retreat to looking on, to give Kate some time to think and respond. Then, if she still doesn't react we move to directive statements: "Tell Mark what you want." After a period of "wait-time" we move to modeling: "Tell Mark, 'No, that is my shovel. I was using it, I want it back!'"

At this point, if Kate does not respond, we might say: "You are having a difficult time using words with Mark. Would you like me to tell him for you this time?" If she indicates yes, we repeat the language model directly to Mark: "Mark, Kate wants me to tell you that she was using the shovel and wants you

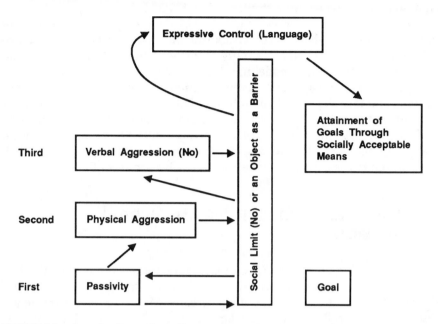

FIGURE 8.3 **Impulse Control as a Developmental Process**

to give it back to her." We do this for the child only once. From that time on, we will continue using the TBC techniques, but after verbal modeling we will simply leave, telling the child that she must use language to get what she needs.

Some teachers feel that this is unfair and that Mark is getting away with something; but there will be many other occasions to deal with Mark, and right now Kate needs a lesson in asserting herself. If we relieve Kate of all the stress in the situation, getting what she needs *for* her, she will have no need to learn to act for herself. If our overdeveloped sense of "fairness" pushes us to play judge and jury, to return all objects to the rightful owners, we will be continuously exhausted because all the children in the class will be pulling at our skirts or pants to have us settle a thousand and one conflicts daily! Rather, when clashes over possessions occur, we will continue to intervene using the TBC techniques, until one day "Kate" will assert herself and gain the power to use language in the context of conflict. There can be no more valuable lesson; and, developmentally, 3-year-olds should be ready to begin learning this skill.

Backtracking a bit, if Kate *does* respond or simply says, "No, stop. That is mine!" the target child becomes Mark. Mark must learn to respond to the language of peers, and we help teach him this by using the TBC. First we simply look on as the children stand face to face, giving Mark time to think and act.

If a sufficient period of time brings no action on Mark's part, we move to nondirective statements, such as, "Mark, it is hard to give up toys that you want so much to keep." After thus encoding his probable feelings, if there are no results from Mark we move to questions: "Mark, do you need my help to return the shovel?" If he says yes we take the shovel from his hand and return it to Kate. If he says nothing we give him "wait-time," and then move to directive statements and modeling: "Mark, Kate said give it back, she was using the shovel." Finally, after some "wait-time" we move to physical intervention, and take the shovel and return it to Kate. If Mark then has a temper tantrum or attempts to strike us we would use mirroring and diversion (body to the toy, etc.), as previously explained. Notice in this resolution there is no attempt to discuss guilt or improper behavior. Our ultimate goal is to teach the children to use expressive language to resolve social conflicts.

SWEARING, BATHROOM TALK, AND VERBAL AGGRESSION

It is Thanksgiving dinner and Grandma and friends are at the table. William states, "Mommy, I want my dessert." "No, not now, dear, you may have it after dinner." "Now, Mommy, now!" William screams. Mother ignores and William resorts to name calling and swearing. Hearing this unacceptable language coming from a 3-, 4-, or 5-year-old sends our pulses rushing! At first we feel helpless and then angry at the child.

If our middle class values cause us as teachers to "flood" when such language is used by a child, we have unknowing played into the child power trap. The developmental stages of impulse control (see Figure 8.2) move from an attempt to use expressive language (I want dessert now) to verbal aggression, to possibly physical aggression or passivity.

We will look at the problem of children's swearing from two aspects: (1) making a moral judgment and (2) preventing disruption of the social situation.

MORAL JUDGMENT

If the child should pick up some rocks, or perhaps some peas from his dinner plate, and throw them at another person (physical aggression), the emotional response he would get from adults would be dramatic. If he were verbally aggressive (using, for example, the "F" word) he would get the same dramatic effect. So, for the young child, still a transductive thinker, swearing has the same concrete meaning as direct physical aggression. When one child screams at another, "I going to cut off your head," the other may scream and run, truly afraid that the words might make this happen.

When children are verbally aggressive with other children, it is our belief, they talk this way because they cannot call up, under the emotional pressure of the moment, the correct language to get their needs met. We as teachers, then, do not make a moral judgment, but simply provide them with the correct language model to express what they want to say. For example, if Kate screams at Mark after he takes her shovel, "You butt face!" the teacher responds: "Kate, Mark can't understand what you want with those words. Tell him to give it back—you were using it." Thus, when one child is aggressive to another, we simply provide the child with the socially acceptable language model. We are teaching her to move from aggressive language to expressive language.

When aggressive language is directed to us we do not fall into the power trap set by the child: Carol was asked to leave the sand play and come inside immediately because of the threat of rain and dangerous lightning. When she refused, her teacher picked her up and carried her into the classroom.

Carol: "I hate you, Mrs. Anderson. You're a @#*%@#!"
Teacher: Carol, I need to bring you in quickly to keep you safe from the lightning. It is OK to be angry with me. Maybe you will want to be friends tomorrow."

The teacher makes no moral judgment on the child's behavior, gives her permission to have the strong feelings that she does have, and promises that the adult friendship will still be there.

The second aspect of the swearing, or verbal aggression, is the disruption of the social situation. Repeated verbal attacks coming from a child may make it difficult for a class to carry on with an activity. When this happens, give a preparatory command (from directive statements on the TBC) and then follow through with a logical consequence if the misbehavior occurs again: "Bill, if you disrupt our lunch with those words once more I will have to move you to the kitchen to eat so we don't have to be interrupted." Again, no moral judgment is made, and we are attempting to teach the child the logical consequences of his actions.

At a later time, in a knee-to-knee relationship with the swearing child, we would go back through the TBC much as we have described in the previous use of the relax-chair. "You have had a difficult time at lunch." (nondirective statements) "What is the rule at the table?" (questions) "The rule is . . ." (directive statement)

Many of the ideas in this chapter dealing with discipline and child guidance will be new to beginning teachers; most of us are much more familiar with the methods applied to us by our own parents and teachers. Thus, when we are in conflict situations with young children, those familiar, even ingrained methods will come to us as knee-jerk responses. But what we tend to want to do immediately is usually just what we should not do, because it would lead us into power traps.

We view children as gradually developing impulse control and the ability to handle frustrations. With the above ideas and techniques we have the perspective to look at the actions of children and then to intervene in a nonjudgmental and nonhostile manner to help them. To set appropriate goals for each child, we use the Adjustment Behavioral Profile found in Chapter 12.

Activities

1. Spend a morning in a classroom with 3-, 4-, and 5-year-old children, observing one child that in the first half-hour has looked like a possible difficult child. Do the SYC Adjustment Behavioral Profile found in Chapter 10, by observing closely the child's departure and reuniting with parents, eating a snack, rest time, circle time, and general play activities.
2. Select one discipline incident that you have recently observed, and with the TBC design a strategy for setting appropriate limits with this child if this incident would occur again.
3. Visit a young children's classroom. First interview the teacher requesting the five best-behaved children, and the five most difficult children in the room. What are the methods by which the well-behaving children get attention and power? What are the methods that the difficult children use to get attention and power? Try to determine, for the difficult children, what is their motivation: attention, power, revenge, or helplessness (Dreikurs, 1972).
4. Observe an experienced teacher working with young children, and watch for a discipline incident. Try to record the teacher's language responses with children. Number them in the sequence in which they occurred. Classify them with the use of the TBC as visually looking, nondirective statements, questions, directive statements, reinforcement, and physical intervention. What percentage was in each category of behaviors? Is this a Relationship-Listening, Confronting-Contracting, or Rules-Reward-and-Punishment teacher?
5. Read one of the books from the Literature with Special Meaning (Figure 8.3), possibly one about sibling relationships, and discuss the story with the children using questioning techniques of fact/labels, convergent, divergent, and evaluative.

References

ALBERTI, R.E., *Your Perfect Right: A Guide to Assertive Living.* San Luis Obispo, California: Impact Publishers, 1982.

CANTER, LEE, and MARLENE CANTER, *Assertive Discipline: A Take-Charge Approach for Today's Educator.* Seal Beach, California: Canter and Associates, 1976.

DREIKURS, RUDOLF and PEARL CASSEL, *Discipline Without Tears.* New York: Hawthorn Books, 1972.

ERIKSON, ERIK, *Childhood and Society.* New York: Norton, 1950.

FREUD, ANNA, *Normality and Pathology in Childhood: Assessment of Development.* New York: International University Press, 1968.

GLASSER, WILLIAM, *Schools Without Failure.* New York: Peter H. Wyden Publishing, 1969.

GORDEN, THOMAS, *T.E.T.: Teacher Effectiveness Training.* New York: Peter H. Wyden, 1974

HARRIS, THOMAS A., *I'm OK You're OK: A Practical Guide to Transactional Analysis.* New York: Harper and Row, Publishers, 1969.

PIAGET, JEAN, *The Moral Judgement of the Child.* Marjorie Gabain, trans. New York: Free Press, 1965.

WOLFGANG, CHARLES, *Helping Aggressive and Passive Preschoolers through Play.* Columbus, Ohio: Charles E. Merrill, 1977.

WOLFGANG, CHARLES, *Solving Discipline Problems: Strategies for Classroom Teachers.* Boston: Allyn and Bacon, 1986.

CHAPTER NINE

DAILY SCHEDULE

In other chapters we discuss methods for organizing space, objects, and materials for successful teaching through play. Another essential element in planning the daily activities for our classrooms is time. The following is a look at how some of the events of the school day can be scheduled and managed to avoid placing unnecessary stress on children, parents, and teachers.

ARRIVALS

The movement from home to school or from parent to teacher and classroom seems to adults a simple matter, but for young children, especially for 3-year-olds (A. Freud, 1968, 1971; Mahler, 1970, 1975), these changes may be considered "culture shock" (Speers, 1971). If you, as an adult, were transported suddenly to a foreign country with a different language, different foods and ways to eat it, different clothing, and the like, you would be under great stress—culture shock (Toffler, 1971). The school, a new place to live and work with others, places similar stress on the young child, who must be asking himself: "Where do I go to the potty if I need to? Who will keep me safe here when my mother is gone? Will others take my toys from me? Where do I sleep and eat?"

This fear of the school as an unknown will produce a variety of behaviors on the child's part. Here is an example of a successful preschool adaptation, with the child progressing through various stages of adjustment (Speers, 1971).

Lap Period

"Three-year-old Kate enters the classroom door, tightly holding her mother's hand. After child and parent are warmly greeted by the teacher, silently observed by the other children, the full meaning of "going to school" and "mother leaving" begins to come to Kate, and she climbs on her mother's lap and buries her face in her mother's chest. For a few minutes she refuses to look at this new world." We call this the lap period of adjustment. The teacher encourages the mother to take the rocking chair to a large upright mirror mounted on the wall, and suggests that when Kate feels more relaxed, her mother might demonstrate some of the toys to her. Then the teacher leaves, stating that she will be back shortly to help.

Customs Inspection Period

Next, we see Kate stop her crying and begin peeking over her mother's shoulder to watch the classroom activities through the mirror. Kate begins to point things out to her mother, and the two chat about what is occurring. We call this the customs inspection period (Mahler, 1970; 1975).)

Practicing Period

After looking about the room for a while, Kate suddenly slips from her mother's lap, runs out into the classroom to grab a toy, and brings it quickly back to her mother. Then, standing at her mother's knee, she watches to see if anyone will intervene—making eye contact with the teacher. The teacher smiles an OK at her.

"Oh, this is a toy dog," Mother says, "It goes 'ruff-ruff' and walks like this." Three or four times Kate runs out, grabs an object, darts back, and puts it in her mother's hands; her mother responds by telling her the name of the object and demonstrating its uses. We call this the practicing period—practicing being separated from mother for short periods (Speers, 1971; Mahler, 1975).

Teacher-Approach Period

We noticed that the teacher did not "throw" herself at the child, but permitted the child and parent time to relax and gradually separate physically.

During the gradual separation the teacher was observing the parent-child interaction, noting the sense modalities employed by the mother (see cueing in Mahler, 1971.):

Hearing—Is the mother trying to reassure the child by using language to explain, this is what we are doing, "This is what will happen next . . . . "? (If so, this may be a verbal mother.)

Touch—Is the mother cuddling and caressing the child, as well as exploring objects with her own hands and encouraging the child to do likewise? (This may be a tactile mother.)

Visual—Is the mother signaling the child with her eyes, telling her to "go ahead and pick up the object," just by using her eyes and facial expressions? (She may be a visual mother.)

The teacher has just learned something about the sense modality or combination of modalities that she may now use to make this child begin to feel comfortable in her new preschool world.

Hearing-verbal child: The teacher tells what is happening or going to happen (we are going to read a book about . . .; you will sit near me so that you may hear the story," etc.)

Tactile-physical child: The teacher brings a furry puppet, or takes the child to the classroom rabbit, encouraging her to touch.

Visual child: The teacher signals with her eyes that there is a free chair, toy, or materials available, and encourages the child to use them.

We may see that if the child and mother communicate well verbally, but there is little or no touching, an attempt on the teacher's part to cuddle with or physically cue that child may be seen by the child as frightening or intrusive.

We may ask why it is that when there are two or three teachers in a classroom each child seems to gain a solid emotional relationship with one or two teachers and will shy away from or reject a relationship with another teacher. It may sometimes be that a certain child and teacher share a form of sensory communication, while the rejected teacher may be unknowingly attempting to communicate in the child's weak or underdeveloped modality. We as teachers might attempt to decide which are our own strong modalities, and begin to practice ways of "shifting gears" deliberately, moving into different modalities, in order to try to communicate with different children. Later in the child's school years his favored modality may become his best learning style.

Parent Departure

Once communication is established between child and teacher, the parent may depart with minimal stress for the new child. The example above demonstrated initial fearfulness and a demand for mother to remain. These stress indicators are viewed as positive, because they tell us that there is a healthy attachment between child and parent. The crying and demanding are simply an indication of love (Speers, 1971). If we have given the child time to regress to more infantile behaviors, such as a lap baby, she should gradually emerge from the arms of mother and be able to join the other children.

Surprisingly, the children who act like "little men" or "little women" and show no emotional stress when mother departs, often have greater difficulty in making good long-term adjustments in the classroom. These "I don't need mother" children often refuse later to be cuddled or comforted by the teacher, need excessive teacher attention, behave in "run-and- chase" fashion, putting themselves in dangerous situations, and engage in stereotypic play—failing to progress developmentally (Speers, 1971).

The point is that signs of stress, crying and demanding, are normal. Our role is to find ways of bridging the child gradually from home to school. One way this can be done is by giving the parent time to stay with the child in the first hours or days of school. Another way is to pin Mother's handkerchief with Mother's perfume on it to the front of the child's clothing, so the child may finger it and smell "Mother" all day long. Or, we might permit the child to call her Mommy by telephone during the day, hearing in her mother's voice reassurance that she will return. Or, the parent could bring a family photo for the child to keep and to show around; or, the teacher could let the child bring a "transitional object"—a blanket ala the "Peanuts" character Linus or a cuddle toy—to carry about for the first few days. These "transition objects" give

**FIGURE 9.1   Young Child Gradually
Separating from Mother**

sensory reminders of home, permanence, and Mother, helping the child make the adjustment from home to school (A. Freud, 1971; Winnicott, 1971).

Another help in this transition is having the teacher and child play "mommy and child" with the use of a toy telephone. Remember our previous illustration of the value of make-believe play for helping children digest difficult emotional experiences (the child making her own ice cream cones in fantasy in the sandbox). With the toy telephone, the teacher carries on a conversation with the new child, reassuring him that his mother is thinking about him and will not forget to pick him up at the end of day (Peller, 1959).

Similar dramas may be played out with puppets, making one puppet the child and the other the parent. In the puppet modeling by the teacher the child puppet pleads, "Please don't go Mommy." The mother puppet explains that she must leave in order to do such and such, and that Mrs. Anderson will keep him safe until she returns. A teacher puppet now appears and helps the child puppet to "go potty," eat, sleep and play. Finally, a knock is heard at the door and mother puppet has returned to reunite warmly with the child puppet.

Here are some further suggestions for helping children make initial adjustments to school:

1. Have the teacher visit the child's home, watch for parent- child cueing modalities, and learn to communicate with the child on familiar ground.

2. Have parent and child make a visit to the classroom when no other children are there, possibly after school or on weekends. Have mother encourage the child to use the small toilets, be seated with teacher and mother for a quick snack, and take toys from the shelf and play with them. Have the child take some object home with him that he will bring back the first day, such as an inexpensive toy, piece of play dough, or crayon with paper. Label the child's storage cubby or cot with his name and, if possible, a photo.

(Note: Some children when visiting a store where things are on display shelves have been told not to touch and even disciplined harshly. The classroom, with things stored on shelves, will appear similar to children and they will be fearful of touching or taking things from shelves. Parents and teachers must communicate that it is safe to take and use the classroom objects.)

3. With a small group of already adjusted children play a series of imitative games, such as "thumbkin," or Simon Says. The object of the play activity is for the new child to be directly introduced to a group of children, so they will at least know each other's names.

4. Cut a large silhouette of the new child, paste a photograph of him on it and display it in a prominent place so all can see it, including parents arriving in the classroom.

5. Prepare the parents on what routine they should follow when they bring in the child for the first time. Explain to them that the school views the early signs of stress as positive, and that they should expect the periods of separation, lap, customs inspection, and practicing before the teacher-approach period. Remind the parent, though, that some children might not go through these separation processes the first day of school, but may wait until later in the school year, after a long weekend or holiday period.

Some parents say, "He did so well the first two weeks, but now he doesn't want to come to school and makes a fuss!" The child is now just beginning truly to separate; if the parents are aware of this beforehand they will not be disturbed by these new behaviors. Parents may consider removing the child from the school, if they have not been previously warned to expect some stress.

THE MESSAGE BOOK

A very good communication aid is a message book (Phelps, 1984) placed on a stand inside the arrival door, high enough so that one may stand and write. The parent writes a message in this book each morning, and also tells it to the morning teacher or head teacher. All staff members arriving to work throughout the day are required to read the message book as they come in. Also on the stand should be an enrollment roster with spaces after each child's name for initialing the child in and out, so that there will be a written record of the child's departure. Children may slip away to another classroom, to the bathroom, or to the playground; the initialed record tells us if they are actually in school. Also, if one parent comes at the end of the day wishing to pick up the child, not knowing that the other parent picked her up just before lunch, and now demands, "Where is my child?" the sign-in sign-out sheet is a lifesaver-literally.

A parent message bulletin board near or above the message stand is another must. Besides messages to parents, all requests to give children medication can be posted (on a standardized form). The forms should be filled out each morning by the parent, and the medicines stored in only one location familiar to all staff and parents. Since it is impossible to give medication to two or more children at staggered times throughout the day, the school should make known to all parents the established times when medications are given. Parents can then inform the physicians or pharmacists, and dosages can be adjusted based on these time periods. It is recommended that only one staff member be in charge of giving medication (with a back up person), and that this staff member initial the parent medication request, creating a record of the transaction.

SNACKS AND EATING

Mid-morning and mid-afternoon snacks provide not only bodily nourishment for highly active young children, but also bring them together to further a sense of group belonging. Business people take clients to lunch, families gather for holiday dinners—sharing food in pleasant settings creates belongingness. It is critical that snacktime be a pleasant experience for children because, if not, the situation may give rise to competition and aggression. Eating periods are not times for teachers to have breaks, leaving behind the less-trained and less-experienced teachers or aides to carry on. If negative instances occur at home between parent and child they will most likely occur at the dinner table or when going to bed at night. Therefore, eating at snacktime and lunchtime in preschool, and later, naptime are prime periods for the child to become "difficult," expecting to carry out power struggles with teachers just as with parents at home.

Group Snack

In organizing for snack, the concepts of control of error and degrees of freedom are used. We do not want the children to play with food, but we do want them to become accustomed to a routine which is nonrepressive and easy to follow.

Snacktime: what *not* to do
In classroom X the teacher instructs a mature child to set out the napkins and cups before each chair at the table. The children come to their seats, which have their names taped on. The teacher, seated at the end of the table makes an announcement or, when permitted, says grace. Then, extending a wicker basket of a food such as celery or cookies, not permitting the children to pass the basket, the teacher instructs each child to take one. (If any food remains the basket is removed from the table so the children will not fight over it.)
The children are instructed to set the snack on their napkin and wait until all are ready to eat. Next, the teacher appears with a pitcher of milk or juice and, moving behind the children, fills their 7-oz. paper cups. After the teacher is again seated, the children are told that they may begin. They are required to eat and drink everything they have been given, and to wait at the table until everyone else is finished. Then one child travels around the table gathering the used cups and napkins. Such is the classroom "kingdom" where the teacher rules in a regal manner.
Such a rigid snacking procedure indicates that the teacher does not believe that children can learn responsibility, and has an overriding fear that an accident will occur. The teacher shows a limited understanding of control of error as he plays food server to passive children.

Snack materials should be engineered to allow children to eat with minimal pressures from adults. First, two plastic cups with pouring lids, holding approximately three cups of juice or milk each, are placed on a cafeteria tray, along with two snack-filled wicker baskets lined with napkins and a stack of 3 oz. drinking cups. The lidded pouring glasses will keep spills to a minimum. Also on the tray are napkins in a weighted holder, which keeps the napkins from being blown about. Approximately 30% more snacks than there are children should be provided. These items are previously prepared by the teacher—or cook, if the school is lucky enough to have one.

The responsibility for bringing the filled cafeteria tray to the table belongs to the children who have finished cleanup from previous activities and have washed their hands. They bring the tray carefully from the kitchen to the center of the snack table.

Round tables, each seating eight children, so that each child can see the face of all the others and have equal access to the cafeteria tray, are ideal. Rectangular tables always seem to leave the end child out of conversations and access.

After washing up, the children seat themselves as desired, select napkins and cups from the center of the table, pour their own juice or milk and pass the container to a neighbor. Snack items are then taken from the basket with plastic prongs (for health reasons), and passed from one child to another.

Children are permitted to take more than one food item, and the small, 3 oz. cups make it necessary that they refill their cups repeatedly. The teacher is seated at the table or at a nearby table and models behavior by carrying on light conversations and eating and drinking the snack as she or he wishes the children to do. Coffee cups and soda cans used by the teacher at the snack table would be inappropriate modeling.

When children have had enough food and conversation they may get up at will, drop their napkins and cups in a number of plastic-lined waste cans nearby, and move to some quiet activity, such as reading or looking at picture books. This procedure gives the children freedom and control. The teacher is not a food server or "boss" but an equal member of the group.

Open Snack

At some child-centered programs the children are all "herded together" for snack, regardless of whether they are ready to eat. Why not give the children total autonomy over eating by arranging an open snack? From 9:00 A.M. until 10:30 A.M. a child-sized table with two chairs is placed in the corner of the classroom, arranged with snack materials as described above, with 3 oz. cups, lidded pouring cups, and snacks in baskets—but this time covered with a see-through plastic lid with a handle. A child is free during this open snack period to find a friend, wash hands (a container with soapy water and paper towels are nearby), and eat a snack when desired. The only rule is that the child bring a friend. If she can't find a friend that morning, the teacher may eat with the child—and then "engineer" socially to help that child make a friend in the next few weeks.

On the wall near the open snack table is a class roster where the teacher keeps a record of the time each child eats snack, and with whom. Open snack is especially useful during the beginning of a school year when many children are making an initial adjustment; it may be alternated with group snack for variety, and in order that the children may benefit from the advantages of both methods.

EATING DIFFICULTIES

Some children become "Mr. Hyde" or "the Hulk" when they come to a group setting to eat. These carryover behaviors from home (Dreikurs, 1964) are rooted in power struggles, and generally are seen in the form of the "child who will not eat," or the "child who becomes aggressive, verbally (calling others names) and physically (jabbing others with his/her finger), harassing others, and hoarding snacks when passed to them."

Our attitude toward such children should be to consider this "misbehavior" a sign of basic insecurity and fear of the eating and group situation. We should not view them as simply bullies or as "just being mean." Our goal is to have the child become comfortable, to eat and socialize with others.

We may start by permitting the difficult, passive, or aggressive, child to eat in a one-to-one relationship with a friend or adult at a small table. This should not be done in such a manner that the child views it as isolation or punishment, but as a special time with a friend or teacher. Later, a second child can be invited to the small table, with others gradually joining over a period of days or weeks until the child finally is eating with a group. Even after the child has adjusted to the large group setting, there may be "bad days" when she might be permitted to revert to a smaller group for eating.

While she is making these initial adjustments, few eating demands should be made of the child, and we will depend on the other children to be good models of behavior for her. If she refuses to eat, we will make no demands, simply cleaning up when snack is over and moving on to other activities. Some teachers worry that if the child has not eaten she will become malnourished; however, the failure to eat at school will only occur over a two- to three-week period, and with a well-balanced day of active play the child will develop a healthy appetite. When the "non-eating child" knows that the pressure is off, she will eat. We as teachers must have faith that this will occur (Dreikurs, 1964).

It is not surprising to discover that it is the "non-eating" child's parents who demand at the end of the day a full report of the child's eating performance: "Did Jon eat all of his lunch today?" This is symptomatic of a power struggle between parent and child at the eating table. The parents' emotional intensity may be strong and possibly intimidating to the teacher, attempting to get us into the power struggle. We must resist. Our response to the parent would be an encouragement statement: "He did better today!" "He is becoming more comfortable at snack and gradually eating more; we are confident that in a few days he will be eating a full serving." We then move on to other positive topics with the parent, telling her or him of the other activities in which the child is doing well. Modeling positive expectations for the child is the best support we can give to parents who appear to us to be over-concerned.

We attempt always to be truthful with parents; however, in one incident a parent inspected his child's lunchbox at the end of the day and, finding items not eaten, verbally exploded, reprimanding the child for not eating. As a result, the child's teacher, for a period of two weeks during initial adjustment, deliberately removed uneaten items from the lunchbox. The parental reprimands stopped and, without this parental pressure, the child began eating his lunch and asking for more—much to his parent's delight. Deciding whether the teacher was "right" or "wrong" in this case presents a moral dilemma exemplary of those which must sometimes be faced by teachers of young children.

For the hoarding child who takes far too much from the shared snack basket, we provide for the initial period items that are very small: nuts, dry cereals, or trail mix rather then one large blueberry muffin. The teacher states, "Take all that you can eat and leave in the basket all that you cannot eat. You may take seconds, and I will always make sure that everyone gets enough to eat." Remember in our chapter on discipline and child guidance our rule is to "tell the child what to do, not what not to do." We resist the natural tendency to state, "Don't take so much, Tommy. You are not going to eat all of that." We permit the child, for a period of days or even two or three weeks, to continue to hoard without any comment. For the hoarder there is a basic "not OK" view of the world, and his "life-stance" is that the world is denying him and he must fight to get his needs met (Harris, 1969).

At the end of snack, during cleaning-up procedures, we will appear before the hoarding child (who will have a large pile of trail mix in front of him uneaten), make eye contact, touch the remaining food with our hand to focus his attention on what we are talking about, and then reassuringly state: "Take all that you can eat and leave in the basket all that you cannot eat. You may take seconds, and I will always make sure that everyone gets enough to eat."

Over the next weeks we begin to "back down" the TBC with the child:

Modeling

Eating with others who exhibit good eating behaviors.

Directive Statements

Before the child takes from the basket of food, the teacher states directly, "Take all that you can eat and leave in the basket all that you cannot eat. You may take seconds and I will always make sure that everyone gets enough to eat."

Questions

Again, just before the child takes from the shared basket, the teacher poses the question, "Jim, what is our rule about 'snacks from baskets'"?

Nondirective Statements

The teacher states to the group in general, as the basket is passed, "We have a rule for taking snacks." Such nondirective reminders simply bring to the child's awareness the desired rule before he acts.

Looking On

Such difficult children need the teacher nearby during snack, radiating a zone of safety and control. If a teacher must supervise a number of tables he or she may choose to eat at the table where the target child is seated for a number of weeks. This "looking on" is not done with an attitude of, "I have to keep an eye on him every moment or he will get out of hand" but rather, our attitude must be that we want a close positive relationship with the child: supportive, helping, and related.

ACTING-OUT WHILE EATING

Once the child has become relaxed and adjusted to eating with others, there will be times when she, or other members of the class, might begin to disrupt the eating situation in a manner which necessitates direct action by the teacher. This will be done, again, by escalating up the TBC.

Carol has been "silly" all morning, giggling, challenging the teacher's limits, and generally refusing to fit into routines. At snack time she is excessively loud, prevents the child next to her from eating by calling her "bathroom" names, and makes the entire eating atmosphere unpleasant.

Looking On

The teacher changes her seating, moving into the direct view of Carol. If need be, she touches Carol or uses any other nonverbal actions to get her aware that she is present. Just looking might get Carol back on track; if not, the teacher escalates up the TBC.

Nondirective Statements

The teacher announces in a nondirective statement, "At snack time we need to remember to use our 'inside' voices."

Questions

Increasing the intervention by moving up the TBC to questioning: "Do you need my help to remember rules at snack?" Or, "Do you need to move to a smaller, quieter table to be able to eat your snack this morning, Carol?"

Directive Statements

With directive statements we tell the child exactly what we want them to do, not what not to do. If the child continues to be defiant, we follow with a preparatory command or promise to take action in the form of a consequence. "Carol (uses name, touches her on shoulder, and makes direct eye contact), I want you to turn around, sit up in your chair, put your food in your mouth, and use an 'inside' voice that does not hurt ears" (Canter, 1976). She remains defiant. "If I see that done again it is telling me that you do not know the rules for eating snack with others and I will ask you to move to another table, or leave snack time this morning" (logical consequence, Dreikurs, 1964).

Modeling/Physical Intervention

If the child continues to refuse, we now intervene physically, if need be, to move the child away from the situation in a nonpunitive manner. (See Chapter 8 on discipline and child guidance for techniques in handling temper tantrums, which are likely to occur when we use very strong intervention.)

RECOMMENDED MEAL PATTERNS

As we plan meals for 3-, 4-, and 5-year-old children the total daily food needs of the child must be considered. What to serve and how much depends upon the ages of the children and their length of stay at school. Children in the school for four to eight hours will require one nutritious, well-balanced meal with one snack for mornings and one in the afternoon. This provides one-third to one-half of the Recommended Dietary Allowances. Children spending more than 8 hours, such as with day care, would be provided additional food, in the form of two meals and two snacks, providing two-thirds to three-quarters of their daily dietary requirement.

The framework in Table 9.1 may be used in planning nutritious, well-balanced menus.

REST/SLEEPING TIME

It is recommended, that for all-day programs, 3- and 4-year-old children might require at least two hours or more of afternoon rest or sleep, while 5-year-olds might need a minimum of 45 minutes' quiet, lie-down-on-a-mat, rest. Resting is another area where power struggles are fought out between parents or other adults and the child, and these patterns will often be brought into the school during sleeping and resting periods. Dreikurs, 1964)

TABLE 9.1   Recommended Meal Patterns*

FOOD COMPONENTS	CHILDREN 3 TO 6 YEARS
BREAKFAST	
Milk, fluid	3/4 cup
Juice or fruit or vegetable	1/2 cup
Bread enriched or whole grain	1/2 slice
or cereal	
cold dry	1/3 cup
hot cooked	1/4 cup
MID-MORNING OR MID-AFTERNOON	
(Snack supplement)	
(select two of these four components)	
milk, fluid	1/2 cup
meat or meat alternative	1/2 ounce
Juice (full strength) or fruit(s)	1/2 cup
or vegetable(s)	
Bread or cereal	1/2 slice
cold dry	1/3 cup
hot cooked	1/4 cup
LUNCH OR SUPPER	
Milk, fluid	3/4 cup
Meat or meat alternative (lean	1-1/2 ounces
meat, poultry, or fish, cooked)	
or cheese	1-1/2 ounces
or egg	1
or cooked dry beans or peas	3/8 cup
or peanut butter[2]	3 tablespoons
Vegetable(s) and/or fruit(s)	1/2 cup(total)
Bread	1/2 slice

(*)From the guidelines of Dept. of Health and Rehabilitative Services, 1317 Winewood Blvd., Tallahassee, Fla. 32309-0700
[2]Caution: Peanut butter on dry bread and popcorn are items that cause many choking deaths in centers for young children.

Again, children—and we adults—live in three worlds: an inside world of thought and feelings, where our focus of attention is internal; a body world, when we enjoy activities such as swimming, running, or simply relaxing in a bathtub; and an external world in which we play, work, and focus on the world around us. A healthy form of regression (A. Freud, 1965) for the adult at the end of a very busy day is to crawl into a large comfortable chair, kick off tight shoes, and feel one's tired body relax (the body world); then, take time to daydream or think over the day (the inside world). Adults and children move in and out of these three worlds throughout the day.

In order to sleep, young children must give up being attuned to the external world of others and objects, move through the body world, feeling themselves physically relax, and then move into an inner world of thoughts that finally lead to unconscious sleep. Overactive children, children frightened by the new school situation, or children who have patterns of engaging in power conflicts centered on napping, will not be able to move back normally through these three worlds. Thus, rest period is not a time to be left to inexperienced staff; teachers need to be present—to rub backs, talk to children, and reassure them with their presence that the children are safe and secure.

The difficult child, when asked to lie on a cot, cannot give up an external awareness because his perceptions are outward and defensive. To help counter this, each child should have a cot labeled with his or her name, located at the same spot each day (for health reasons children should not sleep on each other's cots). This is truly a private space, and other children should not be permitted to invade it by putting their hands or feet on the cots. The teachers should scatter themselves over the sleep area, kneeling near the children who are having difficulty relaxing, helping them with appropriate sensory measures. Soft music without words can be played to mask inside and outside noise. Some children we permit to wear headphones to listen to soft music to screen out external sounds. We must be careful, especially if wires are connected to the headphones, to remove them once the child is asleep.

The child who is visually stimulated may be placed near a wall, shelving, or small movable screen, so that distractions will be kept from view. For some tactile children, gentle back-rubbing will help bring on relaxation. Once the children are relaxed and quieted, teachers may depart the sleeping room, leaving behind one adult, who will always be seated in the same location during rest. This is important, because children will awaken, look to the "adult chair," see the teacher, be reassured, and return to sleep. If that chair is deserted, the child sits up to look for the teacher, and will have a very difficult time getting to sleep again.

There are rare children at this age who seem not to need sleep. Their behavior and personality are productive throughout the school day, and being on a cot is, for them, like being in jail. We require such children to attempt to rest and sleep, but if, after 15 to 20 minutes and our best attempts to help them relax, they cannot, we give them picture books or miniature toys to use quietly on their cots. Then, if the child still acts as if he is in jail, we permit him to leave the sleeping room quietly and do some tabletop activities (clay modeling or drawing, for example) in another room. What we would not want to do is harshly reprimand, causing the child greater tension and making it even more difficult for him to relax. This would be a real contradiction of our action and goals.

CIRCLE/STORY TIME

Bringing together a group of 5's, 4's, and especially, 3 year-old-children and getting them to focus their full attention on one adult takes great care and technical understanding. It might be helpful to reread the concept of "three spheres of communication" described in Chapter 8.

ONE TO ALL

Group time provides third-sphere communication (one to all), whereby the teacher requires all attention to focus on him while his emotions and responses are diffused to all members of a group—generally not to one child. Thus, each child is required to inhibit his own egocentric desires and become a part of the collective activity. This is socially very demanding for the young child, who is still quite self-centered. We must carefully regulate the amount of time children will be required to maintain themselves in nonpersonal, directly controlled situations. Circle/story time is one such situation. If well-managed, this activity can lead the child toward a greater ability to handle direct instruction.

The transition into and out of group time is critical. If all 15 or 20 young children run into the rug room, trying to grab a favorite spot, pushing and shoving will occur with some danger of minor injury.

Let us look at a better way of making a transition from, for example, snack time to circle time (see Table 9.2): The teacher in charge of circle time collects three to six children who have finished with their previous activity and have cleaned up. She directs them to follow her to the rug. Once at the rug the teacher must take a power position, much like a judge in a courtroom, placing herself higher than the children, on a piano stool, rocking chair, etc.

Circle time must be engineered with an understanding of "control of error." Each child should know the rules about what he should and should

TABLE 9.2   Good Transitions

SUGGESTIONS:

1. Generally, never have a young child stand in line to wait.
2. Move children in groups of three to six, with the first group accompanied by the "point" teacher, who has these children get the new area ready for those to follow.
3. The last teacher to leave the space, such as the rug room where story-time was occurring, uses the remaining three to six children to clean up, before moving them to the new location.
4. When children are making transitions to a new space, before they leave their present space, they should know where they are going and what they will do when they get there.

not do, and there must be some definition of individual seating space. Two large half-circles, taped or painted, or a circle design in the rug, indicate where each child is to be seated with legs tucked under. The first children will take the inner circle, closest to the teacher, while the later children will take the back circle, refraining from trampling over children already seated. The motor rules and circle on the floor are structured to control error; if there is no structure the children will be randomly scattered over the rug, rolling over, lying down, and getting up and down.

The teacher should not wait until everyone is present and ready (this would cause the waiting children to find negative ways of amusing themselves), but should simply jump off into a finger game, songs with physical actions, or something similar. Once everyone has come in, a storybook can be begun.

While circle time is in progress, other teachers or aides need to be present at the back of the circle. If certain children cannot relax, and begin to disrupt the story, the helping teachers would move closer to them, touching them on their backs, or drawing them into their own laps, generally helping them to relax. Or these teachers may, in the case of very physically active children, move them to child-sized chairs at the end of the circle. These children literally hold themselves onto the chairs until they gain control of their bodies.

If repetitive disruptions by one or more children do occur, the in-charge teacher who is reading or carrying on the activity must take some action, and that action will based on the TBC.

Looking On

The teacher may simply signal with her eyes to the off-task child that she wants his or her attention. This is also a signal to the helping teacher on the sidelines to move in and help with this child.

Nondirective Statements

At this point it is important for the teacher to understand the concept of high profile and low profile correction in a directive teaching situation. If we stop our activities and reprimand one child directly, we are disrupting the shared fantasy of the story for all others, as well as possibly making the other children feel empathetically tense and uncomfortable. "Johnny, you are not listening and you are disrupting the story for everyone." The eyes of all other children now turn to Johnny. This is a "GI"ing, or guilt inducing, statement. The reprimand has probably disrupted the story more than Johnny's original actions.

In using low profile correction the teacher simply looks at Johnny, says his name, and points out some aspect of the book or object she is sharing: "...

Johnny, you will notice (pointing to the picture) that the troll is hiding under the bridge . . . ." Using low profile corrections we can use the child's name, our hand, and visual focus, and continue with the rhythms of the story.

Questions/Directive Statements

If disruption by the "difficult" child continues we will move up the TBC to questions and to even more directive action which will require a high profile. But, let's keep in mind that when two or more adults are teaching in the classroom, the in-charge teacher can depend on the sideline teacher to help with children who need "looking on." The teacher then questions all children, "What are our rules of behavior at circle time?" Then she directs; "Show me that you know the rules!" Finally, a preparatory command to the off-task child: "John, you are showing me this morning that you have not learned the rules for story-time, and if . . . occurs again, I will ask you to go to the next room and choose something else to do."

Modeling/Physical Intervention

If the misbehavior continues, the in-charge teacher will have the sideline teacher remove Johnny from circle time. Since a very high profile correction is needed, the teacher may choose to stop the story and play or sing a finger- or hand-game, and then reintroduce the story.

Later, in a nonpunitive manner the in-charge teacher will approach Johnny, moving through the TBC again, with child and teacher seated in chairs facing each other, knee-to-knee. "You have had a really difficult time in circle time this morning." (nondirective statement) "What are the rules for circle time?" (questions) "In circle time I want you to sit on your spot on the line, look at me, and listen to the story." If the teacher feels that the child truly does not understand the rules, the two of them could go to the rug room and the teacher could reteach the rules. (modeling) This knee-to-knee follow-through lets the child know, in a nonpunitive manner, exactly what is wanted.

Departing from circle time can be done quickly and in an orderly manner. At SYC we generally dismiss children in groups of six to eight. The in-charge teacher may continue with a simple hand-game, while the sideline teacher signals a small group of children and leads them to a definite location. The in-charge teacher dismisses another group of six to eight that will "go to Mrs. Anderson" at snack or her location. Finally, the in-charge teacher has the remaining children clean up the room and then follow her to the new location. Notice that no one has had to stand in line. Waiting in lines should be a real "no-no" in early childhood practice. Children at this age do not move well in herds!

DEPARTURE

There are some children who do well all day long until the first parent appears at the end of the day to pick up their child. Then the Dr. Jekyll and Mr. Hyde syndrome appears, with crying, temper tantrums, and defiance toward the teachers. Why is this so? We speculate that after the first parent of the day comes for her child, the "Mr. Hyde" child worries about whether he will be picked up by his own parents. For him the question is, "Will my mom forget me?" This is not an extraordinary worry, but will be a concern for all children at this age.

Our goal is to occupy their minds (perhaps with a story) and possibly hands (using structured-construction materials such as puzzles) in some activity that keeps their minds off their worry and separation fears. This can be done by having a small, intimate circle time with the six to eight children who are picked up late. Find a comfortable corner on a rug where children can be on your lap, and physically close to you. Read stories, play hand-games, and carry on lively conversation, permitting individual children to depart from the circle at natural break points when you are aware that the parent has arrived. This should be done whenever the parent is truly late. If we simply leave the last child to be picked up on her own while we go about cleaning up, she will have a real feeling of loss. We should engage her, if possible, in helping us clean up; or take time for some one-to-one communication with her until the parent arrives. We need to involve that child in our own cleanup activity or take time to maintain a first-sphere (one-to-one) relationship until the parent arrives.

SUGGESTED SCHEDULES

The rule of thumb for arranging the daily schedule of activities is to balance physical-activity time with quiet time. Some additional rules:

Active/Passive Times

Consider the amount of physical activity a child is doing and try to balance this with a passive activity. We suggest that children tend to get "stuck" in outside or physical worlds and can't slow down and relax. Some young children, if permitted, would continue to be drunk with running and movement until they were so exhausted they would actually "drop in their tracks." Once we sense that children have had enough activity, we move them to story time, puzzles, or similar sedentary activities.

TABLE 9.3   Schedule

7:30	Arrival
	Play-Activity Curriculum with one table set of Thematic-Project supervised by one available teacher.
8:30	Playground
	Play-Activity and Thematic-Projects Curriculum available
9:15	Circle Time
	(music, hand games, book reading, or general sharing)
9:45	Toileting/handwashing
	(transitioning into snack)
	Snack
10:30	Thematic-Project Curriculum
11:30	Playground
12:00	Circle Time
	(Story reading with transition to toileting, to noon meal)
12:20	Noon Meal
1:00	Toileting (with transition to rest)
	Rest
3:00	Toileting
3:15	Thematic-Project Curriculum
	1/3 of children on screened porch or screened outside area)
	Play-Activity Curriculum
	2/3 of children inside
	(Note: children will rotate in thirds to outside porch.)
4:45	Playground
5:25	Circle Time
	Clean-up and Depart
5:45	Close

Note: Half-day programs would simply follow the above morning schedule.

Outside Climate and Weather

To balance outside and inside activities, we must be aware of our general climate and be prepared to make daily adjustments. In tropical climates during the summer months we may wish to have the outside time in the early mornings when it is relatively cool, and stay indoors in the afternoon. The opposite is true for cold climates or winter months, when we may wish to stay inside in the mornings and go outside in the afternoon in the warmer sun.

MOTOR RULES AND "MARS" DAYS

We watch a 4-year-old child get up from snack time: He stands with the backs of his legs pushing out the chair, takes three steps to the wastepaper basket, throws out his trash, and begins to walk to the playground door. He suddenly stops; it is apparent that an idea has entered his mind. He returns to his seat and pushes it in under the table, so that no other child will trip over it. This "pushing in the chair" is a learned "motor-rule" (Piaget, 1932). Adults as well as young children go through their days as if on automatic pilot, moving from one motor action to the next. "Collect your papers from the snack table, stand and move to the trash basket, push in your chair" are all motor-rules that this child has internalized. Once these motor-rules are learned after entering a new school, the child "understands" the structure of the school and gains a sense of security that he can master such a world. This world is predictable; but if, for example, a photographer appears unexpectedly to take group photographs, the schedule of activities is dramatically altered. The children become demanding, whining, wanting to know "why are we not going to do so and so, Mrs. James? When are we going to have snack?" This shows tension and confusion. What is important, then, is to have the children learn quickly the motor-rules for all of the materials and rooms.

Spatial location in our adult world communicates to us motor rules and behavior, and because we are well-socialized we respond appropriately. In a movie theater we act with certain defined motor-rules; at a football game these rules change; at the dinner table they change again. This is equally true for the School for Young Children. The motor-rules and behavior for the playground, rug-story room, toilet area, snacking, and during our rest time; all demand changes in both child and teacher behavior, and this must be learned.

When new children enter our school for the first time, then, we "teach the walls and objects." By this we mean that the teacher would start at the front door of the school and begin to move around the walls, teaching the motor-rules of using the child storage cupboard, blocks and block shelves, sociodramatic play area, etc., until objects are "taught." With these new children we would also do this at each change throughout the day—the movement to outdoor playground, movement to story time, etc. This teaching of "walls and objects" is done using the direct-instruction procedure of say, show, check (Bereiter, 1966; Engelmann, 1980). For example:

Say: "Friends, these are the blocks and block shelves; watch as I take out these three blocks. You will see that there is a paper block shape, here on the shelf, which tells me that this size block and shape goes here."

Show: "Now I am going to ask one of you to put this block back in its 'home'. Look closely—where·does this one go? (Teacher holds up wooden arch.) Mike, put this block on the right shelf. (Mike does it correctly.) Friends, is Mike correct? (Children respond yes.)"

Check: "Now, watch closely! I'm going to put these three blocks back one at a time. See if I do this correctly. Is this right?" Children: "Yes!" "Is this right?" Children: "Yes!" "Is this right?" (places it incorrectly) Children: "Nooo!" "Why not?" (Children explain why not.)

"Now I am going to give each of you three blocks, and let us see whether you can put them back on the shelves, where they will "sleep in their homes." The teacher watches the actions of each child to see if he knows the concept;

if not, the teacher reteaches the child who made an error, again in the three-step lesson of say, show, check. Notice in the "check" step above, once the teacher felt that the children knew the concept, she used the negation (she did it "wrong") to see if the children could make the correction (Engelmann, 1980).

Through of direct-instruction, we teach the motor-rules of all our play center's objects, rooms, and space. At the end of this orientation the children can answer questions such as: "How are the pencil sharpeners to be used? How do I go to the toilet?" The understanding of these motor-rules gives the child a sense of security in the school world.

Once the children gain an understanding of the use of the classroom components, activities will proceed almost effortlessly. However, after a two- to three-month period, both the children and the teachers begin to neglect the motor-rules, especially if new, improperly oriented, staff are added. We now find puzzle pieces scattered among the Lego storage boxes, housekeeping equipment from the sociodramatic play area lying on the floor, trash left on tables after snack time, etc. These are all signs that the structure of classroom order is falling apart; an "accident waiting to happen."

The rule of thumb in open play environments, especially for visitors who are inspecting a new school, is that if teachers and children do not take care of school objects, it is likely that the children are not taken care of properly either.

The results of disorder and disarray are increased whining and aggression from children, low levels of play, with children simply wandering about looking for something to do, destruction of property, teachers becoming tense and overdirective with children—wanting to impose more verbal rules. At worst, injury may occur. The solution is to call for "Mars Days."

By "Mars Days" we mean that the teacher starts the school "anew," pretending that the children have just arrived on a rocket ship from Mars. In groups of six to eight the children go around the school with the teacher, learning walls and objects as before, as well as the changes in space and time throughout the daily schedule. The new teacher who is unsure of the motor-rules may join one of these groups and learn the motor-rules right along with the children.

SUMMARY

In summary, techniques have been presented for smoother handling of arrivals, snack eating, meal patterns, rest/sleeping, circle/story time, transactions, departures, schedules, and teaching motor-rules. The SYC takes the position that children can be trusted, that their inappropriate actions stem from lack of ability to behave as we desire. We aim to give them a secure environment where they can learn.

To accomplish this task, the teacher needs to understand how to arrange a well-balanced classroom, allowing for freedom and control of error. Once a well-designed play environment is created, and the child understands the motor-rules and time schedules, the classroom runs smoothly without the need for excessive teacher control. The teacher is then free to facilitate the children's ongoing play, usually with the Teacher Behavioral Continuum, to further their journey toward effectiveness, autonomy, and increased maturity.

Activities

1. Visit three classrooms and collect their schedules of activities for the day. What percentage of time is divided between the three methods of teaching: Play-Activity, Thematic- Project, or Direct-Instruction? Based on the age of the children in this class are these time divisions appropriate? Consider the three spheres of relationship: (1)one-to-one, (2) one-to-eight, and (3) one-to-all. Does the schedule permit all forms of spheres of relationship or is it heavily weighted to one to the deficit of another? Is there an appropriate division between indoor and outdoor time?
2. Observe three classrooms with young children having snacks. Analyze whether this is child-centered or teacher-controlled? Which form has more misbehavior by children?
3. Observe an experienced teacher doing circle time and, with the TBC, tally a mark regarding the types of teacher behavior used for children that might disrupt. Is this high or low profile, or appropriate? Is there a structure that gives children security (control of error) during story time? How do they arrive and depart?
4. Interview two experienced teachers, asking them for their list of classroom rules for young children. Take each one and see how you might reorganize time, space, objects, or children to eliminate each of these rules.
5. Interview a parent who is having a 3-year-old or younger child go off to school or day care for the first time. What are their concerns? How do they view the child's protesting when they depart? How does the child reunite? What advice can you give them? Observe the parent-child interaction. Can you find a strong modality of communication between the parent and child? Try to communicate with that child in that modality. Interview the teacher and see his/her view of this stressful time. Ask the teacher what actions they take to help with separation.

References

BEREITER, CARL, and SIEGFRIED ENGELMANN, *Teaching Disadvantaged Children in the Pre-school*. Englewood Cliffs, N.J.: Prentice- Hall, 1966.

CANTER, LEE, *Assertive Discipline*. Los Angeles: Canter and Associates, 1976.

DREIKURS, RUDOLF, *Children: The Challenge*. New York: Hawthorne Books, 1964.

ENGELMANN, SIEGFRIED, *Direct Instruction*. Englewood Cliffs, N.J.: Educational Technology Publications, 1980.

FREUD, ANNA, *The Ego and the Mechanisms of Defense*. New York: International Universities Press, 1971.

FREUD, ANNA, *Normality and Pathology in Childhood: Assessments of Development*. New York: International Universities Press, 1968.

HARRIS, THOMAS A., *I'm OK—You're OK: A Practical Guide to Transactional Analysis*. New York: Harper and Row, 1969.

MAHLER, MARGARET S., *On Human Symbiosis and the Vicissitudes of Individuation*. New York: International Universities, 1970.

MAHLER, MARGARET S. and others, *The Psychological Birth of the Human Infant*. New York: Basic Books, 1975.

PELLER, LILI E., "Libidinal Phases, Ego Development and Play," in *Psychoanalytic Study of the Child, no. 9*. New York: International Universities Press, 1959.

PHELPS, PAMELA, *The Creative Preschool*, Tallahassee, Fla.: personal communication.

PIAGET, JEAN, *The Moral Judgment of the Child*, trans. Marjorie Gabain. New York: Free Press, 1965.

SPEERS, REX W., and others, "Recapitulation of Separation- Individuation Processes When the Normal Three-Year-Old Enters Nursery School," in *Separation-Individuations, Essays in Honor of Margaret Mahler*, John McDevitt, ed. New York: International Universities Press, 1970

SPEERS, REX W., *Variations in Separation-Individuation and Implications for Play Ability and Learning as Studied in the Three-Year-Old in Nursery School*. Pittsburgh: University of Pittsburgh Press, 1970.

TOFFLER, ALVIN, *Future Shock*. New York: Bantam Books, 1971.

CHAPTER TEN

THE SPECIAL NEEDS CHILD

Matthew, a precocious 4-year-old, is organizing a group of children in the housekeeping area. "I'm the dad, and it's time for me to go to work. Becka, you be the mommy, Shawn is the baby, and Emily is Grandma," says Matthew. Becka replies, "It's your day to take Shawn to school. Here's your hat and briefcase."

Matthew takes the hand of Shawn, who has been rocking back and forth on the floor at the edge of the group, and leads him over to the chairs that become the car. Shawn throws himself on the floor and screams, biting at his hand and kicking his legs in the air. Mrs. Davis, the teacher, intervenes, drawing Shawn into her lap, gently rocking him and saying into his ear, "You can say *No!* Shawn. You can say *no* to Matthew." Shawn seems to withdraw into his inner world, shaking his head back and forth, repeating to himself, "No, no, no, no, no, no. No. No."

Shawn has come to our school at his pediatrician's recommendation. His speech and language development are at least two years behind his chronological age of four years. His typical behavior is passive and withdrawn. When any social demands are made on him, he falls apart in what looks like a temper tantrum. He has an older brother at home with autistic characteristics, some of which Shawn has picked up, such as echoing speech, head rocking, and hand shaking. Shawn is mainstreamed into our classroom and we wish to make a significant contribution to his developmental progress—while continuing to provide a high quality program for the rest of the children.

About six weeks after Shawn started at preschool, his mother approached the director and said, "I'm going to take Shawn out of this school. When he first came, he was a little behind in language, but at least he was well-behaved. Do you know what he did last night? He got a fluorescent marker and drew scribbles all over the walls in his room. He has just gotten worse and worse since he came here." The director discussed with Shawn's mom that what she was seeing was two-year-old aggressive behavior in a four-year-old body. For Shawn, this was progress. What he had shown earlier was aggressive behavior more commonly observed in infancy.

The director discussed how children's development moves through stages of passivity, aggression, and verbal expression—before self-control and using of language to get needs met and to solve problems begin to emerge. Shawn's body had kept growing, but some other areas of development had slowed down or gotten off track. The mother got some tips on channeling that "terrible two"-year-old type of aggression into acceptable forms of behavior; for example, she got some big pads of paper and gave them to Shawn for specific use with markers.

When Grandma came to visit Shawn, she brought a large, very expensive picture book. Shawn grinned with delight, took it to his room, and later proudly returned to show it to her. She called out aghast to her daughter, "Look what he's done!" Shawn's mother, after seeing that he had scribbled all through the book with marker, said, "Shawn, I am glad to see you remembered that markers are for paper." Shawn's mother had begun to understand about development, and acceptable alternatives, but she had a lot of explaining to do to Grandma! Now she knew that it was time to begin to teach Shawn which paper is appropriate to write on and which is not.

During the next month, Shawn was out on the playground riding a tricycle, which had become one of his favorite activities. The wind blew his hat off, and when he got off the tricycle to retrieve it, another child got on. Shawn stood in front of the tricycle growling and grimacing at the other child; the teacher, observing, called out, "Shawn, use words." Shawn responded in his loudest voice to the child on the trike, "USE WORDS!" The teacher realized that Shawn still needed her to model for him what words should be used, so she said, "Say, 'Mine. That's my bike.'" He said, "My bike"—and he got it back through the use of words.

Gradually, Shawn got to be friendly with Stephen, who was a great "pretend" player. Shawn began to play and talk a little more, first with Stephen, and then with other "good players" whom the teachers encouraged to play with them. Everyone was pleased with Shawn's progress, and eventually he was able to attend a small individualized kindergarten class in the local public school.

Shawn's story exemplifies some of the benefits of integrating a child with exceptional needs into a child-centered program which uses the TBC teaching strategies. Shawn can learn appropriate social behaviors through imitating the other children. Some of the social attitudes and skills a child like Shawn can learn are sharing, cooperating, respecting the property of others, and modifying aggressive acts and impulses. The teacher can help Shawn move through the social stages from unoccupied to onlooker, to solitary play, to parallel play, to associative play, and to cooperative play. Figure 5.6, the observation record of a teacher's play facilitation, can help the teacher plan an intervention strategy.

Children with developmental disabilities and delays generally move along the same developmental track as children who do not have such difficulties, but at a slower pace in some areas. The teacher will probably have to start at the more structured end of the Teacher Behavior Continuum. She needs to externally provide structures which the child does not yet have internally. With Shawn, she provided the external model of the appropriate language he needed to use to get his trike back. Like a child with a broken leg, who must wear a cast until the inner leg is healed and strong enough to function, the developmentally disabled child's internal structures need to be strengthened to function effectively, as in impulse control, or in the use of language. The teacher must provide external support, through modeling and physical intervention, until the child has internalized the needed skills and these become strong enough to function without the teacher's direct help.

As the child makes developmental progress, the teacher can move back from modeling to directive statements, questioning, nondirective statements, and eventually simply providing the visual support of looking on. With Shawn, the teacher made the mistake of using a directive statement when what he needed was modeling. She quickly self-corrected and modeled, "That's my bike."

MAINSTREAMING

Mainstreaming has become an increasingly popular approach to educating children with disabilities. Mainstreaming can be defined as placing children with disabilities into educational programs for and with nondisabled children (Odom & Karnes, 1988). This trend toward educating disabled children in the least restrictive environment, i.e., in close proximity to normally developing peers, began in the 1970's with a keystone piece of legislation, PL 94-142. The benefits of mainstreaming for the child with disabilities could include the following:

-improved social interactions
-more normal behavior
-improved language development
-more independence

-possible educational/developmental benefits, depending on the program and the teacher's intervention. (Odom & McEvoy, 1988)

Not only does the handicapped child benefit; the nondisabled children benefit as well. They learn, at an early age, to live with children who are "different." The differences become less important as the children begin to play together and learn one another's individual strengths, and that they can be truly friends and co-players.

Public Laws 94-142 and 99-457

Until the late 1960's, children with noticeable disabilities either stayed at home or were sent to institutions to be educated. In 1975, Public Law 94-142 was passed, requiring that each state provide access to a free educational program within the public school system to all "handicapped" children between the ages of 3 and 18. This right was further expanded for special needs children, focusing on infants and toddlers, with the later passing of PL 99-457, which gave parents clear rights in designing and guiding the intervention or educational program for their special needs child. These programs are required to promote the highest degree of self-sufficiency possible and must be provided in the "least restrictive environment" or as close as possible to normal children and normal environments. PL 94-142 requires school programs to have the following components: (1) identification of children who may need services; (2) evaluation of the kind and degree of need; and (3) intervention. Each eligible child within the public school services area would have an Individualized Educational Program (IEP). This IEP would involve the parents, child, teachers, and administrators and would include an assessment of the child's present level achievement, long- and short-term educational goals, services to be provided, and the degree of integration with the normal program.

The rationale behind PL 94-142 and the legal imperative to provide education in the least restrictive setting stems from the view that the child's civil rights are violated when he or she is segregated form normally developing children and thus presumably form a more effective program (Odom & McEvoy, 1988). A further rationale is that children with disabilities might be helped developmentally to acquire more advanced skills when they can observe and participate with children who are modeling age-appropriate behaviors.

WHO ARE THE CHILDREN WITH SPECIAL NEEDS?

Many labels are used to try to categorize children with special needs. Some of the terms which can be helpful to the teacher of young children in gathering information and planning for each child include retarded, physically challenged, cerebral palsied, emotionally disturbed, mentally disabled, hearing impaired, visually impaired, learning disabled, autistic, and developmentally delayed.

The words we use are often rooted in outdated concepts of dependency and helplessness, and perpetuate negative attitudes and expectations. The following guidelines are helpful for thinking about and planning for children with disabilities:

1. Emphasize the uniqueness and worth of all children rather than differences between children.

2. Keep the individual in perspective: Avoid emphasizing the disability to the exclusion of individual achievements.

3. Think about ways the child with a disability can do something independently, or for another child.

4. Provide an environment where the child with a disability participates in activities with children without disabilities in ways that are mutually beneficial and inclusive rather than in those that foster the attitude of "one of them" vs. "one of us."

(Adapted from National Easter Seal Society Guidelines)

THE TEACHER'S ROLE

The preschool teacher may identify a child with a learning difficulty, or may accept and integrate into the classroom a child with an already determined disability. In either case, the child with a disability should be viewed and treated first as a child, like other children. Typical patterns of child development, and the SYC teaching strategies based on knowledge of that development, will apply to children with disabilities, while disability-related information may provide some unique insights and techniques to add. The teacher must tap into all available sources of information, including parents, doctors, local experts, the library, and community resources and associations, to find out what to do to help that particular child.

If a child's behavior is outside the teacher's sphere of expertise, he or she will need to refer the child and family to community resources for some specialized kinds of diagnosis and treatment.

Young children generally exhibit a great variety of individual differences. Early childhood materials and activities are designed to be used at varying skill levels. For example, easel painting can be done to some extent by any child, disabled or not, who can hold a paintbrush. The levels of skill and symbolic development are sophisticated nuances which the teacher well-trained in child development can best understand, analyze, and facilitate. The Teacher Behavior Continuum (TBC) provides the ideal structure for the teacher to individualize both educational and social interventions with children who have disabilities as well as with those who do not.

At a practical level, there are three processes which can help the teacher provide for a special needs child in the classroom: (1) a staffing process, (2) a written Individualized Educational Plan (IEP), and (3) curriculum design.

INDIVIDUALIZED EDUCATION PLAN

The staffing process would bring together specialists such as teachers of young children, administrators, and psychologists to create an Individualized Educational Plan (IEP). In doing so, much time may be spent in determining "who is in charge" or who is chairing the meeting, what are the roles of individuals around the table, and in listening to anecdotal evidence for the correctness of certain members' "personal wisdom." For an effective working staff meeting, SYC suggests a preestablished structure based on the following six steps:

1. Statement of Problem(s),
2. Generating Possible Solutions,
3. Evaluating Solutions,
4. Deciding on Solutions,
5. Implementing, and
6. Evaluation. (Gordon, 1976)

For each step an arbitrary set of rules is established regarding who may speak, time allotted, and purposes. (Note: The classroom teacher chairs the meeting and, in the seating arrangement, places himself or herself at the end of the table in a power position. Administrators attending the meeting are considered the teacher's staff and assistants, not authorities.) A timekeeper should be appointed by the teacher.

Step 1. *Statement of problem(s)*: Overview of the student's behavior (time: 15 minutes).

Purpose: To gather all necessary information about the child *before* moving to solutions.

Procedures: The chair ascertains that all members are informed about data that has been collected. If formal test data is available, all members should have received and read copies before the meeting. The following information is then presented: Teacher's Statement (teacher only) regarding the behavior of the child; Teacher Background Information (teacher only, or specialist that has collected background information); All members' contributions to background information (all staff).

a. The teacher who is chairing the committee opens the discussion or overview of the child's needs and behavior. If the teacher has had previous experience with the child, she or he would discuss typical behaviors or incidents that have occurred, and describe what type of intervention has taken place and the results.

b. The teacher or any other specialist who has collected any form of data reports it at this time. This data might be results on any packaged program checklist or formal test, the Adjustment Behavioral Profile, Behavioral Play Profiles (Parten's social stages, developmental level in the classification of play, use of play materials), etc., which are found in Chapter 1.

c. The meeting is now open for input from any other members who have information such as profile, testing, or baseline data. No solutions are to be proposed at this time.

Guideline for timekeeper: Let the group know when the 10-minute mark occurs.

Step 2. *Generating possible solutions* (time: 10 minutes).

Purpose: To facilitate the entire group's "brainstorming" of possible actions to help this child, and to draw on the techniques available in the Play of Thematic models.

Procedures: Each staff member should quickly outline on paper his/her ideas for solutions, answering the questions, what time, space, and object changes are need by this child to meet his special needs? Then all members would present orally their suggestions, one at a time around the table. Criticism is not permitted during this step, as it might inhibit the creative idea exchange.

Step 3. *Evaluating Solutions* (time: 10 minutes).

Purpose: To open critical evaluation of the range of possible action, and to gain consensus.

Procedures: Staff members now discuss what their suggestions have in common. As much as possible the chair should draw on the constructs and techniques discussed in this book, asking such questions as, "Can the child's needs best be served by play-activities experiences, or through direct instruction? "Can we use techniques from these models?" (Note: It is important in this step that the teacher and staff have progressed from "personal wisdom" and speculative thinking to designing intervention using a more scientific basis. "Personal wisdom"-based speculation, is where teachers try to solve and design intervention by "stabbing in the dark." The enclosed techniques provide a framework for more scientific problem solving.

Next, the five to six suggestions with the most support could be listed on a chalkboard.

Step 4. *Deciding on solutions* (time: 20 minutes).

Purpose: In this step an orderly plan, including goals, must be agreed upon in writing.

Procedures: The staff comes to a written agreement on steps, procedures, goals, and a plan by using the IEP form (Figure 12.2). Responsibilities are accepted by staff members, and the IEP signed. Also required is an agreement as to when the committee will reconvene for step 6, evaluation.

Step 5. *Implementing* (time: pre-established in Step 4).

Purpose: The intervention is carried by all members with responsibility.
Procedures: The intervention is carried out.

FIGURE 10.2   Individualized Educational Plan

Student's Name_____

Birthday _____/_____/_____

School_____   Date   _____/_____/_____

Teacher_____

Staff Members   _____
                     _____
                     _____

I. Student's Behavior

a. General Concern:_____
_____

b. Developmental Level of Functioning:_____
_____
_____

c. Specific Improvement Desired:_____

II. Goals and Action(s) to be Taken:

a._____

By Whom:_____

Teaching Strategies:_____
_____

Success Criteria_____
_____

Date
Start_____/_____/_____   Accomp._____/_____/_____

b._____

Staffing Members (signature):

Teacher: _____
                _____
                _____
                _____

Step 6. *Evaluation* (time: 20 minutes).

Purpose: To meet to re-evaluate the success of the plan.

Procedure: This meeting would take place after a reasonable amount of time has gone by, permitting everyone to fulfill his or her role in the IEP—or at the end of a teaching unit, or any other reasonable break in time. Any member of the committee may call for an earlier date if it becomes obvious that the IEP is not working as intended.

Activities

1. Visit a classroom where disabled children have been successfully mainstreamed. Ask the teacher for suggestions for working with disabled children.
2. Visit an Exceptional Education Classroom where the children are not mainstreamed. List the pros and cons of mainstreaming vs. specialized classes/facilities.
3. Visit an early childhood site where mainstreaming is done. Tactfully find out the reasons. See if you can observe their most difficult child, and their manner of intervening with him/her. Is it possible that this child might have a developmental delay or disability and that a referral for specialized services might help?
4. Observe three young children with disabilities in a play or art setting. Plan how you would use the TBC to help them move toward the next developmental level. (Use the teacher-observation record, Figure 5.6.)
5. What are the advantages and disadvantages of labeling children "developmentally different" at an early age?

References

GORDON, THOMAS, *T.E.T.: Teacher Effectiveness Training.* New York: Peter H. Wyden, 1974.

ODOM, S.L. & M. KARNES, eds., *Early Intervention for Infants and Children with Handicaps: An Empirical Base.* Baltimore: Paul H. Brooks, 1988.

ODOM, S.L. & M.A. MCEVOY, "Integrating of Young Children with Handicaps and Normally Developing Children," in *Intervention for Infants and Children with Handicaps: An Empirical Base.* Baltimore: Paul H. Brooks, 1988.

CHAPTER ELEVEN

WORKING WITH PARENTS

The day-to-day life of the teacher is almost never free of questions or problems stemming from relationships with parents of students. Parents' statements, questions, and behaviors—sometimes seemingly destructive behaviors—are signals which alert us to their needs and those of their children. How can we make sense of this continuous parental input, prioritizing needs and making reasonable responses? On what basis would you make a decision to take action as a teacher in the following situations?

Situation 1 "The 'hole' in the donut"

Holly's parents would be called *Yuppies* today. They want to do all the best for their daughter. Her father is personable, greets you warmly, and is always ready to question you about the latest "how to parent" book, public television program on children, or articles on "how to raise your child smarter" that he has found in an "in flight" magazine. His attitude was described by one teacher, with some frustration: "He always sees the 'hole' in the donut!"

He wants the school to provide him with a curriculum whereby he and his daughter would have specific hours set aside for instruction. Holly's mother is a volunteer for a host of social actions in the city, and is first to respond when parent help is called for. She is well-liked by teachers, but periodically brings questions from her husband, "Jim wants to know. . . ."

There is always an urgency and intensity to their demands, though they are grateful and positive toward teacher observations and suggestions. After a school pageant they were very displeased that their daughter did not have a more central part to play.

Situation 2 "New role demands and family separation"

Jason, a new student, is 3-years-old and has a brother, apparently much preferred by the parents, who is 8. His father has opened a new sales business located near the school, and his mother has just returned to a full-time job on the opposite side of the city. Father's new responsibilities include getting the boys up, getting breakfast, making lunch, and dropping the boys off at school. He is at the school gate 15 to 30 minutes before the school is to open. When teachers arrive early to make preparations, he requests that Jason be allowed to enter early, so he can get to his business. Normally, Jason enters the school carrying a bag containing an Egg-McMuffin and orange juice.

During the first three weeks of school, Dad forgot Jason's lunch on four occasions. On the first and second occasion, he returned a 11:45 AM with a pizza and a cola for Jason, to the envy of all the other children. On the third occasion he appeared after lunch was half over and children were napping, with a fast-food hamburger and soda. The fourth time he forgot completely. Because of father's morning haste there is no time to talk to him, and when mother is informed at the end of the day, when she picks him up, her response is, "That's his responsibility. Tell him about it, not me." Jason is a personable child, greeting you with a warm smile, much like that of his salesman father, which makes you feel special; but at times, especially when requested to do a task, his expression becomes flat and emotionless. He usually responds to a new activity, no matter how simple, with, "No, I can't do it." During these times, when he seems to pull inside of himself, he also pulls at his hair on one side of his head, until now he has a number of bald spots.

Situation 3 "Aggressive behavior"

Robert is the only son of a rugged, athletic, chain-smoking father, and an attractive primary teacher mother. Because of recent moves he has been in and out of a number of daycare centers. He is a thin-featured, pale-complexioned (to the point of looking anemic), tense child who appears as tightly coiled as a spring. He cannot look a teacher directly in the eyes, and usually turns away when invited to join activities. At lunch or snack he seats himself with the more excitable boys, and uses bathroom talk in a whispered, covert manner, whipping the boys into a giggling frenzy which usually ends with their throwing food at each other. When the teacher approaches to stop this behavior, Robert puts his head down, smiles slightly, and acts as if he is totally innocent.

His most productive behavior is during story time, when, for the first time his eyes are focused on the teacher and the book. It is rare that the teacher finds a book to read to the group that his parents have not already read to him. His answers to questions after story reading are insightful and animated, and show understanding as well as enjoyment of books (recall that his mother is a primary teacher).

During play-activity curriculum he is like a caged tiger, normally crouched in a protective corner in the block room, wanting to use the materials but not feeling free to do so. His attitude stems from fear that if he starts a block structure someone will destroy it. This nearly total fearful and untrusting view of his peers causes him to lash out with sharp fingernails, sometimes directly at the other children's eyes, and to repeatedly bite peers for the most minor contact. After his aggression he tells the teacher that the other child was hostile to him; but upon investigation it usually turns out that the other child merely bumped him accidentally, or inadvertently stepped on one of his toys. During conferences his mother refuses to discuss this behavior, changing the topic to his performance in our more academic curriculum.

On the rare occasions when the father picks him up he seems impatient to get in and get out. Robert complicates this by refusing to come when called, running to the opposite side of the playground, causing his father to move after him. The frustrated father, when he feels no teacher is looking, strikes Robert sharply on the backside and departs with Robert crying and being dragged by one arm. Robert also refuses to depart with his mother. She reacts by whispering in his ear bribes of candy or gifts that she has for him in the car. Last week the mother and father separated and when school closed yesterday there was no one to pick him up. The home and emergency numbers provided by parents at registration time were called with no results. Robert was taken home by the head teacher, repeated telephone calls were made with no success, and Jason spent the night at the teacher's house.

Incident 4 "Sexual actions and apparent injuries"

Carol's mother's new boyfriend now brings Carol to school, normally an hour to two late each morning. She appears wearing black leotards, a tank top, and, on one occasion, a red lacy garter belt. The boyfriend does not come into the school, but leaves Carol at the school gate with a kiss that appears passionate and adult-like. Carol is a beautiful child with long black hair and large round eyes, but a nervous smile. She often drops her eyes when spoken to by the teacher and turns away looking over her shoulder in a coy manner. She is not defiant but simply passive and noncompliant to teachers. She has for the last two weeks been preoccupied with masturbation, and repeatedly attempts to enlist others to join her in parallel fashion or to masturbate her.

Female teachers first talked to her in a supportive manner, asking her not to "do that." This counseling escalated to outright demands that she stop inviting others to join her. She repeatedly gets the children who are more easily controlled to go behind the storage shed, where they are found with their dresses up and fingers in their panties. The behavior is so repetitive and excessive that a teacher is assigned to watch her at all times, but she is expert at concealing her lower body behind the toys, or the sand table, or the block shelves, while she signals a nearby child to watch what she is doing. She was seen having the boys place their fingers in her, as she and they giggled. One of the boys reported this to his mother, and she came to school and announced: "My child is being sexually abused by this 4-year-old girl and I want something done immediately, or I will call the child abuse number." The following day Carol came to school walking "as if in pain," and was found to be bruised and bleeding in her anal area.

Most teachers will realize that some of these parent situations are clearly not serious, while others might call for consulting or legal action. However, each situation does demand a degree of teacher intervention; each situation requires the teacher to make a reasoned decision.

To respond effectively to these situations, we must determine what degree of power would be appropriately used in our intervention. Various incidents might call for simply a relationship-listening response by the teacher, others a confronting-contracting response, a logical consequences response, or even a legalistic-coercive approach, which would go beyond the teacher's and school's authority. The following construct may be useful in determining appropriate teacher responses to particular parent situations.

NEEDS OF STUDENTS

The four examples previously mentioned concerned Holly's parents (with their competitiveness and "hole-in-the-donut" questions), Jason's father (new role demands and family separation), Robert (aggressive behavior and parent difficulty in handling him), and Carol (excessive sexual actions and apparent injuries). Obviously, each of the situations is related to a need of the parent or child. An analysis of this need by using a construct such as Maslow's (1970) hierarchy of needs (see Table 11.1) can give order to what might appear to be unrelated behaviors of parents and children.

From a Maslowian position, before parents or children can gain self-fulfillment, their lower needs must be met: One must first meet the **physiological**

TABLE 11.1   Maslow Needs Hierarchy

LEVELS

4	self-actualization
3	belonging
2	security
1	physiological

needs of food, water, and basic physical health care (needs which were not met in situation 4, when Carol was physically injured).

Once these physiological needs are attained, **security** can become a focus for a parent's or student's energies. The teacher can attempt to help establish these feelings of security. (Robert, in situation 3, exemplified a child with fears of others' aggression.) The next hierarchical need is **belonging**: attaining a degree of respect from one's peers and those to whom one is related (situation 1, Holly's parent's competitiveness).

Within the context of Maslow's theory, it is suggested that a teacher can analyze the behavior of the parents and identify what need of the child is being blocked and where this would fall in the Maslowian hierarchy. The teacher is then ready to evaluate the degree of severity of these problems.

DEGREES OF CRISIS

When looking at the human needs underlying some of the problems portrayed in the situations above, it is apparent that the degree of seriousness of the situation may vary from life or psychologically threatening (sexual abuse, physical injury) to limited seriousness (social competitiveness of Holly's parents). As we move through Maslow's needs hierarchy we see a classification of crises: (a) imminent crisis; (b) developing crisis; and (c) potential crisis (McMurrain, 1977).

Imminent Crisis

An imminent crisis would be a situation in which the level 1 **physiological** needs are involved, and there is a life-threatening situation. If Carol's injuries are not immediately treated with medical care, irreversible damage *will* occur. Time is of the utmost importance with this incident.

Developing Crisis

The **developing** crises are generally related to the blocked needs of Level 2 **Security**. The consequences are serious but there appears to be more time to head off the event. Robert's loss of home and of his home stability constitute a **developing** crisis. If changes do not occur, we might speculate, his behavior will continue to regress, with the potential to become an **imminent** crisis. In the situation of Jason and his busy parents, another blocked need is **belonging**, which also suggests a **developing** level of crisis.

Potential Crisis

With the desire of Holly's parents for their child to be always special, the need level is **esteem**, and there is a **potential** crisis. The situation might be strongly felt by the parent, but the seriousness is related to a blow to self-esteem.

THE TEACHER'S HELPING BEHAVIOR

With the understanding of the two correlated constructs above, Maslow's levels of need, and levels of crisis, we come to the question of what responding actions the teacher should take. The answer is found in the continuum of human relationship models, which can be classified under the headings of relationship-listening, confronting-contracting, contingency-consequence, legalistic-coercive. The degree of power of the teacher's intervention would escalate or de-escalate with relationship to the level of needs and the severity of the crisis (see Table 11.2).

TABLE 11.2   Needs, Crises, and Relationship Models

NEEDS	CRISES	MODEL

Level 4
Esteem
	P
	  O
	    T
	      E
	        N
		RELATIONSHIP-
		    LISTENING

Level 3
Belonging
	D T
	  E I
	    V A
	      E L
	        L
		CONFRONTING-
		    CONTRACTING

Level 2
Security
	O
	        P
	          I
	            N
	              G
		RULES, REWARD, AND
		    PUNISHMENT

Level 1
Psychological
	I
	  M
	    M
	    I
	      N
	        E
	          N
	            T
		COERCIVE-LEGALISTIC

TABLE 11.3   Techniques for use with Holly/Competitive Parents

NEED: LEVEL 4-ESTEEM

CRISIS: POTENTIAL

MODELS: RELATIONSHIP-LISTENING

T.E.T
Critical listening
Acknowledgement responses
Door-openers
Active listening
Method 3 "no lose"
  or Six steps to problem
  solving
"I"-message
    TA
Respond with the adult ego state
Give strokes

Value Clarification
Value clarifying discussion
Question based on
  valuing
  choosing freely
  choosing from alternatives
  choosing after considering
  consequences
  prizing
  affirming
  acting
  repeating

In the case of Holly's parents, with their social competitiveness, the need level is esteem, and we have a potential level of crisis. The helping techniques for the teacher are found in the relationship-listening model. Gordon's **Teacher Effectiveness Training-TET** discusses problem ownership and how to establish an accepting relationship to help the parents gain some emotional control and do some problem solving to meet their own needs (see Table 11.3).

The case of Jason's parents with their busy schedules, the blocked need is belonging and suggests a **developing** crisis. The techniques of confronting and contracting seen in Glasser's or Dreikurs' books would be most useful for the teacher in dealing with such situations. Both models place a high value on getting needs met in a social context and give clear suggestions as to how to accomplish a positive sense of belonging (see Table 11.4).

TABLE 11.4   Techniques for use with Jason/Can't depend on Parents

---

NEEDS: LEVEL 3-BELONGING

CRISIS: DEVELOPING

MODELS: CONFRONTING-CONTRACTING

Dreikurs
Confronting
Question motivation
   attention-getting
   power
   revenge
   helplessness
Make a plan based on
   motivation
Use encouragement
Design class activities or
   class meetings
Do sociogram
   Glasser
Ask "what" questions
Help child develop a plan
Sign agreement
Intense counseling
Class meetings
With a lack of success,
   bring in principal, parent,
   outside agency

In the case of Robert, with his aggressive behavior and the family separation, the need level is security and the level of crisis can be considered as developing. The teacher in this instance may choose techniques under contingency-contracting. This means that with Robert *and his parents* the teacher would specify actions to be carried out by Robert's parents. If they carried out these actions, every effort would be made by the teacher to be positively reinforcing; if they did not, negative actions, including moving to the **coercive/legalistic** might be necessary. The coercive/legalistic solution of the teacher and school might include using a social service agency to get family counseling, or turning the case over to the legal authorities (see Table 11.5).

In the case of Carol, the injured student, the need level is **physiological** and the crisis is **imminent**. This life-threatening situation calls for very powerful intervention, which we call **coercive legalistic**. When time is of utmost importance the teachers, with school officials, could use the assertiveness techniques as described by Alberti's book, *Your Perfect Right*, to get immediate help and legal protection for the child (see Table 11.6).

TABLE 11.5   Techniques for use with Robert/loss of dependable home

NEEDS: LEVEL 2-SECURITY

CRISIS: DEVELOPING

MODELS: RULES, REWARD, AND PUNISHMENT

Behavior Modification
set up contingency with parents
establish positive and negative
    reinforcers
set up contingency with Robert's father
establish positive and negative
    reinforcers
    Behavior Modification/Punishment
Assertive Discipline
    Establish rules for parents' behavior
    Establish rules for Robert's father
    Use broken-record approach if necessary
    If necessary Robert might be removed
        from school

Usually, in serious cases the legal steps required by the teacher are set by law. The teacher would be ethically bound, if not legally bound, to take

TABLE 11.6   Techniques for use with Carol/An Abused Child

NEEDS: LEVEL 1, PSYCHOLOGICAL

CRISIS: IMMINENT

MODELS: (COERCIVE-LEGALISTIC)

Assertive Model
Establish actions by
    administrators with legal
    authority to protect this
    child
Assertive Nonverbal and Verbal
    action towards officials
Use broken-record approach if necessary
Followup on administrative actions

coercive action for the student's welfare. To clarify, **coercive/legalistic** is not a model, but a process whereby the teacher carries out, using assertive techniques, the actions required by law. What is suggested is that the teacher, as a problem solver dealing with parent-child situations, can reexamine his or her own "personal wisdom response" in the broader perspective of the constructs described above. For our discussion, direct parallels were made between situations, needs, and models; in reality this division might be less clear-cut, and actions would have to be adjusted accordingly.

PROACTIVE WITH PARENTS

The constructs and incidents above place the teacher in a reactive, often emotionally trying position. The greater percentage of parents, however, are trying to be the best parents they can be. Our role with them is one of relationship-listening, and is proactive.

The relationship-listening stance with parents focuses on communication and education. There are many parent-related activities which help to maintain this communication, some of which are newsletters.

With an Apple computer, printer, and easy-to-use software, a classroom teacher can create with minimal effort an attractive newsletter that may go out once a month. Departments in such a newsletter might be:

-current themes being studied

-staff changes

-procedures from the parent handbook

-personal announcements of staff or parents (Mrs. Walker has had an 8-lb baby girl)

-the arrival at school of a new child or one departing

-community events of interest to parents and children

-board decisions

-books for this months lending library.

Lending Library

Mounted inside the front door at adult eye level is a small bookshelf, labeled Parent Lending Library. Stock this shelf with five child-related books or videotapes that would be helpful to parents. If there is one that most parents find useful, a parent evening could be held to discuss it. This discussion could be taped, so parents who couldn't attend might listen to it at their leisure. The teacher could chair the discussion or invite a local child expert to do so.

Covered-dish Dinners

Every other month plan a parent evening, preferably at the end of a unit when you have many children's products to share with them. A sign-up form with certain food groups listed may be used. You may want to entertain with a short, 15- to 20-minute children's drama, or with singing related to the completed unit.

Art and Product Display

At the end of a unit, having saved and labeled children's paintings, books, and similar products, get from your local appliance dealer large upright refrigerator boxes, which stand up easily, and tape the children's products to it. Have a two-day art display in an indoor hallway, or an evening display on your playground.

Saturday Work Day

Both mother and father might enjoy getting some hands-on experience building structures on your playground. This needs to be planned well, with all equipment and materials at hand. We had one very proud child say, "My daddy built this bench!" Many evenings he would ask his father to sit with him on "their bench."

Parent Survey/Discussion Evening

Survey your parents to find out what their special interests are, and hold parent evenings to discuss such issues.

Drop In/Planned Lunch

Invite parents to drop in for lunch with their child once a month. Or, at the end of cooking units throughout the year invite manageable groups to come, with the children serving their parents as in a restaurant. Tablecloths taped on, a menu printout from the computer, and uniforms for the "waiters" could be used. This would be planned for the entire year so that all children could have a chance to "do lunch" with their parents.

Breakfast

Plan certain mornings throughout the year to have nourishing cookies, or fruit, coffee, tea, or juice, so parents may stay for 15 minutes to have breakfast and carry on casual conversation with teachers.

Grandparents Day

Once a year, giving plenty of advance notice, invite all grandparents to come for a morning, presenting some musical or dramatic entertainment by the children.

Parent Message Book

The parent message book has been described in the chapter on schedules. It permits parents to write in it any message they wish to give to staff each morning.

Family/Child Entertainment Day

Pick one entertainment day, such as when the circus is in town, and buy a block of seats where all the families and children from your school may be seated together.

Adopt a Grandparent

If we discover that one child's grandparents has time to spare, we may adopt that grandparent, asking him or her to regularly come and join in classroom activities.

Parenting Course

Many of the adult education programs in the public schools, or a local community college's continuing education department, might send an instructor to teach a parent course, if enough parents are interested.

Holiday Celebration

Use a season holiday to get parents together for a social event.

Toddler-Morning

If we have space, possibly on the playground in good weather, we have a toddler day where siblings ages 1 to 3 might experience our school.

Parent-Teacher Conferences

Parent and teacher conferences should be scattered throughout the school year, not all in one month. Use exhibits to demonstrate changes occurring in the child's development.

Parent Handbook

A parent handbook is an excellent way to inform both teachers and parents about your classroom and school. It could contain information under the following headings:

-teachers and their background (training and experience)
-clear financial agreement and cost, and ways of payment
-heath and safety matters
-what to wear (girl's "jelly" shoes are very dangerous on the playground)
-carpool formation procedures
-nutrition
-toys from home
-arrival and pickup
-overview of program philosophy
-normal daily schedule

Telephone List

Children make friends at school and wish to have a class roster with the child's and parents' names, addresses, and telephone numbers.

Babysitting List

Some schools, as a service, give lists of people who will babysit on weekends or evenings. These names could be obtained from local Girl Scout troops, high schools, or from the older siblings of your students.

School Gate Parent-Teacher Discussion

When a child is picked up by a parent at the end of the day, the brief teacher-parent contact presents a critical opportunity to reassure parents. They want to hear that everything is OK. Assign one teacher, normally the head teacher, to be free from child supervision during the first hour in the morning and the last hour of "pick-up."

When Accidents Occur

In a classroom of young children accidents will occur. Most parents know that bumps and scrapes are normal, but will be upset to find a severe mark on their child which they weren't made aware of. They feel that if you don't know about the scratch or bruise you must not have been supervising properly; thus, the teacher should tell the parent at the end of the day about any mark and what was done about it. It is advisable to keep a small, fairly inexpensive ($200 for 75 children) school accident policy. If a child's tooth is knocked out at school, the policy pays all medical expenses. If there is a severe accident, the head teacher, or director, should always call that evening to see if everything is OK.

Handling Parents' Complaints

Make sure that staff understand that all parents complaints must be reported, and set up a system for getting that information.

Parent Conferences

Here are some guidelines for parent conferences:

1. Be prepared for the conference. Take all the data you have, even if you do not use it all.

2. Open and close on a positive note.

3. Do not alarm parents by listing small, unimportant negatives.

4. Encourage parents, through your questions, to talk about their concerns.

5. Help parents come to solutions to problems that really belong to them, rather than opinionating. Read the explanation of problem ownership in Thomas Gordon's book, *Teacher Effectiveness Training*.

6. Set conferences at a time and place where you will not be interrupted, and encourage the parents not to bring siblings, older or younger, with them.

7. At the beginning of the meeting, set a time for closing the conference—and stay with it.

8. At the end of the conference, summarize the agreements made, write them down, and put them in the child's folder. (Cherry, 1987)

FIGURE 11.1   Parent-Teacher Conferences

Home Visits

Home visits before the child comes to the center give us much information about how to make the child feel comfortable. These could be done at any time through the year, as well.

Evaluation Survey of Parents

It is advisable to survey parents every six to eight months to hear their concerns and views of your classroom.

Teacher Attitudes

Research on successful American companies, chronicled in the best seller, *In Search of Excellence*, points out that these companies understood how important it was to "go the extra mile" for consumers. A parent is not impressed that you have many children to be concerned about; for that parent there is only one child. If a parent forgets the child's lunch in the morning, find something nourishing from the snack foods to give him. If parents forget to send a bathing suit for their child, have an extra one for her.

The principle of the **tyranny of fairness**, which states, "if we do it for them, we will have to do it for everyone" is a destructive attitude. It says, "You must fit into our box because we are unwilling to spend any more energy to permit children or parents to have special needs." In the relationship-listening position towards parents and children, we do listen to their needs and, if humanly possible, will accommodate them. If "we will have to do it for everyone" is true, then we *should* be doing it for everyone.

Activities

1. Survey three early childhood centers or schools in your area, and attempt to analyze what proactive steps these schools take in regard to parents, and parent involvement. Then, attend one of these parent-school functions.
2. Interview five experienced early childhood teachers, and get vignettes related to the top three most difficult problems that they face in working with parents of the children in their school. Select three of these "difficulties" and analyze them based on Table 11.2: Needs, Crises, and Relationship Models. What advice could you give to the teacher related to these three problems?
3. Collect five to ten back-copies of newsletters that have been sent to parents by your local centers or schools. Analyze them as to what are the subheadings and then design your own letter with subheadings as categories that you would use in your own classroom.
4. Interview three to five early childhood specialists or five to ten experienced teachers and request them to list parent-oriented books that they feel would be best to place in a parent lending library.
5. Design a parent survey form in cooperation with a local early childhood center or school, mail it, and tabulate the results. What actions could this school take to eliminate the negatives in such a survey?

References

ALBERTI, ROBERT, and MICHAEL EMMON, *Your Perfect Right*. Obispo, Ca.: Impact Pub., 1978.

BERNE, ERIC, *Games People Play*. New York: Ballantine Books, 1964.

CANTER, LEE, *Assertive Discipline*. Los Angeles: Canter and Associates, 1979.

CHERRY, CLARA, *Nursery School & Day Care Center Management Guide*, 2nd ed. Belmont, Ca.: David S. Lake Publishing, 1987.

DREIKURS, RUDOLF, and PEARL CASSEL, *Discipline Without Tears*. New York: Hawthorn Books, 1972.

GLASSER, WILLIAM, *Schools With Failure*. New York: Harper & Row, 1969.

——*Reality Therapy*. New York: Harper & Row, 1967.

GORDON, THOMAS, *Leadership Effectiveness Training: L.E.T.*. New York: Wyden Books, 1977.

HARRIS, THOMAS, *I'm OK—You're OK: A Practical Guide to Transactional Analysis*. New York: Harper and Row, 1969.

HOMMES, LLOYD, *How to Use Contingency Contracting in the Classroom*. Champaign, Ill.: Research Press, 1970.

MCMURRAIN, THOMAS, *Intervention in Human Crisis*. Atlanta: Humanics Press, 1975.

MURIEL, JAMES, *The OK Boss*. Millbrae, Ca.: Celestial Arts, 1979.

PETERS, THOMAS, J. and WATERMAN, *In Search of Excellence: Lessons from America's Best-Run Companies*. New York: Harper & Row, 1982.

SIMON, SIDNEY, LELAND HOWE, and HOWARD KIRSCHENBAUM, *Value Clarification*. New York: Hart, 1972.

SMITH, MANUAL, *When I Say "No" I Feel Guilty*, New York: Dial, 1975.

WOLFGANG, CHARLES H., and CARL D. GLICKMAN, *Solving Discipline Problems: Strategies for Classroom Teachers*. Boston: Allyn and Bacon, 1980.

CHAPTER TWELVE

ASSESSMENT AND EVALUATION OF LEARNING

The classroom teacher is faced with the task of demonstrating that the students have grown developmentally, or that they have learned skills. When child-centered teaching methods are used, assessment and evaluation are made through direct observation of the child's self-initiated actions in the regular classroom setting. In contrast, the teacher-directed models use criterion-referenced tests, which focus on the child's attainment of one key skill which can be related to a scope-and-sequence chart. The child-centered methods (open) and teacher-directed methods (closed) would be at the extremes of a continuum illustrating methods of data gathering for assessment.

CHILD-CENTERED ASSESSMENT

The primary assessment tool of the play-activity (child-centered) curriculum is the direct observation of children, or specimen record. The teacher becomes a "potted plant"; that is, he withdraws from classroom activity and finds a corner where the children can be clearly observed and notes taken. Usually the teacher focuses on one child for a period of 20 minutes, recording all

TABLE 12.1   Method of Data Gathering

Open	Closed
No Selectivity	High Degree of Selectivity
No Inference Required	High Degree of Inference

Specimen Records (observations)
      Diary
            Anecdotal Records
                  Time Sampling
                        Criterion-Referenced Test

actions of the child in longhand, or with the use of a tape recorder. The observational recording is placed into the format shown on the next page.

After filling in the top three blanks on the observation form, the introduction is completed—much as if it were a program for a Broadway play:

> Introduction:
> This is the monthly observation of James Anderson (age 3-8) at 10:12 A.M. on Friday. We find James in the block corner with Bill Womack, Paul Henly, and Sara Weiner. He is dressed in blue jeans, flannel shirt, and sneakers. This is the second day he has been back after missing school for seven days with the chickenpox.

A map is drawn of the classroom or the corner area where the observation takes place. Label furniture and play materials, and locate the other peers or adults with a circle around their names.

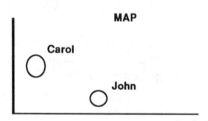

MAP

The page is divided down the middle with a line that separates the observation side and the theory/comment side. On the observation side record the actions of the target child for a period of 20 minutes, putting time references every 4 to 6 minutes whenever there is a natural break in the activities. If the child makes products, such as painting a "bird" or building a block structure, sketch them in on the observation side so that the reader can see the shape or form. Use detailed descriptions of the gross and fine movements of the child and, as much as possible, the visual and verbal actions of

FIGURE 12.1   Child Observation Form

Child's Name _____   Date _____   Time _____

Observer's Name _____

Other people in general area (list) _____

_____

Location _____

_____

Introduction _____

_____

_____

MAP

_____

Observations | Theory/Comments
                                     |
                                     |
                                     |
                                     |
                                     |
                                     |
                                     |
                                     |
                                     |
                                     |

Summary

_____

_____

_____

Educational Recommendations_____

_____

_____

_____

the child. Leave out interpretations and comments or, if necessary, put the comments or explanations in brackets to set them apart. Try not to use general words: "He played with the toy truck." We want to know what exactly he did with the truck. A form of shorthand can be used during the actual recording and later transcribed into more understandable written form. (See Carbonara, *Techniques for Observing Normal Child Behavior,* for examples and suggestions for recording.)

Observation:

10:05: James reaches out with his right hand and grabs the red tow-truck, as he crawls across the floor on hands and knees. He makes roaring noises with his mouth (like a truck motor) pushing the truck up to a toy gas station and says to Paul, "Fill it up with unleaded gas."

Getting no response he takes off the toy gas hose, places it to the back of his truck, and makes hissing noises. The pump hose is 'hung up' and he pushes the truck across the room moving on hands and knees until he stops in front of the rocking chair."

Puts finger in his mouth and looks around the classroom at each child's activity (appears to be thinking). His face lightens up with a smile and he crawls quickly to the block shelves.

James takes from the shelf six 1-unit blocks, building two parallel walls; using four 1/2-units, he makes a roof between the two parallels, and closes one open end with two more 1/2-unit blocks.

10:10: With "motor" sounds he backs the tow-truck into the open end of the block structure, selecting two more 1/2-units and placing them before the open end to close in the truck.

He stands, walks quickly to the shelf, takes down the woven basket with two hands and brings it to his block structure. Sara is now kneeling before the structure, looking intently. James shouts firmly at Sara, "No, no!" Sara smiles and responds, "I have a flat tire." James says, "What?" Sara replies, "I have a flat tire." James asks, "Where?" Sara points to a small car at the opposite end of the room which is missing a tire. James looks at Sara and smiles. James quickly removes the two blocks from the structure's entrance, drives out the truck with motor noises, selects a male doll from the basket, places it on top of the cab of the truck, and both children crawl across the floor with great speed and giggles with James pushing the truck before him, stopping before Sara's car. James states, "Which tire is flat?" Sara says and points, "Here." James says "That's not flat, there's no tire, where is it?" Sara shrugs her shoulders.

10:15: James mumbles, takes male doll from top of truck, "walks" doll to Sara's car, directs doll's hands at the missing tire area, and makes clicking noises with tongue. James drops male doll, runs to opposite side of room returning with a similar size car, pushes Sara's car aside, and replaces it with a new one with the wheel intact. James states, "It is fixed now." Sara replies, "Thanks." Sara makes motor noises, pushes her car across the room towards James's block structure with James following, pushing his truck. . . .

On the right side of the paper, the theory/comments section is used to explain in developmental terms what is occurring on the observations side.

Theory/comments: James is symbolically representing a truck, and is beginning to elaborate dramatic play. He attempts to engage John in the activity without success; as a result his play can be classified initially as isolated social play.

He now builds a "garage" with blocks (structured-construction). When approached by Sara his first response is a verbally aggressive *no*, but Sara responds with role-playing and their play progresses into the beginnings of sociodramatic play (beginning of associative).

This observation and theory/comments are, of course, based on the 20-minute observation period. Once these are written, a line is drawn separating the main data from the summary section. In the summary the observer-teacher looks back over the entire 20-minute period, attempting to label predominant activities, perhaps commenting on age-appropriateness. Also, comments based on the teacher's knowledge and experience can now be added to give greater meaning to the summary.

Summary:

The observation this morning shows 3 years 9 month-old James primarily enjoying wheel toys such as cars and trucks. His first building is a detailed and elaborated block structure of a garage, house, and gas station, and with the wheeled vehicles and miniature mother, father, and sister he has played out dramatic themes of getting a car repaired, going shopping at the mall, and a chase by a policeman. This dramatic play was isolated with James making seven overtures to John to join him, without success. For the first time he was able to pick up the role and cues of Sara and they were able to play an elaborate theme of cars, trucks, and domestic home life. James was enrolled at SYC one month ago and was ill seven of these days. This was his first attempt at associative/cooperative play with another child, Sara. Sara has made repeated attempts in the last two week to befriend him by showing him where to store his painting, sitting near him at circle time, and running freely with him in large motor play on the playground.

The last section on the observation form, Educational Implications, allows the teacher to make specific recommendations, such as formal testing, or raise questions which she or he feels need to be discussed with other staff members:

Educational Implications:

This morning it appears that James is able to accept Sara's overture of friendship and can be a co-player in sociodramatic play. I will make this known to other staff members and we will take actions to help this friendship continue, possibly: (1) put James into Sara's group for projects, (2) move Sara's and James' storage lockers together, (3) tell James' mother, who has been asking if he has made friends with Sara, and she might be invited over on the weekend.

UNDERSTANDING SPECIMEN OBSERVATIONS

The evaluation of all of the instruments that follow can be understood with relationship to their open vs closeness, degree of selectivity, degree of inference required, advantages, and disadvantages. (Bentzen, 1985)

Open vs. Closed

The specimen observation, as seen above, is considered the most open data gathering instrument because it attempts to capture a slice out of the daily life of the child as fully as possible without initial interpretation, allowing the data to be read and interpreted—and reinterpreted. The setting and context in which the behavior occurred is also recorded. Videotaping could be an even more complete form of data gathering.

Degree of Selectivity

The observation is not selective; all action and behavior are recorded.

Degree of Inference Required

At the time the recording is being done no inferences are made. These may come later.

Advantages

Child-centered advocates see behavior as a holistic process; that is, it cannot easily be directed into small pieces; all domains, social, cognitive, etc., are important. The specimen observation captures the whole child at a point in time, and can be revisited for reinterpretation.

Disadvantages

Specimen observations are very time-consuming, and great skill is needed to "get on paper" all the child actions. Videotaping could be helpful, but a person with technical skill would be needed. Also, the specimen observation is not quantifiable and can't be used for summary comparisons. Thus, it might not meet specifications for certain funding sources which require number-based data as demonstrations of effectiveness.

DIARY

In a diary the teacher makes daily written summaries of a child's behavior, focusing on a selected aspect, e.g., use of materials; hence the name "topical diary." This permits a long-term overview of the child's actions and requires that the writer-observer-teacher be in daily contact with the child over many weeks or months.

September 5-

This is John's first day at school. He cried and demanded that his mother not leave him. Mother remained until mid-morning, and when she did depart he cried for 3 to 4 minutes, and cuddled on the teacher's lap. After the initial cry, he used the paint easel and puzzles for the remainder of the morning. Ate well at snack, but was demanding at lunch, refusing to eat anything. He cried again at cot-time, but was able to get comfort by using his "blankie" and teacher's cuddling. He fell asleep and slept deeply for the entire period. He wandered aimlessly, after rest, and did not play. He was flat and expressionless with his mother when she picked him up.

September 6-

Refused to get out of the car this morning, causing great concern by mother, who had to depart for work immediately. He cried at the gate as she departed, refused affection from the teacher, but went to the paint easel and puzzles, which he used age-appropriately for the entire morning. At snack he seemed very hungry and ate all of his lunch. He went immediately to his cot at rest, using his blankie for comfort. After rest he attached to Mark, and followed him around doing large motor activity with laughter and joy. When mother arrived he ran to the gate, smiled and called her name. They hugged affectionately, but he insisted on carrying his artwork to the car, and refused to give it to mother.

(The diary would continue for many more days in a similar manner.)

Open vs. Closed

The diary is considered open because it contains a wide range of data and general observations, notes behavioral changes over time and in context, and preserves data for later comparison and interpretation.

Degree of Selectivity

The dairy is unselective because is not restricted to one narrow, pre-defined behavior; but, it is not as selectively open as a specimen observation because it specifies a "topic," such as initial school adjustment, as above.

Degree of Inference Required

A moderate amount of inference is required because the teacher must decided what is related to the topic; this is not as limiting as the more restrictive instruments.

Advantages

The advantage of the diary is that behavioral information can be collected over a very long period of weeks or months without the great expenditure of time required for the specimen observation. The behavior is placed in context, is permanently recorded, and can document the nature of the child's growth and behavior.

Disadvantage

The major limitation to the diary is that it can be kept only by teachers or parents who are in daily contact with the child over a long period of time. For the teacher with 15 to 20 children, this would require a defined focus on one particular child, and might be prohibitive.

ANECDOTAL RECORDS

Anecdotal records of unusual events are written by the teacher after the fact. They are done sporadically throughout the year and can be continued the next year. The records are made by the teacher from direct observation and written with as much detail as possible, including context and setting.

October 13 (4:35 P.M.)

Carol was climbing the large tower on the playground in a game of "run and chase" with Allen. As Allen climbed the steps toward her, she began to flee, running to the fireman's pole. Her flimsy "jelly" shoes caught in the space between the platform boards causing her to fall face forward off the climber platform into the sandpit. She cried intensely, was pick up by Mrs. Barker, sand wiped from her face, and her face and body physically inspected by this teacher. She was taken to the shaded bench and an ice pack was brought and applied to her face. Mrs. Barker talked to her softly, attempting to comfort her and stayed on the bench with her until her mother arrived at 5:25. Mother was told what occurred, and instructed not to permit Carol to fall asleep when she got home and to watch for indications of a head injury, such as rolling eyes, throwing-up, cramps, and other discomfort. The parent was requested to take Carol to a doctor if any symptoms occurred and the school would pay any medical expenses (school has an accident policy). The mother's response was that "these things occur as part of life experiences," and she indicated that she was capable of watching Carol at home in the next few hours. The teacher called Carol's home at 8:00, talked to the father, who indicated that all was well with Carol. Carol returned the next day with a 2-in. bruise under her left eye. No other negative reaction was seen from Carol as the result of this fall. (Note: "Jelly" shoes were declared not approved for school wear in the next school newsletter, and the rule put into the parent handbook.)

Open vs. Closed

The anecdotal record is considered open because those data can be saved for reinspection.

Degree of Selectivity

The anecdotal record is highly selective because the teacher records only unusual events.

Degree of Inference Required

The written anecdotal record calls for a high degree of inference, but the recording itself, especially if the teacher adheres to factual description, can be viewed as requiring minimal inferring.

Advantages

The anecdotal record is a running record of unusual events, in context, of a child's life over a long time period. Compared to other forms of data, it is easy to gather with a limited time commitment.

Disadvantages

Because the recorded incidents are unusual, they may be emotionally loaded for the teacher, and the records may therefore be written with bias. Unreliability is therefore a major disadvantage.

TIME SAMPLING

Certain categories of behavior are preselected in the time sampling procedure, such as Parten's social stages, or play classifications. A time sequence is preestablished, and then, every five minutes, for example, the teacher-observer will record what is being seen. This time procedure must be followed consistently over a fairly long period of time, so that the behaviors may be considered typical. The observer-teacher will make tally marks in each of the well-defined categories at each of the times established; thus, the name time sampling.

The Social Observation System (Figure 12.7) is a time-sampling instrument requiring the teacher to record a slash mark on a chart which scores the child on Parten's social stages. After a sufficient period of recording, totals and percentages can be obtained for the subcategories above. These percentages could be graphed for a visual display of the child's behavior.

Open vs. Closed

The Time Sampling system is considered closed because at the time the observation is done only one category or a few categories are accounted for, and all of the other behavior is lost.

Degree of Selectivity

The time sample is highly selective because only one predetermined behavior is recorded.

Degree of Inference Required

Time sampling with an instrument such as the Social Observation System requires an immediate inference by the teacher: a decision as to what behavior is being seen, and in what category it should be scored. It is therefore important that the categories be clearly defined. To make the Time-Sampling instrument reliable, two or three teachers could score the same children at the same time, and their scores be compared. If there is a 90% or higher agreement, we may say there is inter-observer reliability.

Advantages

The advantage of Time Sampling is that the teacher may choose before-hand the type of behavior on which to focus (incidents of aggression, friendship patterns, use of equipment, etc.). This method can be done with much less time and effort than specimen observations. The teacher can compare his or her recording to another teacher's to check reliability. The score, a total number of marks in each category, can be used to make group comparisons or be displayed on graphs.

Disadvantages

Time sampling requires categorizing schemes, which means the loss of context and other behaviors. For example, if we were making a comparison of a child's usage of different types of play materials (symbolic, fluid-construction, structured-construction, etc.), and for a few days the water table was broken and the paint pots empty, the category of fluid-construction would show a depressed usage.

RATING SCALES

At times we may wish to have a teacher act as an expert witness who has had a great deal of experience working with a child. Rating scales, such as the Child-Play Behavioral Rating Scale (Figure 12.4) and the Adjustment Behavioral Profile (Figure 12.6) indicate at what level in a certain category a child might be functioning. A number scale from 1 to 5 (highest to lowest) is used. Rating can be done after directly observing a child, such as setting up a testing situation where we ask the child to walk a balance beam, but is usually done from recall. To make the rating more reliable two or three teachers could discuss each item and come to a group agreement.

An example of a Rating Scale item might appear as:

Never		Always			Question
1	2	3	4	5	a. Can use language to express basic needs (example: toileting)

Open vs. Closed, Degree of Selectivity, Inference Required

The rating scales are considered closed and a high degree of selectivity is needed. The degree of inference required is extremely high because usually the judgment is made from memory. Thus the reliability of the teacher response may not be consistent. Inter-observer reliability would need to be established on any such instruments.

Advantages and Disadvantages

The major advantage is that the teacher can complete the rating scale in a matter of minutes if done by memory. Also, the data can be reduced to numbers to make statistical comparisons, so that we may obtain answers to questions such as, "What is the average age at which a child can do this and how early or late is this particular child?" A disadvantage would be that the rating could be influenced by a teacher's feelings; if a parent were critical of a teacher, for example, and were threatening to "go to the director"—and it was time that very afternoon to rate this parent's child, the teacher might have difficulty making objective judgments.

CRITERION REFERENCED TEST (CHECKLIST)

The following are criterion reference tests widely used in early childhood programs. The reader will notice that many of these tests have been designed for identifying special needs of children with developmental delays.

Alpern-Boll Developmental Profile, Dr. Gerald Alpern, PO Box 3198, Aspen, CO 81611
Assessment Programming Guide for Infants and Preschoolers, Developmental Services, Inc., PO Box 1023, Columbus, IN 47201
Bayley Scales of Infant Development, Psychological Corporation, 304 East 45th Street, New York, NY 10017
Beginning Milestones, DLM Teaching Resources, One DLM Park, Allen, TX 75002
Behavioral Developmental Profile, Marshalltown Project, 507 East Anson, Marshalltown, IA 50158
Behavior Maturity Checklist II, Psychology, Research and Evaluation Section, O'Berry Center, Goldsboro, NC 27530.
BKR Development and Trainability Assessment Scale, BKR Educational Projects, PO Box 16986, Plantation, FL 33317
Brekken-Drouin Developmental Spotcheck, Children's Developmental Services, Casa Colina Hospital, 255 East Bonita Avenue, Pomona, CA 91767
Carolina Developmental Profile, Kaplan School Supply, 600 Jonestown Road, Winston-Salem, NC 27103
Cassel Developmental Record, Psychologists and Educators, Inc. 211 West State, Jacksonville, IL 62650
Cattell Infant Intelligence Scale, Psychological Corporation, 304 East 45th Street, New York, NY 10017
Classroom Behavior Inventory, Earl S. Schaefer, Frank Porter Graham Child Development Center, University of North Carolina, Chapel Hill, NC 27514
Denver Developmental Screening Test, Ladoca Project and Publishing Foundation, East 51st Avenue and Lincoln, Denver, CO 80216
Distar Instructional System (includes assessment instrument), Science Research Associated, Inc., 2590 East Erie Street, Chicago, IL 60611
Early Independence, Edmark Associates, PO Box 3903, Bellevue, WA 98009
Early Learning Accomplishment Profile for Developmentally Young Children, Kaplan Press, 600 Jonestown Road, Winston-Salem, NC 27103
HICOMP Preschool Curriculum and Test, Charles E. Merrill Publishing Co., Columbus, OH 43216
Kahn Intelligence Test, Psychological Test Specialists, PO Box 1441, Missoula, MT 59801
Koontz Child Developmental Program, Western Psychological Services, 12031 Wilshire Boulevard, Los Angeles, CA 90025
Peabody Developmental Motor Scales, IMRD Publications, Box 154, George Peabody College, Nashville, TN 37203

Portage Guide to Early Education, Portage Project, Cooperative Educational Service Agency 12, 412 East Slifer Street, Portage, WI 53901

Preschool Developmental Profile, 839 Greene Street, PO Box 1104, Ann Arbor, MI 48106

Prescriptive Learning Accomplishment Profile, Kaplan School Supply, 600 Jonestown Road, Winston-Salem, NC 27103

Slosson Intelligence Test for Children and Adults, Slosson Educational Publications, Inc., PO Box 280, East Aurora, NY 14052

Vineland Social Maturity Scales, American Guidance Service, Publishers Building, Circle Pines, MN 55014

Criterion Referenced Tests nearly always come with the direct-instruction programs. These tests contain a series of behavioral items—such as "child counts to 5" or "can use under/over when told to place a block in position"—which are answered by the teacher with a *yes* or *no* response after directly testing the child. (See list of often-used criterion referenced tests.)

Open vs. Closed

The criterion referenced checklist is closed, because only one very narrow behavior is being observed, and the context and all other behaviors are lost.

Degree of Selectivity

The degree of selectivity is high because a judgment has been made that a particular behavior is important for every child to learn, as in the direct instruction curriculum. An instrument is needed to document that the teaching has been effective, so the test items are deliberately selected to cover the pre-selected behaviors.

Degree of Inference Required

The Criterion Referenced Test requires a high level of inference on the teacher-observer's part, but many of the packaged tests have gone through rigorous processes to ensure that each item is related to a behavioral objective. Since the behavior is very narrow, there is little question about whether or not the child can perform the skill.

Example of criteria referenced item

Yes	No	Item
( )	( )	1. Matches 2 colors
		Materials: 8-2' paper squares (2 red, 2 blue, 2 yellow, 2 green)
		Procedure: Place 1 square of each color in front of child. Give child stack of matching

colored squares arranged in random order. Demonstrate matching response with red card and return it to stack. Say, "Put each piece of paper on the one that is just like it." Credit if child matches at least 2 colors. Spontaneous corrections of errors are acceptable. Allow 1 trial. If child matches all 4 colors, credit item. (Learning Accomplishment Profile,Chapel Hill Training-Outreach Project, Cognitive skill 36 (item 12), page 47.)

Advantages

This system requires little recording skill. The items are directly related to the teaching curriculum and the results provide a guide for reteaching. Number comparisons can be made, permitting a statistical evaluation of the children and program.

Disadvantages

Only narrow behaviors are considered, usually cognitive skills, with all other aspects of the child's growth being lost or ignored.

A Wider Point of View

We have looked at commonly used forms of assessment and evaluation, from "open" observation to "closed" Criterion Referenced Tests (checklists). All of these can and should be used in the classroom. At times, direct observation of one child or a group of children is needed—perhaps to enlighten us as to sources of a continuing intra-group conflict, or for a similar purpose. At other times, diaries recording behaviors centered on certain topics might be the most useful tools, or anecdotal records might best serve a certain purpose.

If we want to know how many of the children in the class are using certain play materials, or at what social level they are functioning, time sampling would give us answers. Criterion referenced tests might be used to assess the results of teaching.

For the teacher, then, it is necessary to ask good questions about children's growth and learning, and to then make judgments about what assessment instruments might best be used to find answers.

Activities

1. Attempt to carry out each of the methods of data gathering found in this chapter. Which was the most time-consuming? Which gave you the widest variety of data or the narrowest?
2. Find, evaluate, and contrast three of the Criterion Referenced tests. What justification would you give for selecting each? Give one of these tests to three young children. What have you learned after the application? What other information, not provided by the test, would you like to have about this child?

Reference

BENTZEN, W. R., *Seeing Young Children: A Guide to Observing and Recording Behavior*. Albany, N.Y.: Delmar Publishers, 1985.

CARBONARA, N. T., *Techniques for Observing Normal Child Behavior*. Pittsburgh: University of Pittsburgh Press, 1982.

SANFORD, A. R., & J.G. ZELMAN, *LAP: The Learning Accomplishment Profile* (rev. ed.). Winston-Salem, N.C.: Kaplan Press, 1981.

SPIVACK, G., & J. SPOTTS, *Devereux Child Behavior (DCB) Rating Sale*. Devon, Pa.: Devereux Foundation, 1966.

WILLOUGHBY-HERB, S. J., & J. T. NEISWORTH. *HICOMP Preschool Curriculum*. Columbus, Ohio: Charles E. Merrill, 1983.

FIGURE 12.3   Child-Play Behavior (CPB) Rating Scale

Date Scored	Rating 1st	2nd	3rd	4th
Starting	____	____	____	____
Ending	____	____	____	____
Color Used	____	____	____	____

Birthdate_____

Age: Yrs_____Ms_____

Child's Name   _____

Teacher(s) 1st   _____

2nd   _____

3rd   _____

4th   _____

Directions
1. Observe child in wide variety of play situations for six to eight weeks, before rating.
2. Make rating on most recent behavior.
3. Some items will require setting up a test situation in the classroom context, and requesting performance by the child.
4. Base rating on your experience only.
5. Consider each item separately from all others.
6. Use extreme high and low rates when warranted.
7. Rate every question.

Profile Scoring Sheet
1. Move number score from each item to the item number found under the heading FACTOR ITEM RAW SCORES on the scoring sheet.
2. Add all numbers in that row and put total in space under the heading TOTAL RAW SCORE. Circle the raw score number to the scale to the right under the heading APPROX.AGE. The number under approx. age-2, 3, 4, 5, and 6, represent the score most children at this age would score in the row for sociodramatic play, dramatic play, fluid construction, etc.
3. Children who score one and one-half ages below their approximate age, might require play facilitation by the teacher.

Creative use of materials and activities.

Score the following based on:
(a) the degree to which the child uses the materials or uses action in an appropriate manner, showing an understanding symbolic growth and development.
(b) the extent to which the child does not limit himself to the obvious use of the materials itself, but use it in a creative manner.

Score each item on a five-point scale in regards to the following:
___1. The material is used without regard to its physical or representational properties in a manner recalling the play of infants.
      e.g.   Examine the material superficially. Picks up a toy and bangs it on the ground or on own body. Stirs the sand with his finger
___2. The material is used with some regard for its properties, but these are not exploited to the full. There is an element of lack of vision in the handling.
      e.g.   Shovels or rakes at the sand without making anything. Clicks a toy pistol in an aimless kind of way. Hammers a piece of wood without inserting a nail. Daubs paint on paper or wood.
___3. The material is used with regard to its properties, (symbolic use), but in an obvious way. There is no coherent play theme which transcends the given materials and within which their appropriate use figures (symbols) as meaningful behavior.
      e.g.   Fills the bucket, or makes a sand-pile without naming it. Paints waste wood with the intention of coloring it, but without any further imaginative or constructive intent. Puts the doll to bed in the cot provided, without extending the imaginative theme to other aspects of the domestic situation Hammers a nail in wood.
___4. The material is used in a manner transcending its merely obvious properties.
e.g. Builds an elaborate block structure. Makes a recognizable human figure of plasticine. Makes or attempts to make a sword or an airplane of waste wood.
or The material is used appropriately within the meaningful context of a larger imaginative whole
      e.g.   Uses the doll tea-set in the context of a fairly well organized tea party. Plays with the sand, giving a representation of a store or shop.
___5. The materials is used in a highly insightful manner. adapted to a context which clearly transcends it.
      e.g.   Builds a "ship" on the sandbox, inverting a table on it and wedging this with a blanket, using the clothes horse as ships ladder, and so on. Plays at a "tea-party" using sand as a birthday cake, which he decorates, perhaps using small pieces of wood as candles, or perhaps wrapping small bits of plasticine in paper to make candies, and so on.

FIGURE 12.3   Continued

Child-Plan Behavioral Rating Scale

Sociodramatic Play (Macro)
1 2 3 4 5 | | | (1) | Imitative role play
1 2 3 4 5 | | | (2) | Make believe with objects
1 2 3 4 5 | | | (3) | Persistence in role play
1 2 3 4 5 | | | (4) | Interaction
1 2 3 4 5 | | | (5) | Verbal communication

Dramatic Play (Micro)
1 2 3 4 5   (1)   Imitative role play
1 2 3 4 5   (2)   Make believe with objects
1 2 3 4 5   (3)   Persistence in role play
1 2 3 4 5   (4)   Interaction
1 2 3 4 5   (5)   Verbal communication

Fluid Materials
1 2 3 4 5   (6)   Water Play
1 2 3 4 5   (7)   Sand Play (dry)
1 2 3 4 5   (8)   Finger-Painting
1 2 3 4 5   (9)   Easel Painting
1 2 3 4 5   (10) Sand Play (wet)
1 2 3 4 5   (11) Clay
1 2 3 4 5   (12) Drawing (crayon)
1 2 3 4 5   (13) Drawing (pencil)
1 2 3 4 5   (14) Drawing (markers)
1 2 3 4 5   (15) Drawing (chalk)

Materials Requiring Restructuring
1 2 3 4 5   (16) Carpentry
1 2 3 4 5   (17) Box/Cardboard Construction
1 2 3 4 5   (18) Paper/cut & paste
1 2 3 4 5   (19) Other_____

Structured Materials
1 2 3 4 5   (20) Pratt Blocks
1 2 3 4 5   (21) Interlocking Cubes
1 2 3 4 5   (22) Lego
1 2 3 4 5   (23) Octons
1 2 3 4 5   (24) _____
1 2 3 4 5   (25) _____
1 2 3 4 5   (26) _____
1   (27) Puzzle (four pieces)
   2   Puzzle (six pieces)
      3   Puzzle (eight pieces)

4			Puzzle (ten pieces)
	5		Puzzle (more than ten pieces)

Representational Ability
Symbolic

			(28)	Best Flat (two dimensional)
1				Random/Controlled Scribbling (circle)
	2			Circle/face (circle)
		3		Arms-legs/body appears (circle)
			4	Float House (or substitute)/bottom line (circle)
				5 Base Line Supports/two-dimensional (circle)

Sensorimotor Abilities

Fine Motor
Draw-a-design

1				( )	Vertical line (4')
	2			( )	Horizontal line (4')
		3		( )	Circle
			4	( )	Backwards L
				5 ( )	3 line asterisk

Barrage Catch Game (three attempts)

1				( )	Catch with both hands
	2			( )	Catch with one preferred hand
		3		( )	Catch with one other hand
			4	( )	Toss in air (3'plus),catch with both hands
				5 ( )	Toss in air (3'plus),catch with one hand

Barrage Throw (three attempts)

1				( )	Hits 15' target hole (10' distance)
	2			( )	Hits 10' target hole (10' distance)
		3		( )	Hits 5' target hole (10' distance)
			4	( )	Hits 10' target hole (20' distance)
				5 ( )	Hits 5' target hole (20' distance)

Large Ball Bounce

1				( )	Large ball, 2 pounces (preferred hand)
	2			( )	Large ball, 5 pounces (preferred hand)
		3		( )	Large ball, 2 pounces (other hand)
			4	( )	Large ball, 5 pounces (other hand)
				5 ( )	Large ball, dribbles forward 7 feet

Gross Motor
Walking

1			( ) Walking on tiptoe
	2		( ) Walking a straight line
		3	( ) Standing on one foot

FIGURE 12.3   Continued

	4				( )	Standing on the other foot
		5			( )	Skipping

Climbing
1					( )	Climbs rope ladder
	2				( )	Climbs pole
		3			( )	Fixed Rope Climb, 6"knots
			4		( )	Fixed Rope Climb, 12'knots
				5	( )	Unfixed Rope climb

Balance
1					( )	Walks balance beam
	2				( )	Walks balance beam holding 5 lb. object
		3			( )	Walks backward on beam
			4		( )	Walks backward on beam holding 5 lb. object
				5	( )	Walks beam, bending under barrier at child shoulder height

---

FIGURE 12.4   Child-Play Behavioral Rating Scale Profile

Child's Name_____

Age_____
Birthday_____
Sex_____

Rater's Home_____
Rater's Relationship to Child_____
Date of Rating_____

Play Form
    Factor Item   Approx. Age
          Raw Scores   2   3   4   5   6
                       Total Raw Score

1. socio-dramatic
    role   1___   2___ objects
    persist 3___   4___ interact   _____   4 6   8 10   12 14   16 18 20
    verbal   5___

2. dramatic play
    role   6___   7___ objects
    persist 8___   9___ interact   _____   4 6   8 10   12 14   16 18 20

3. Fluid-construction
    water   11___   12___ sand (dry)
    finger   13___   14___ easel pt   _____   4 10   16 22   28 34   40 46 50
    wet sand 15___   16___ clay
    crayon 17___   18___ pencil
    marker 19___   20___ chalk

4. Restructuring-Const
    carpt   21___   22___ cardboard
    paper/ 23___   _____   3 4 5 6 7 8 9 10 11 12 13 14
    paste

FIGURE 12.4   Continued

Play Form Factor Item Raw Scores	Total Raw Score	Approx. Age 2	3	4	5	6

5. Structured-Const
   block   24___   25___ cubes
   Lego   26___   27___ Octons   _____   4 6   8 10   12 14   16 18 20

6. Puzzles (item 28)   _____   1   2   3   4

7. Symbolic/flat const (item 29)   _____   1   2   3   4

8. Fine Motor
   draw   30___   31___ catch
   throw   32___   33___ bounce   _____   4 6   8 10   12 14   16 18 20

9. Gross Motor
   walk   34___   35___ climb
   balance 36___   _____   3 4 5   6 7 8   9 10 11 12 13 14

FIGURE 12.5   Adjustment Behavioral Profile

DIRECTIONS:
1. Observe the child in a wide variety of play situations for six to eight weeks before rating.
2. Make a rating on the most recent behavior.
3. Base rating on your experience only.
4. Consider each item separately from all others.
5. Use extreme high or low rating when warranted.
6. Rate every question.

Profile Scoring Sheet
1. Move each score from the question statements on the Profile to the Scoring Sheet under the heading FACTOR ITEM RAW SCORE.
2. Add all numbers in that category and put a total in the space under the heading TOTAL RAW SCORE. Circle the raw score number to the right on the scale and heading-ADJUSTMENT. NEEDS INTERV suggest that an intervention is needed, and WELL ADJ is indicated good adjustment.

Adjustment Behavioral Profile

Child's Name_____

Rater's Name_____   Date of Rating_____

Based on your recent knowledge of this child, rate him/her on the five point scale to follow, based on what is considered normal for this age child.
Rating Levels:
Never 1, 2, 3, 4, 5, Always   Compared to normal children, How often does the child...

Self Control
1 2 3 4 5   1   Carries an art assignment to completion

Detachment
1 2 3 4 5   2   Cuddles with teacher responsively after moments of positive affect
1 2 3 4 5   3   Allows cuddling and comforting by teacher after being accidentally hurt

Language
1 2 3 4 5   4   Uses language to express needs
1 2 3 4 5   5   Engages teachers in conversation
1 2 3 4 5   6   Engages peers in conversation

Social Isolation
1 2 3 4 5   7   Hides in corner or takes steps to avoid peers
1 2 3 4 5   8   Exhibits an expression that is flat and lifeless

FIGURE 12.5   Continued

Social Aggression

1 2 3 4 5   9   Swears, name-calls, and uses bathroom talk toward peers
1 2 3 4 5   10   Swears, name-calls, and uses bathroom talk toward teacher
1 2 3 4 5   11   Bite, strike, attach other children in a free-play situation
                          with peers, without apparent cause.

Conflict over Possessions

1 2 3 4 5   12   Act passively when others take his/her toys
1 2 3 4 5   13   Act physically aggressive when others take his/her toys
1 2 3 4 5   14   Act verbally aggressive when others take his/her toys
1 2 3 4 5   15   Has temper tantrums when others take his/her toys

Critical Times

1 2 3 4 5   16   Shows fear of loss of parent when he/she departs, but
                          recovers with teacher's help
1 2 3 4 5   17   Refuses most food during snack
1 2 3 4 5   18   Fights for and hoards food at snack
1 2 3 4 5   19   Not rest or sleep fully after a period of settling
1 2 3 4 5   20   Wets cot at rest time
1 2 3 4 5   21   Stays at circle for more than 10 minutes
1 2 3 4 5   22   Re-unites without conflict with parents

FIGURE 12.6   Adjustment Behavioral Profile Score Sheet

Child's Name_____

Age_____   Birthday_____   Sex_____

Rather's Name_____
Rater's Relationship to Child_____
Date of Rating_____

Behavioral Category	Factor Item	Raw score	Total	Adjustment				
				Needs Interv			Well Adjust	
1. Self control	Completion	1. ___	___	1	2	3	4	5
2. Detachment	Cuddling positive Cuddling negative	2. ___ 3. ___	___	2	4	6	8	10
3. Language	Language needs Teacher conversat. Peer conversation	4. ___ 5. ___ 6. ___	___	3	6	9	12	15
4. Social Isolation	Hides Flat expression	7. ___ 8. ___	___	10	8	6	4	2
5. Social	Swears at peers Swears at teacher Attacks	9. ___ 10. ___ 11. ___	___	15	12	9	6	3
6. Conflict over possessions	Passive Aggressive Verbal aggressive Tantrum	12. ___ 13. ___ 14. ___ 15. ___	___	20	16	12	8	4

FIGURE 12.6   Continued

7. Critical Time	Departure	16.___	___	35	28	21	14	7
	Food	17.___						
	Hoard	18.___						
	Best	19.___						
	Wets	20.___						
	Circle	21.___						
	Re-unites	22.___						

FIGURE 12.7   Social Observation System

Directions

It is suggested that the classroom teacher mount the Social Observation System form on the back of a solid supply cupboard door at eye level in a central room where most children would be playing. At the same time period each day for a two-week period, the teacher would take a few minutes to score her way down the list of children on the left side of the form. First she observes the child's activities and then puts one tally mark in the space under the substage of the social development in which the child is performing.

After a two-week period (longer if the teacher decides) totals for each child are obtained by adding down the columns under each category. A grand total is obtained by adding left to right all totals. The total number each social category is then divided by the Grand Total to get a percentage for that social level. The percentages can now be graphed on the Individual Social Graph (Figure 12.8) for each child.

The information permits us to know where each child is functioning socially, and could call for intervention if the results are not age-expected.

Observer's Name_____

Dates: Began_____   Ended_____

Child's Name	unoccu-pied	on-looker	solitary	parallel	associa-tive	coopera-tive
1.						
2.						
3.						
4.						
5.						
6.						
7.						
8.						
8.						
9.						
Total Grd Tot Div						
Percentage						

FIGURE 12.8   Individual Social Graph

Child's Name_____

Date: Began_____   Ended_____

	unoccu-pied	on-looker	solitary	parallel	associa-tive	coopera-tive	
100							
90							
80							
70							
60							
50							
40							
30							
20							
10							
0							
oberv	1 2 3 4 5	1 2 3 4 5	1 2 3 4 5	1 2 3 4 5	1 2 3 4 5	1 2 3 4 5	1 2 3 4 5
%							

CHAPTER THIRTEEN

1ST GRADE READINESS AND PLAY CURRICULUM

SYC has accepted the belief that the play-activity curriculum follows the child's "natural" way of learning, provides the best school environment for day-in, day-out living and learning, and is developmentally appropriate. Therefore, when the question is asked, "Will this play curriculum develop school readiness? Or, when is my child ready for first grade?" we must reply with the question, "What kind of first grade?" Will the classroom be based on a continuation of the play-activity curriculum—or on direct instruction? In first grade, children usually spend most of their time at desks involved in paper-and-pencil tasks.

In Chapter 3, Understanding Young Children's Play, we suggested that near the age of 7 a child moves from being a "player" to a "worker." A "worker" is a psychological term for the child who has moved out of an egocentric fantasy-based form of thinking and behaving, and can carry out socially agreed-upon tasks and activities with others (A. Freud, 1971; Piaget, 1962). He can also inhibit earlier drives to destroy, to use up, and to demand his own childish needs. Most developmental theory sees age 7 as pivotal in growth and development. Near 7 the child moves to a new cognitive stage (Piaget, 1952) and social-emotional stage (Erikson, 1950), and experiences physical changes (Gesell, 1946). Again, the child moves from being a player to a worker.

When we talk of "readiness" for the first grade, we are usually referring to reading readiness. A study (Wolfgang, 1974) in this area was conducted on 400 first-grade boys who were tested on reading performance at the end of the school year. Some of the boys did extremely well; others did very poorly. The tested IQ's of the participants did not predict reading performance. What, then, the researchers asked, was the reason for the diversity in performance of the students?

Reading, according to developmental theory, is the use of signs. And the developmental precursor for signs is representation in play (e.g., a child imagines that a block is an electric shaver) (Piaget, 1962). Thus, wondering about the representational play their subjects might have experienced, the researchers brought many of them individually to a testing room and asked them to play symbolically, that is, to use miniature life toys in "make-believe" play.

The results were that all of the advanced readers could play "imaginatively" for three to four minutes as the experimenter had requested—but after two or three short dramatic play sequences they seemed to see no point in continuing and were uninterested in doing so.

The nonreading boys divided into two groups. One group took the miniature life toys and got "lost in play." Their themes were about monsters, domestic situations, and "shoot-em- up." The play was rich with imagination

TABLE 13.1   The Value of Sociodramatic Play for School Success

---

"The following school-related behaviors, activated, learned and practiced in the context of well-developed sociodramatic play, illustrates the relevance of this type of play behavior for school adjustment and success." (Smilansky, 1990)

-gathering scattered experiences and combining them in new ways.
-selective drawing on experiences and knowledge according to a fixed frame of reference.
-discerning and enacting the main characteristics of roles and themes; grasping the essence of things.
-concentrating around a given theme.
-controlling himself in relation to an internalized sense of evolving order.
-controlling himself and disciplining his own actions within a context.
-flexibility in approaching various situations.
-respect for the individuality of others.
-the intrinsic satisfaction and extrinsic reward for being creative.
-developing the child from being predominantly egocentric into being capable of cooperation and social interaction.
-observing reality (the surroundings) with a view to utilizing these observations in relation to himself.
-moving from the particular and limited to general and more inclusive concepts.
-developing the use of abstract thought.
-vicarious learning utilizing the experience and knowledge of other children.

---

and fantasy. The other half of the nonreading boys could not play dramatically. They stood up the pieces of furniture and walked the miniature people about, but they did not seem to be able to pretend that the miniatures were real or to dramatize events using them. In regard to this, Smilansky (1968) discovered during early Head Start research that there were, surprisingly, many children ages 4 to 6 who could not and did not engage in sociodramatic play. She discovered that these same children later had not become "workers" in first grade, that apparently they could not "play the role" of student or the "game" of school. (See Table 13.1 for Smilansky's defense of sociodramatic play and its value for school success.)

The research described above, although only one limited study, suggested that the advanced readers had moved out of play and had made the developmental shift to "worker" which, as discussed, usually comes at the approximate age of 7. We may further hypothesize that the group of excellent dramatic players who were nonreaders had not made the shift to "worker" and were still in the fantasy-egocentric stage of early childhood.

The nonplaying nonreaders at the end of first grade are of much concern, because not only do they still need to play, but they need an intervention program described in the play-activity methods to facilitate that play, and then gradually bridge them into direct instruction. According to developmental theory, these nonplayers/nonreaders should not be in a direct instruction program that is heavily based on paper-and-pencil tasks related to "signs." This would be casting seeds on rocky ground.

Questions regarding readiness for first grade can only be answered when "first grade" is defined. If it is oriented toward reading skills and pencil-paper-tasks, large numbers of 6- to 7-year-old's who are "on time" developmentally and have moved to using "signs" would be ready; some children would not. If the first grade is one where children have hands-on activities and involvement in elements of the play-activity curriculum, then the classroom might serve "nonworkers" well.

We must not, however, simply say of the nonworkers: "let them wait a year." Rather, an activity-based first grade or pre-first grade would pick these children up where they are developmentally, and provide experiences which would prepare them for a skill-based curriculum. For children who have been unsuccessful, the "dragon" that must be slain in school philosophies is named the "tyranny of fairness." As mentioned previously, this means in practice that in order to be fair to all children we must treat them all "the same." If we teach the same well-defined skills to everyone in first grade we are "fair." This is, of course, as nonsensical as would be purchasing clothing of the same size for all first graders on the basis that it is unfair for one child to get a larger size than another.

Children in first grade differ developmentally just as they do in clothing sizes. We need a variety of classroom models which cover the continuum from activity-based to direct skills in order to meet the individual needs of each child fairly. "Wars" between philosophies and education models must be forgotten; what matters is which is the best model for this particular child at this particular time.

For the beginning teacher who is about to journey into the land of teacherhood we hope that SYC has given you a map and signpost to guide you in your quest. May your dreams and realities be good ones; our sons and daughters are depending on it.

References

FREUD, A., *Normality and Pathology in Childhood: Assessments of Development*. New York: International Universities Press, 1971.

PIAGET, J., *The Origins of Intelligence in Children*. New York: International Universities, 1952.

PIAGET, J., *Play, Dreams and Imitation in Childhood*. New York: Norton & Co., 1962.

SMILANSKY, S., *The Effects of Sociodramatic Play on Disadvantaged Preschool Children*. New York: John Wiley and Sons, 1968.

SMAILANSKY, S. & L. SHEFATYA, *Facilitating Play: A Medium for Promoting Cognitive, Socio-Emotional and Academic Development in Young Children*. Gaithersburg, Md.: Psychosocial & Educational Publications, 1990.

WOLFGANG, C.H., "An Exploration of the Relationship Between the Cognitive Area of Reading and Selected Developmental Aspects of Children's Play," in *Psychology in the Schools* (July 1974), 338-43.

Index

DATE DUE

NOV 2 8 1992			
JAN 0 4 1999			
FEB 2 0 2000			
FEB 0 2 2002			
JAN 3 1 2003			
MAR 2 1 2003			

GAYLORD   PRINTED IN U.S.A.